PRAISE FOR
The Hero's Choice

"*The Hero's Choice* is a compelling story about a rather ordinary man, who finds his voice, transcends adversity and elevates his life to a whole new level of existence. It will teach you to live from the inside out rather than the outside in; to make choices, day in and day out, consistent with who you really are—your highest self. I highly recommend it for anyone committed to living with purpose and meaning." -**Dr. Stephen R. Covey**, author of *The Seven Habits of Highly Effective People* and *The 8th Habit*

"Dr. Allen has written a powerful story about a man who sheds his preoccupation with ego and learns to live from integrity, courage and love. It beautifully illustrates how a person who discovers his soul can bring out the best in everyone around him. It's a story of true leadership." -**Dr. Lance Secretan,** award winning columnist, speaker, coach, consultant and author of *One: The Art and Practice of Conscious Leadership*

An inspiring tale that celebrates the power of possibility and human potential. A must-read for anyone traversing the whitewater of involuntary career transition." -**Jan Austin**, founder of Coach U. training program and author of *What No One Ever Tells You about Leading for Results*

"Pure delight! *The Hero's Choice* is a timeless metaphor. A mysterious stranger guides the hero with practical wisdom, in the tradition of Obi-Wan Kenobi in *Star Wars* and the master in *Illusions* by Richard Bach. Textured with layers of insight, this fictional drama resonates with a depth and beauty comparable to *The Celestine Prophecy* by James Redfield. *The Hero's Choice* thoughtfully lifts not only the spirit, but reveals a way to live decently, compassionately, and happily." -**Charol Messenger**, a book doctor, and author of *The New Humanity* and *I'm Dancing As Fast As I Can*

"The Hero's Choice teaches a new way of being within the workplace—a way of being based on authenticity, accountability, honesty and love. It will teach and inspire each of us to make our companies great places to work." -**Larry Wilson,** founder of Wilson Learning and author of *Play to Win: Choosing Growth over Fear in Work and Life* and *Changing the Game: The New Way to Sell*

"Getting fired can be one of the most positive experiences and turning points in your life. This book shows how to benefit and grow when this and other trials happen to you." -**Brian Tracy,** internationally known authority on leadership, personal development and goal setting and author of 40 books and more than 40 best selling audio and video learning programs

"Dr. Allen's story follows the personal growth of Hal, as he evolves from a self-absorbed real estate wheeler-dealer to a forgiving, accountable, family man with a greater purpose and perspective. I thoroughly enjoyed the book and would recommend it to anyone who is searching for more in their own life." -**Karl Mecklenburg,** motivational speaker, author, and Denver Bronco Ring of Fame inductee

"Brilliant! I got chills reading it. Dr. Allen's engaging story reveals simple steps that transform enormous, stressful trials into peaceful and productive encounters. I wish I had been exposed to these invaluable principles long ago. This is a powerful book that will change lives." -**Alfred T. Zirkle,** international speaker and president of IndustryPro, past president two public corporations and past president of International Business Brokers Association and Association for Corporate Growth/Utah

"Roger Allen has written some of the best training and consulting products on the market today. I know because I continually receive feedback from the users of those products. And I'm glad that Roger has now turned some of the concepts he's so passionate about into a book that can be enjoyed by tens of thousands of people. *The Hero's Choice* will inspire you to live the life that is right for you instead of living a script given you by someone else." -**Chip Wilson,** Founder and CEO of 360 Solutions

"If you are a boss or have a boss, own a small business or work in a Fortune 500, this book is for you! Roger Allen shows you how to make tough choices to reach new heights of success." –**John Ward**, Business consultant and founder of BusinessWorks

For Trisha,

Your growth is your single greatest intention & investment.

Much Love,

Judy

7-8-10

the

Hero's Choice

Choice

Living from the Inside Out

Roger K.
Allen

 Leadership Press

ISBN: 978-0-9797831-2-8

PRINTED IN CANADA

In loving memory of my father

C. Kay Allen

Acknowledgments

Life is a journey we travel together, and I have long believed that the source of meaning and richness in our lives comes from our relationships. Countless people have inspired and supported me in my personal journey, and I would like to acknowledge just a few of them. I would not be who I am, or where I am today, if not for each of you.

First, my wife, Judy, who has always loved me deeply and unconditionally. And of course my children, Melinda, Jonathan, Cheryl-Lynn, and Cris, who are truly examples of living by higher principles. How grateful I am, as a father, for your devotion to God and willingness to exercise positive and strengthening choices in your lives.

I am grateful to my loving parents, C. Kay and Doris Allen, both of whom, sadly, have passed away. However, I am proud of their legacy and proud to carry on the work of my father. He was my personal mentor and is, even to this day, the inspiration for all that I do. I'm also very grateful to my siblings—Connie, Rolayne, Paul, and their families—for our ongoing friendship, love, and support. They are my best friends.

Many colleagues and friends have influenced my career—most notably Randy Hardman, my good friend and partner at The Human Development Institute, and Preston Pond, my mentor and partner at The Center for Organizational Design. I also want to acknowledge Chip Wilson and the staff of 360 Solutions, who have made our consulting and training products available to hundreds of consultants and many thousands of leaders, employees, and people around the country.

I'm grateful to many good friends who have loved me and helped shape my life: Kent Bott, Larry Burk, Blaine and Katherine Porter, Fred Zirkle, and many more, too many to mention, within my church community who accept me despite my imperfections.

Finally, there are many who have inspired and contributed to Hal's story. I'm grateful to Garth Scovil for our long talks about Hal's journey as well as the restoration of the '59 Coup de Ville. A special thanks to Rob Jaussi for letting me tell a portion of his story, and to John Ward, who encouraged me to write this work as fiction. Thanks to Torben Welch for his advice on legal matters. I'm grateful to Andy Wolfendon for help with editing and Charol Messenger for her final edit and help tightening the story and making it more visual. And many thanks to Carroll Morris, who continually challenged me to make the story better. The story would not be what it is without her coaching, editing, and assistance with the writing.

Chapter 1

Fired!

Hal Stratton caught himself holding his breath as he pulled his antique Chevy pickup into the parking lot of Western Realty. The company he'd started seven years earlier. His baby.

Looking at the August sun over Denver's Rocky Mountains, he guessed it was 6:45 p.m. He looked at his wristwatch to see how close he'd come to the actual time. A little game he played. Spot on this time.

He was early—just as he liked. He took a couple of deep breaths, willing himself to relax and gather his thoughts. It was crucial to be his sharpest this evening for the most important board meeting since he'd created the land development company.

The friends Hal had brought into the business trusted his instincts and supported the deals he'd made as managing partner. Their small investments had grown impressively as he built Western Realty into a $60-million company. However, purchasing the McFee Ranch a few months earlier had caused considerable friction. The partners disagreed with the decision, because he had taken money out of the business when revenues were dropping. They had even gone as far as to seek another partner, one with deep pockets and business acumen.

Hal looked into his rearview mirror and smoothed his short

brown hair. He almost wished he hadn't as he saw the concern in his hazel eyes and frown line between his straight brows. The look startled him and he shook his head, trying to recapture his natural optimism and confidence. He took another deep breath and slid his six-foot, solid frame out of his 1950 red pickup.

"Darn that Charlie White."

The partners had been excited when White came into the business back in June in a land for stock trade. Hal had reluctantly agreed, knowing that White's abrasive temperament would alter the balance on the board.

He'd been right. From the start, he and Charlie White were on the opposite side of every issue.

In his lucky blue-gray "closer" suit, Hal walked briskly into the lobby of his company offices. The décor, a dark brown leather couch, large upholstered chairs, coffee table, and a tall cherry wood reception desk, conveyed excellence and professionalism. The original paintings by up-and-coming Western artists made the space distinctive. Not only a good investment, they symbolized what Western Realty was all about.

"Hi, Janine," Hal said, greeting his long-time office manager and executive assistant with a warm smile. Her engaging personality, intelligence, and efficiency made her indispensable. "Time for the tribe to gather. Anyone here yet?"

Always an ally in the past, Janine Markham attemped a pleasant smile but Hal noticed how her eyes skittered away from him and her hands fumbled aimlessly with a stack of papers. "All of them." She tipped her head toward the conference room. "They're already here."

"I didn't think I was late." He checked his wristwatch against the clock on the wall.

"You're not. They're early." She raised an eyebrow. "They came a half-hour ago."

Hal nervously adjusted his gray silk tie. "Really? Who arranged that?"

"I don't know. I wasn't asked to set it up." She stood, agenda in hand, ready to follow him into the room. "Watch your back, okay?"

The board members were in a huddle when Hal and Janine walked in. They quickly broke apart, like schoolchildren caught doing something wrong.

"I see the meeting's already started," Hal said with forced heartiness. "What did I miss?"

The response was telling. Patricia Harmon, tall and striking with shoulder-length chestnut hair, shifted nervously from one foot to the other. Keith Mickelson, broad and bald, tugged at his tight sports jacket and muttered a greeting. Larry Greenwald, one of Hal's best friends, straightened up to his slender 6'2" height and, avoiding eye contact, shook his head.

Only Charlie White held Hal's gaze, looking every bit the influential man he was. In his mid-sixties, he still had a full head of gray hair. His eyes were piercing and his mouth bore a slightly sardonic turn. His imposing physique was emphasized by an impeccably tailored, custom-made suit.

"Let's get this show on the road," Charlie announced, taking a seat at the dark cherry conference table.

Hal sat at his usual spot at the head of the table and opened the meeting. Janine handed each board member a copy of the agenda. Charlie quickly tossed it aside. "Let's not beat around the bush, Stratton," Charlie said, slapping both hands down on the table. "It's time for straight talk. Since these fine folks—" he gestured toward the other board members "—aren't willing to bring up the predicament you've gotten us into, I will."

"Bear with me," Hal said briskly. He knew Charlie White was pitting the board against his decisions and Hal needed to set him straight. He leaned forward, his elbows on the table, his hands folded before him. "As we go over the agenda, I'm sure all of your concerns will be addressed—"

"Stratton," Charlie interrupted, "you've steered this company into a huge mess. We're losing money hand over fist. I want to know why … and what you're doing about it."

Hal kept his voice businesslike despite the verbal assault, and reached for the handouts he'd so carefully prepared. "That's at the top of my agenda. I know the numbers haven't looked good lately," he continued, "but I've put together some information I

3

think you will all find encouraging. I've also come up with some steps we can take to keep the company going until revenues pick up."

"We need to do something drastic before we all lose our shirts," Charlie declared, ignoring Hal's comments. "You do realize that, don't you?"

"Now, wait a minute," Hal said, bridling his gut reaction. Western Realty had acquired many desirable properties under his leadership—shopping centers, office buildings, apartment complexes, a warehouse, and several parcels of vacant land. "We're not in danger of that, and you know it."

"*You* may not think so," Charlie cut in, "but the rest of us aren't so sure." He turned and thrust a finger toward Keith Mickelson. "Tell Hal what you told me."

Startled, Keith looked from Charlie to Hal, then back to Charlie. He stammered. "I, uh … you've made some questionable deals lately, Hal. They're draining our resources. I know there's always risk in this sort of business, but … um … I have to wonder if we'd be in a better position now if the board as a whole had been more involved." Keith cleared his throat nervously. "Or if we had different leadership."

"What?" Hal clasped his hands tightly together as heat flooded his face. He hadn't expected to be attacked by an old friend. Certainly not so personally. He forced himself to speak calmly. "Listen. I know we've got some cash-flow problems at the moment, but it's temporary and due to some excellent long-term holdings, properties our competitors would love to own, I might add. And that's the price we pay for *future* revenues. Standing firm is our best course of action." Hal held up a hand, forestalling any comment. "I know you guys want to see steady returns on your investments. I don't blame you." He sat straight up in his chair. "I've spent a lot of time thinking about how to get out of this situation. Let me tell you what I've come up with."

"It's what you were thinking three months ago that's killing us, Stratton." Charlie White shook his head as he stared at Hal. "I'm not up for any more of your ideas."

Hal grimaced and locked onto Charlie's eyes. "The McFee

Ranch was a great buy. You should know that. It'll take some time, but that purchase alone will make us *all* wealthy. I've got the numbers to—"

"Speaking of numbers," Patricia Harmon interrupted, "what does the occupancy rate in our apartments need to be so we break even, on average?"

"About eighty-five percent," Hal responded, still glowering at Charlie. "You know that as well as I do."

"Where are we currently?" she added.

Hal broke Charlie's gaze. "Come on, Patricia. Sixty-five percent."

"Right." She nodded slowly, her mouth turned down grimly. "I agree with Charlie. We need to take action now."

"If you'd just—"

Charlie clasped the side arms of his chair and leaned over the table combatively. "There's a deeper issue here that we're all avoiding. How did we get so many holdings in the southwest part of the city in the first place? That's what *I* want to know."

"We picked them up at a good price," Hal began.

Charlie sneered. "Really? And now we know why. With sixty-five percent occupancy, I have to wonder if you did adequate market research before plunking down our money."

Hal rose to his feet. "Now, wait a minute. No one could have predicted the Computrex layoffs and the effect they would have on the occupancy rates of those units. Not you, me, anyone. I didn't build this company into what it is today by making bad decisions. In fact, up to this moment, no one has questioned my judgment. I've gotten us through challenging times before ... and I will do it again. Most of you know that."

Hal glanced around the table, hoping that one of his long-time colleagues would speak up on his behalf. No one, expect Charlie White, met his eyes. Not Keith, his golfing buddy who had lauded his every move—until Charlie's arrival. Not Patricia, a single parent who had asked Hal to be godfather to her adopted son. Not Larry, a friend going back to high school whom Hal had rescued from a dead-end job to become a partner in Western.

Hal's chest tightened. He was on the wrong end of a power

struggle, and not one of his friends was stepping into the fray. No one was willing to take on Charlie White. He sat back down wondering what—if anything—he could do to salvage the meeting. "What's going on here?" he asked. "I need to know."

"That should be obvious," Charlie said, gesturing like a conductor holding the last note of a symphony. "Your leadership is in serious question. You've made bad decisions, Stratton. And you've incurred considerable debt by purchasing the McFee property." Charlie paused dramatically. "I've checked with our controller. There've been some irregularities that have contributed to this shortfall."

"What?" Hal jumped back to his feet, blood pounding in his head.

"You keep *saying* the company is in good shape," Charlie scoffed, "but something's not right." He shook a mocking finger at Hal. "I'm looking into the company's finances over the last five years." He leaned back hard against his chair. "Looking for assurance that you haven't gone south with some of our money, Stratton."

Hal staggered backward, taking the attack on his integrity like a blow to the chest. It was one thing to be accused of poor management. But outright dishonesty? That was outrageous! Absurd!

He turned to his friends. "Larry, do you agree with this? Patricia? Keith?"

Only Janine looked him in the eye, her expression as devastated as he felt.

Hal noticed that he was trembling. "You can't believe I would do something dishonest. You know me better than that!" He bowed his head and raised both hands above his head. The words came slowly. "If you believe I've done *anything* improper or illegal, conduct an audit. You won't find a thing. I guarantee it."

The silence in the room was deafening.

"One more thing, if I no longer have the support of the people in this room, I will resign as president and managing partner of this company, effective immediately." Hal thought he saw alarm in Larry Greenwald's eyes. "I mean it," he insisted.

Keith spoke haltingly. "Are you, uh, asking us to take that vote *tonight*?"

"I am. Absolutely." Hal nodded, gaining confidence. Okay, sure, some mistakes had been made—but these charges were wildly unjustified. Would his friends allow this new kid on the block to sell him down the river? Or would they step up and put Charlie in his place? In fact, Hal *welcomed* the vote.

Charlie White stood. "How many of you would like Hal Stratton removed as President and managing partner of Western Realty?"

At first only Charlie raised his hand. Hal held his breath. Then Patricia raised hers. Then Keith. Then, after a long moment, Larry.

Hal shook his head, glaring at his partners. "So that's the way it is." His voice was low but intense. "Never mind that I put the deals together that made you all rich. Never mind that I put in seventy hours a week—while you all went on vacations. Never mind that I sacrificed *my* paycheck during the lean times." He looked around the table scornfully.

Seething, he gathered his materials and put them in his briefcase. "Thank you for your time. I'll leave you to your meeting." He turned and left, slamming the door behind him.

Hal was in the parking lot when Janine caught up to him and took his arm. "Hal! You can't just leave. You didn't do this. You have to fight."

He pulled away from her. "They voted me out. There's nothing I can do," he said bitterly.

"But—"

"Call my wife, will you?" He softened his tone. "Tell her what's happened and not to expect me until she sees me."

"Shouldn't you tell her yourself?"

"Janine, please—just call her."

Numb with disbelief, Hal Stratton walked away from the Western Reality building to his pickup. In an instant, his career over, stripped away by a single vote.

The sun was low, suffusing the sky over the mountains with golden light. He climbed in and began driving on autopilot, no awareness of the traffic around him, no thought of where he was going.

He had *not* mishandled the funds.

So why do I feel guilty?

Had he inadvertently done something that could be seen as malfeasance or, worse, criminal? He ferreted out memories of business transactions. What was Charlie White talking about?

He was breaking the speed limit. He didn't care. What was the point? He jammed his foot down hard on the accelerator. He could put an end to this by simply ramming at high speed into a cement bridge abutment. How simple it would be.

He had no idea where he was going until he saw the mountains up ahead. He drove on. Without caring where the road would take him, he left the freeway, making random turns onto smaller roads.

A memory from his boyhood suddenly accosted him. He was 14 years old and on a deer hunt. The sky was overcast and there was not a hint of sun. Hal, his father, and brother set up camp in the usual spot. The surroundings were familiar, except there was a foot and a half of new-fallen snow on the ground. And a little snow changes everything.

Hal, who always loved to be alone out of doors, left camp by himself to search for deer in a steep and rugged canyon. He lost track of time. When he started to get hungry and tired, he decided to head back. But which way? The shadows were lengthening and the temperature was dropping. He spent an hour crisscrossing his own tracks, then felt a desperation that bordered on panic. He was lost.

Hal drove on tonight, gripped by the same desperation. The road narrowed, blacktop to dirt, then ended deep in a canyon. The sun had set, and the canyon was deep in shadow. He got out of the pickup and watched the patterns of light changing, twilight into moonless night. The blackest night he could recall. Devoid of hope.

With a suddenness, something broke inside. He gasped as the pain of his loss flooded his awareness and he let out an animal cry of anguish. It echoed back at him as he sank to his knees in despair.

Chapter *2*

The Stranger

Hal woke before dawn, cold and stiff, disappointed to be alive. He thought of a phrase he'd heard once from a college teacher: "Dark night of the soul." He'd laughed then, thinking it was melodramatic gobbledygook. Now he knew better. He'd just gone through such a night himself, swinging wildly from anger to fear, self-recrimination to blaming others, rage to despair. He'd questioned everything about his life, as he faced the betrayal of his friends, the loss of status and income, and the necessary task of telling his family, especially his father. Drained of hope, enthusiasm, and direction, Hal felt empty. Oblivion seemed a better option.

But here he was, dirty and achy from a night spent underneath a giant pine tree at the edge of a turnaround deep in the mountains. He sat up, leaned back against the tree, and pulled his sleeping bag around him, trying to muster the energy and will to get up.

But his body refused to move. He hugged his knees to his chest and lowered his head, staring at the ground with glazed eyes. He remained in that position until the first rays of sunlight began to creep across the canyon floor. Eventually he would have to move. He would drive home and face Kathy and the kids.

She would be furious, no doubt about it. More because he'd pulled his "disappearing act" than because of being fired. He'd told her when they first met that being alone in the mountains occasionally was very important to him, had been since he was a kid. He was in his late teens when he started staying overnight following an afternoon hike. She had never understood why he didn't plan his outings ahead of time, instead of following his impulses. The fact that he always had basic survival gear in his pickup didn't placate her. His periodic disappearances were a continuing source of discord in their marriage.

This time, he was in for a double dose of Kathy's anger. He'd gone off after being fired—and he'd had Janine call with the news. That was truly out of line, now that he thought about it. He should get on the road, at least try to call her on his cell phone, not that he'd get a signal in these mountains.

The sun reached his side of the valley, warming him. He closed his eyes. He would have to face the music with Kathy sooner or later. Maybe he could put it off. Head for Mexico. No, he couldn't do that, given Charlie White's accusations. He imagined the headline: WESTERN REALTY MANAGING PARTNER FLEES WITH MISSING MONEY!

A surge of anger rushed over Hal at the thought of Charlie White and, with it, the need for action. Muttering, he flung off the sleeping bag and struggled to his feet. A man standing at a nearby trail was watching him.

Hal assessed the intruder. He looked to be in his eighties, large stature, sparse white hair, weathered skin. He wore banged-up hiking boots, faded pants, a well-worn plaid jacket. And a peaceful expression. *No danger. Just an irritation.*

"Don't see many people out here this time of day," said the old man.

Realizing how strange he must look in his rumpled suit, dress shirt, and dusty oxfords, Hal busied himself rolling up his sleeping bag. "Don't imagine you do."

"It's chilly now, but it looks like it's going to be a beautiful day."

Hal huffed. "I wouldn't go that far." He immediately regretted saying anything that might keep the conversation going.

"Mind if I take a load off my size elevens for a minute?" The man sat on a nearby log and let out a satisfied sigh. "You from around here?"

"The city," Hal stated. *Obviously.* "I went for a drive last night and ended up here."

Ignoring the old man, Hal put his sleeping bag in the trunk with the rest of his survival gear. Then he took his cell phone from his briefcase and walked to the middle of the dirt road. No signal, just as he'd suspected. "Kathy's going to kill me," he muttered.

"Need to make a call?" the man asked. "I have a cabin not far from here. You can use my phone, if you like."

Hal hesitated. "If it's not too much trouble. My wife's got to be worried."

The old man nodded. "I'm Donald Millhouse." He extended his hand.

"Hal Stratton."

Donald Millhouse started up the path briskly. Hal followed, ignoring the nagging feeling that he should be on his way home. The smell of pine and sage triggered memories of his childhood. He'd grown up in the western suburbs of Denver. His favorite thing as a boy had been sneaking off to a grove with a creek and a couple of ponds. He'd play in the mud, catch fish with his bare hands, pull cattails to see them burst and scatter their seeds to the four winds. Oblivious of time, he'd hike up and down the creek looking for treasures under every rock, adventure around every bend.

Sooner or later it'd be time to go home—where he'd get a scolding from his mother … for being gone so long, for getting wet and muddy, for being in that stupid creek again, for not getting his chores done, for … for … for … fill in the blank. The grove was the only place where disapproval couldn't reach him.

"Almost there," Donald Millhouse said, pulling Hal back to the present. They turned onto a narrow trail that opened to a clearing and a picturesque log cabin. Donald pointed down a long lane. "If you'd gone left at the fork last night, you'd have ended up in my driveway instead of the turnaround."

Hal followed Donald up the steps of the wide front porch and into a simple yet magnificent room with honey-colored peeled-log walls and a vaulted ceiling. "Wow!" Hal turned around, taking in all the details. Several oil paintings covered the walls. Wood and bronze animals graced tabletops and window ledges. Navajo rugs warmed hardwood floors. A large fireplace in the center divided the room into a kitchen and eating area on one side, and a homey great room on the other. A large leather sofa and two matching recliners made a comfortable seating group, giving the room a tangible warmth and feeling of safety.

"I'd love to have a place like this. It's beautiful."

"Thanks." Donald pointed to a cabinet in the kitchen. "Phone's over there. I'll make some coffee while you're calling."

Hal stood at the phone, feeling like a kid trying to avoid facing his mother. He picked up the receiver and punched in the numbers. It rang several times. No answer. Maybe Kathy had decided to teach her classes today instead of waiting for him. Then her voice came across the line, shrieking in his ear. "Hal! Is that you? Where are you? Are you okay? Why didn't you come home last night?"

He turned his back to Donald and spoke in a low voice. "I'm safe, and I'll be home soon."

"Is it true? They fired you? Did Charlie really accuse you of embezzlement?"

"Yes, Charlie made some wild accusations, and they fired me. I'll tell you all about it when I get home, okay? Now's not a good time."

"Oh, well. If it's not a good time, why don't you tell Janine to call me!"

Kathy slammed the phone in his ear, leaving him standing there, receiver in hand. He replaced it, hoping the old man hadn't overheard the conversation.

"It's okay," Donald said when Hal turned around. "I've been there myself. Life sometimes deals some pretty hard blows."

"You've been fired?"

"Oh, yeah," Donald replied with a thoughtful nod. "Hit me pretty hard. I'd tell you about it, but I'm thinking you're wanted at home."

Hal sighed. "My wife can't get any madder than she is. I'd

really like to hear what happened to you."

"Then how about some breakfast while we talk? You've got to be hungry."

"Starving." Hal had eaten little the day before, and the long night's ordeal had taken a toll. "You sure you don't mind?"

"I haven't eaten myself. Besides, I don't get many visitors, so you're welcome company." He pointed to a cabinet. "Plates and glasses are there, OJ in the fridge, bread for toast on the counter."

They worked together in companionable silence. As Hal buttered the toast, he noticed that being in Donald's easy company was calming. He finished the toast and set plates on the hand-hewn oak table. Then he looked out the picture window that framed a magnificent view of a mountain range. "This is an incredible place, Donald. Lived here long?"

"Moved out here from Chicago some years ago. Always had a yen to live in the mountains." Donald spoke without looking up.

Hal scanned the room, looking for something that might give a clue about Donald. The only personal item was a family picture on the mantel of the river-rock fireplace. A woman and two children. Above the mantel was a plaque with the words, *The Hero's Choice.* A work of art, with intricate calligraphy in the fashion of an old illuminated manuscript. Hal was about to ask about it when Donald carried a platter of eggs and bacon to the table and called him to eat.

"Quite a view you've got," Hal said, motioning toward the picture window.

"There's something about the mountains, don't you think? They renew the spirit." Donald smiled at Hal. "But then, you know that. Why else would you have driven up here last night?"

"I didn't come on purpose. Actually, I'm surprised I didn't end up in a ditch somewhere. I have no conscious memory of how I got here."

"But here you are, and we're having breakfast together. Interesting, isn't it?"

His smile was warm and … *accepting*, Hal thought.

"I was on my morning walk when I saw you," Donald continued. "My early morning walks are a communion with God

13

and nature. Today was a particularly beautiful morning."

"I guess that depends on your perspective."

Donald sat back, his hands resting on the table. "That's true. Life is all about perspective, isn't it?" He paused. "Eat up, before everything gets cold."

Hal was ravenous, and the food was delicious. He wolfed it down, slightly embarrassed at the speed with which he cleaned his plate. As they sat back to enjoy a cup of coffee, Donald told his story.

"Back in the late forties, just after the War, I took a job selling insurance. I was good at it. Eventually became general manager of a region producing around twenty million dollars in annual sales. Not bad for those days. But then the company was bought by a larger outfit, and they wanted their own manager in my position. I was out, unless I was willing to take a position as an account executive."

"That's a tough step down."

"It was. And the new general manager made my life miserable. When I couldn't take it any longer, I decided to leave. That was just fine with them, especially since they had no intention of giving me all that was owed from my stock options and pension. I filed a lawsuit, but it was David versus Goliath, and Goliath won." He shrugged.

Smarting from his own plight, Hal asked, "How did you handle it?"

"Not well." Donald gave a self-deprecating smile. "I was angry and bitter for a long time."

"Angry and bitter doesn't begin to describe how I'm feeling." Hal closed his eyes and ran his fingers through his hair.

Donald put down his fork and leaned back in his chair. "What happened, Hal? If you don't mind me asking?"

Donald's pleasant face and easy manner invited openness. And Hal was surprised to realize how he wanted to unburden himself, especially to someone he didn't have to worry about disappointing.

Despite his intention of making it short, he poured out everything, beginning with how he'd earned a degree in business management and finance, then put in ten years working for a corporation before realizing it wasn't the place for him. "I was trying to show my father I could do what he'd done," he said, shaking his head. "But I felt stifled working for someone else. I like to be the one in charge, the one making the decisions, without having to get them vetted by some muckety-muck." He paused. "Following orders really wasn't my game. I like to do things my way."

"So what did you do?" Donald asked, lightly stroking his chin.

Hal told Donald how, without telling Kathy, he'd taken money from their savings and plunked it down on a piece of prime real estate he'd been eyeing. He believed it was just a matter of time before a big developer would come along and offer a hefty price. Sure enough, he'd sold the property for a sweet profit and, flush with pride, announced to Kathy he was quitting his full-time job and going into business for himself.

Donald grinned. "I don't imagine she took that news well."

Hal shook his head. "You got that right. I thought she'd be thrilled at what I'd accomplished and encourage me in my new venture. Boy, was I fooling myself." Hal flicked his wrist. "'Are you insane?' were her exact words. She accused me of risking our family's future and wanted to know why I thought I could build a business." He looked right at Donald and grinned. "So I had to do it, of course. To prove I could."

"And you were successful?" Donald asked, with raised eyebrows.

Hal nodded. "I achieved everything I'd hoped for and more." He gave Donald an abbreviated history of Western Realty. The words came easily. His early successes, the excitement of bringing his three friends into the business, and his dream of doubling the size of the company every two years and eventually becoming one of the preeminent land development and real estate companies in the area.

The strain in his voice returned as he described the board meeting and events of the previous night. "The worst part is my so-called friends didn't even have the decency to come to my defense when White so unfairly challenged my integrity."

A respectful silence filled the room.

"It had to be a bitterly disappointing night for you, my friend," Donald said quietly.

Hal looked at his hands, embarrassed that he'd revealed so much, though grateful Donald had listened without launching into a lecture about what he should or shouldn't have done. "Yesterday was the most devastating day of my life." He clasped his hands together and looked down at the table. "I'm still trying to make sense of it."

"Any thoughts on how you're going to respond to the board's action?"

"Maybe file a lawsuit and try to stop Charlie White in his tracks. Or move on. Find a job. Start a new business. I don't know." Hal could not bring himself to look Donald in the face.

"You said 'move on.' Do you think you can do that while holding onto the bitterness and resentment you're now feeling?"

The question caught Hal off guard. He had every right to be bitter and resentful! A sharp reply was on his tongue.

But Donald continued. "I only ask because I held onto my bitterness for a lot of years. In fact, I've handled some of the biggest challenges in my life very poorly, in ways that almost destroyed me."

Hal looked up. "What do you mean by poorly?"

"Defending and protecting myself. My ego, I should say. Justifying my own actions and blaming people and circumstances."

The way Donald looked at him made Hal feel totally transparent. He felt the urge to leave … but politeness kept him in the chair.

"I only share this with you, Hal, because I've been there." Donald spoke intently. "It was after many years of suffering that I finally understood I'd created my own misery by the way I handled these events."

Some gall, thought Hal. *How am I supposed to feel after being fired from my own company? Overjoyed?* "What am I supposed to do?" he asked bitterly. "Roll over and play dead? Act like I'm above it all?"

Donald chuckled. "It's not about 'supposed to.' When we're in the middle of a crisis, it's hard to see we have real choices. But

I've found that our choices make all the difference in what happens."

"Are you saying *I'm* to blame for what happened?" His mouth gaped open at the accusation.

"I'm only saying that you have choices, Hal, even in the most difficult of circumstances."

Hal squirmed. *I've managed my life very well up to now, old man.* He pushed his chair back. "No offense. You've been very kind to me this morning, and I appreciate it. But I need to get home. Kathy's waiting, and I can't think much beyond dealing with how she's going to react."

"Sorry if I upset you, friend," Donald said, rising. "I just wanted to let you know that there's life after being fired."

Hal avoided eye contact. "Well, thanks for the breakfast and the use of your phone."

"You're welcome to come back. Call, or just stop by. It doesn't matter. I'm usually here." Donald scribbled his phone number on a piece of paper and handed it to Hal. "Like I said, I can always use the company."

Hal stuffed the paper into his jacket pocket, with no intention of ever retrieving it.

Chapter *3*
Coming Home

Thereafter Hal got to their Littleton home, the slower he drove. He got off the freeway for a route that had lots of stoplights. Since when had he started thinking of going home to Kathy like going home to his mother? They hadn't started out that way.

He'd fallen in love with Kathryn Norberg the moment he saw her at a Greek function at the University of Colorado in Boulder. Her athletic figure and glossy chestnut hair had first caught his attention. But once he started talking to her, he was irresistibly attracted to the humor in her green eyes, her playful attitude, her sharp mind. They spent as much time together as possible, hiking, biking, dancing, studying, and talking into the wee hours of the morning. The spring they were to graduate—he in business, she in education—they'd agreed to play less and study more, in order to keep up their GPAs.

They'd married two days after graduation, saying their vows in front of a justice of the peace, with his parents as witnesses. Her mother had died when Kathy was thirteen, leaving her in the care of an alcoholic father. Her single-minded goal had been to get out of the house and out of Pueblo, where she had few good memories. Her determination had paid off with a scholarship to CU and a

Rotary Club grant. She'd packed her bags for Boulder and never looked back. She'd hardly communicated with her father since.

Now that he thought about it, Hal realized both he and Kathy had been motivated by their relationships with their fathers: him to equal his father's accomplishments, her to create a stable home—one where the electricity wouldn't be turned off or the cupboards empty.

It was around 11:00 a.m. when he pulled into the driveway of their Neo-Mediterranean-style home, *big* Neo-Mediterranean home with a payment to match. He could cover next month's mortgage no problem, *maybe* the one after that, but then? With a heavy sigh, he opened the main garage door and parked his pickup next to Kathy's fully loaded Acura RDX, the main family car. Behind the garage was the add-on that served as his shop, where he was planning to restore the '59 Cadillac Coupe de Ville he'd run across a few years back.

The door from the house to the garage opened, and Kathy stood in the doorway, her body stiff, her chin jutting out. Then she went back inside and slammed the door behind her.

Great. I've lost everything I've worked for, and now I have to deal with her. He got out of the car, brushed grass and small twigs off his trousers, and smoothed the front of his jacket. He looked just like what he was, a man who had slept outdoors in an $800 suit and hadn't shaved for twenty-four hours.

Kathy was in the kitchen, leaning against a cabinet, her face pale, her eyes rimmed red. He dropped his briefcase and went to take her in his arms.

"Don't you dare!" She pushed him away. "What makes you think you can come in here after leaving me to worry all night, not knowing where you were or if you were all right?" She burst into tears, but still refused to let him comfort her. "Did you even think how it would be for me to hear what had happened from Janine? Did you even ask yourself what I would tell the kids when they wanted to know why you didn't come home? They didn't believe me when I said you were on one of your stupid overnights. I looked too upset."

Hal bit back a sharp reply. "Okay … I made a mistake. I get it, and I'm sorry. But considering what happened to me, maybe you could cut me a little slack?"

They stood across from each other, each in their private pain, until Hal couldn't stand it any longer. "I'm sorry," he said again, and this time when he held out his arms, she came into them, sobbing against his chest.

After a few minutes, they went into the family room and sat on the couch. He leaned forward, head in hands, and in a low voice told the story for the second time that day. The longer he talked, the more upset he got, working both of them into a frenzy.

"It's not fair!" she said. "They can't do that."

"Yes, they can." He stood and began pacing. "They did. Charlie White's a Machiavellian crook, and the rest of them are spineless wimps!" He gesticulated wildly. "If I meet them in a dark alley, I'll—"

"Hal, please. Don't talk like that. You're scaring me."

"Well, they'd only be getting what they deserve."

"What are you going to do?" Her voice wavered.

"I don't know." He stopped pacing and stared out the family room window. "I haven't had time to think about it."

"Are we going to be okay?" Kathy's right foot bounced rhythmically. "Financially, I mean?"

Hal returned to the couch and sighed. "Your salary will cover the basics. We've got enough savings to pay other expenses for the rest of this month and September."

Kathy moved close to him and ran her hand soothingly over his back. "I'm so sorry this happened, Hal. I can tell how awful you feel." She brightened optimistically. "But you're a resourceful guy. I'm sure you can get another job before long. And if we need to, you can sell some of your interest in Western Realty."

"What?" He pulled away and crossed his arms over his chest. "Why would I sell my interest? Western Realty is *my* company. *My* dream. *My* future!" He stared at Kathy through squinting eyes and a wrinkled brow. "You really don't get it, do you?" Without a backward look, he left the room, went upstairs, and collapsed on their bed.

Hal was awakened by the sound of voices downstairs. The kids were home from school. A few minutes later Kathy opened the bedroom door. "I've told them what happened. They want to talk to you."

"I'm not ready for that. Give me a chance to …"

She crossed her arms. "They need reassurance from you, Hal. Take a shower before you come down, though. You look pretty scary."

Hal rolled over and groaned. "Thanks a lot." But he felt much better standing under a hot shower, shaving, then brushing his teeth. *Almost a captain of industry*, he thought with sarcasm.

Kathy met him at the foot of the stairs. "They're waiting for you in the family room." She stepped back to let him pass, not wishing him luck or giving him an encouraging hug.

Thanks for the support, he thought as he stepped into the family room. He expected to see his children in their usual positions, slouched on the floor or in the beanbag chair they sat in when watching TV or playing video games. Instead, they were sitting in a row on the couch.

Nicole, fourteen and the oldest, had her arm around Derek on one side and Susie on the other. Her light-brown hair was pulled back in a ponytail, her posture straight like the gymnast she was. Derek, twelve, was dark like Hal and tall. He was at that awkward stage where he never knew how his voice was going to come out, a boy or a young man. Susie, ten, had curly hair and dimples, and an impish quality that reminded Hal of how Kathy used to be.

Hal had no idea what he would say to them. He gave the girls a hug and ruffled Derek's hair, then pulled up a chair. "You all know I lost my job last night," he began. He couldn't bring himself to say *fired*. "So you're going to be seeing a little more of me over the next few weeks while I decide what to do next." He smiled, aware that he'd delivered the message with a positive spin.

"How can you lose a job?" asked Susie.

"He means he got fired, doofus," Nicole said.

"Well, how can he get fired?" Susie demanded. "It's *his* company."

Hal managed a small laugh. "Good question. Have you ever been ganged up on at the playground? Well, that's kind of what happened to me. My partners brought a bully into the company, and he decided to run me off. So he's blamed me for some of the problems we've run into lately. He's a big guy. A very powerful guy. He scared my partners into siding with him instead of sticking up for me."

"What a bunch of wimps," Nicole said.

"My thoughts exactly. Anyway, they voted me out as president of the company."

"Are we going to be poor now?" Susie asked, frowning.

"Absolutely not. I'm still part owner of the company. Your mom's got her job, and we have some money in the bank. We may have to cut back a little, but life won't be that different."

"Really?" Derek's doubtful tone was a carbon copy of Kathy's.

Hal knelt. "Listen, you guys. People lose their jobs all the time. It's not the end of the world, okay? I'll take a few days off, then start job hunting. So go ahead and do your homework and play with your friends. And don't give it another thought. Okay?"

No one moved. Then Susie, of the bouncy curls, said, "Okay." She left the room, and the others followed.

That wasn't so bad, Hal thought as he watched the kids scatter.

Kathy wasn't in the kitchen, so he headed out through the garage to his auto shop—the "Garage Mahal" Kathy had christened it. He'd been so busy with Western Realty over the past few years that he hadn't spent much time working on the Caddy, but today it felt like the right place to be.

He did a slow perimeter walk around the old car, which he had found buried under a pile of hay in an abandoned barn on a property Western Realty had purchased. The car had been covered with dust and bird droppings. Mice and wasps had made nests in the air cleaner and other cavities of the body and frame. The tires and door seals were shot; the oil seals in the engine, transmission, and axles were dried up; the knobs on the dash were discolored and cracked. But the car had low miles and was actually in great shape for its age. Hal had speculated, based on a smashed-in front fender, that the original owner was getting too old to drive anymore. The car had probably been parked in the barn and simply forgotten.

He ran his hand over the hood, imagining how the coupe would look fully restored. Sleek. Elegant. Powerful. He felt a wave of excitement—the same excitement he felt as a boy when starting a restoration project with his father. He'd been twelve when his father first invited him to work on classic cars. To a young Hal, it was like being invited into a sacred space. His father was the priest, and he was the acolyte whose job was to hand over the requested tools. When he was finally allowed to do some work, he was so worried about doing it right that he made stupid mistakes and got an earful from his father.

Shame and feelings of inadequacy surfaced as Hal thought about his father. How would he ever tell him he'd been fired? His illustrious father had put himself through the University of Colorado, then worked his way up to executive V.P. of a medical supply company. When he retired wealthy, he went into state politics and held major political offices for the State of Colorado. His life was nothing short of an American success story. A lot to live up to.

As much as Hal wanted to put it off, he knew he had to tell his father—when they met on Saturday for breakfast, as they had for several years.

"Hey, Dad!" Nicole called, interrupting his thoughts. "Phone call. It's Janine." She handed him the satellite cordless.

He waited until she went back inside the house. "Janine?"

"I've been so worried about you, Hal. You okay?"

"Of course not. How could I be?" He immediately regretted his words. No reason to be rude to an ally—maybe the only one he had left at Western Realty. "How were things today?"

"Awful. I'm not sure everyone's happy about the vote last night. The board members were in the conference room this morning. I didn't hear what was said, but Charlie White did a lot of shouting."

"Janine, you don't believe I've done anything wrong, do you?"

"Of course not." She paused. "Hal, what are we going to do?"

That *we* lit a fire in him. It was wonderful to know someone understood ... and cared. "I don't know yet, Janine ... but your support means a lot to me."

"You know I'm on your side. If there's anything I can do, just

23

ask." She paused. "Anything."

All evening, Hal remembered the painful details of the previous night. Each memory brought anguish. And the more he thought about it, the angrier he got. How could so much have changed in just twenty-four hours?

Family life went on around him. He paced and muttered. The kids talked on the phone, did homework, played video games. Kathy cleaned the kitchen, got the two younger kids in bed, prepared for the next day's classes. It was late when she sent Nicole complaining to her room.

"What was that about?" Hal asked Kathy after Nicole was upstairs.

"We need to talk about how the kids are taking this."

"What's there to talk about? I told the kids what happened, and they took it pretty well. I was honest and matter-of-fact. I think Dr. Phil would have been pleased."

Kathy put her hands on her hips. "What planet do you live on? They came away from your little talk with some pretty serious questions."

"Well, they didn't tell me about them," Hal answered, mimicking Kathy's stance. "What are you talking about?"

"Nicole wants to know if she can continue with her gymnastics and ballet lessons. Derek is afraid we'll cancel our skiing vacation. And Susie ..." Kathy's voice trembled. "Susie wants to know if we'll still have her birthday party. They're scared, Hal."

Hal shook his head. "If they are, it's probably because you're upset and it's rubbing off on them ... besides, they've had it pretty easy. So things will be tight for a while. So what? They'll get through this, and it might even be good for them."

"They don't need you moralizing." Kathy stomped a foot.

"And I'm sure *you're* going to tell me what they *do* need."

She ignored his sarcasm. "You ... you've been gone so much with business that they hardly know you," she said. "Now that you're not going to the office, maybe you can make time for them after school and on weekends. Talk to them. Listen to them."

"Anything else, oh wise teacher?"

"I know you don't want to hear this," she took a step back, "but we have to get specific about how we're going to handle our finances. We're not in terrific shape, you know. My salary barely pays the mortgage. And we don't have enough in the bank to last more than a couple of months."

"Kathy, please!" Hal almost turned to flee the deteriorating conversation. "I'm *very* aware of our financial situation. Remember, I still own equity in the company. The partners can't take that away."

"But what good is that unless we can get at it?" she whined. "You already let me know you're not willing to sell your equity."

"It's not that simple." He tried to maintain his composure. "Western doesn't have enough cash flow at the moment. The money's tied up in properties." He laughed aloud. "That's just great, isn't it? We have all these assets, and we may not be able to pay the bills next month." He jabbed at the air with a fist.

"Actually, *I'm* the one who pays the bills!" Kathy snapped. "I've been saying for years we need to keep a budget, and we need to put money into savings. But you never listen to me."

"Oh, thanks for reminding me." He pointed at her. "Then maybe *you* should be the one to cancel the ski vacation and the country-club membership and cable TV and the kids' sports and music lessons. Oh, and how about trading in your expensive car for something more practical. And—"

"Calm down," Kathy whispered urgently. "The kids will hear you."

"So what if they do?" Deliberately raising his voice, he yelled, "Let them have a dose of reality. I got fired—and you don't care!"

Kathy shook her head in disbelief. "What's the matter with you, Hal? All I wanted is for us to make a plan of action, and you lose it."

"What's the matter with *me*?" He could barely contain himself. "This has been the hardest twenty-four hours of my life, and all you're doing is criticizing me. Would it kill you to give me some support for once?" He kicked a soccer ball that had been left on the floor. It flew across the family room and into the window, cracking the glass.

Kathy let out a cry, then clapped a hand over her mouth, her eyes wide. She whirled around, dashed up the stairs, and slammed their bedroom door behind her.

"That's right!" he shouted after her. "Shut yourself in the bedroom."

He prowled through the house, Kathy's expression haunting him. He came across the soccer ball and kicked it again. This time it bounced harmlessly off the beanbag chair. He dropped onto the sofa and pressed his hands to his temples. How could life have changed so abruptly? How had things gotten so far out of control?

After a while, his adrenaline abated, and the need for sleep overwhelmed him. He trudged up to the bedroom. Kathy was still awake in bed, but she didn't speak. She turned her back to him, and they clung to their edges of the bed.

As he slid from wakefulness into forgetfulness, Donald Millhouse invaded his thoughts. What had that old man said? Something about accepting reality and making choices? *I thought he was talking about being fired. I didn't know he was talking about my marriage.*

Chapter 4

Help Wanted

Hal Stratton woke to the sounds of his family getting ready for school. After the way he had acted last night, he was too embarrassed to face them. He pulled the covers over his head and pretended to be asleep. Still, he strained to hear what was going on. Susie pounded on the bathroom door, demanding that Nicole get out of the shower. Derek wanted to know where his favorite shirt was. Kathy was herding them all down to the kitchen, and going over their schedules while they ate breakfast.

At one point, their voices lowered. He couldn't make out what they were saying, but he knew it was about him. Soon after, he felt the presence of someone at the doorway. He held his breath and didn't move, until a slight noise told him that whoever it was had turned away.

He heard them leave in stages. Kathy first, to be at school early. Nicole a little later, called by a long honk. Derek and Susie after that, calling to their friends as they joined up at the corner bus stop.

Silence descended on the empty house. He'd never been alone in the house during the day. Not only the house but also the neighborhood felt empty. Men and women at their jobs. Children at their school desks. Only stay-at-home moms with preschool children were home. And one jobless man.

An emptiness flooded Hal, and an urge to get out. Go somewhere. He got up and wandered from room to room. He picked up Derek's Denver Broncos jersey from off the back of a chair. How long had it been since he'd watched a football game with his son, or a sports event of any kind? On the kitchen island was a note from Nicole's gymnastics coach. On the refrigerator, a photo of Susie at the horseback-riding rink.

The phone rang. Hal started to pick it up, but pulled back and looked at the caller ID. His parents. *Nope, not ready to deal with them yet.* Breakfast tomorrow with his father would be soon enough. For a moment, he wished Kathy would call them and blurt out the news. Of course, she wouldn't. Besides, he wanted to make sure his father realized how unexpected and devastating the board meeting had been.

But that was tomorrow. What would he do today? He needed to clean out his office at Western. No way. Put that one off a few more days. No business secrets in his computer or anything embarrassing in his files.

Then the thought struck him. Someone had probably been in his office, rifling through his things. The idea infuriated him. He picked up the phone and punched the number, tapping his toe impatiently. When Janine answered, he asked abruptly, "Has anyone been in my office?"

"No," she answered.

"How can you be sure?"

She chuckled softly. "Because I locked the door."

He laughed with relief. "I don't know what I would do without you, Janine. You're the best."

"Thanks." Her voice lowered. "But if any of them asks for the key, I'll have to give it to them. There are files in there they have a right to."

"Not to my personal things, though. Stall them until next week. I'll be in then to get my things."

"I'll be waiting. Take care, boss."

Feeling better, Hal headed to the Garage Mahal and his Caddy. He'd always said he would start renovating it when he had time.

Now he had plenty. But once inside the garage, he couldn't get motivated. He sat on a stool and stared at the car, rehashing the board meeting, worrying about his relationship with Kathy, and wondering what to say to his father.

Around lunchtime, he went into the kitchen to make a sandwich. The Help Wanted section of the newspaper was placed prominently on the center island. He'd not paid attention to it before. "What's this?" he asked aloud, then shook his head. Kathy didn't understand who he was, nor what he'd accomplished. Did she really think he would find a job in the paper?

He wadded the paper into a ball and tossed it onto the kitchen desk where she prepared lessons and managed the family finances. He grabbed his keys and drove to an automotive shop to buy the special tools and parts he needed to restore the vintage Caddy.

With perverse pleasure, Hal picked out bearings, seals, and gaskets; multi-coat, antique-white paint; a paint gun and all the accessories he wanted. The total on the bill was staggering, but he handed over the charge card without a second thought.

Hal spent the rest of the afternoon in the Garage Mahal, until he heard the garage door going up. Kathy was home. *Oh, no.* He remembered his petulant handling of the Help Wanted section.

He set down a tool and hurried into the house, hoping to retrieve the paper before she found it on her desk. He got there just in time to see her face change. "Sorry," he apologized. "I didn't mean for you to see that."

"Of course you did." She stared at him harshly, then turned away.

"Okay, if that's how you want it!" he muttered and went back to the shop.

When Susie called that dinner was ready, Hal told her they should eat without him. He didn't want to interrupt the work of getting the car ready to pull the engine and transmission. He crawled into bed long after Kathy and the kids were asleep.

Chapter 5

Breakfast with Dad

H al glanced at the bedside clock: 7:05 on Saturday morning—three days after the disastrous board meeting. Kathy was still asleep. He crawled out of bed, careful not to disturb her. "I won't upset you if you won't upset me" seemed a good living arrangement.

Moving quietly, he shaved, showered, and dressed. Then he sneaked downstairs and past the family room where Susie and Derek were in their pajamas watching cartoons. Susie spotted him and jumped up to give him a hug. "Are you going to tell Grandpa you got fired?" she asked.

"Yes, I am."

Her smile brought out her dimples. "It's okay, Daddy. I still love you," she said, patting his back.

"Thanks, sweetie." Hal put her down and turned quickly for the garage so his daughter wouldn't see his moist eyes.

He was in his pickup by 7:35, just enough time to make it to the restaurant by 8:00. These father-son Saturday morning breakfasts at the Wellshire Inn had been a tradition for four or five years now, but never had Hal dreaded an encounter like he did this morning. And the string of red lights only intensified the anxiety he'd been trying to ignore.

Hal noticed an empty space next to his father's Cadillac Escalade. What a contrast, his father's luxury SUV and his fully restored 1950 Chevy 3100 pickup with a fuel injected V-8 engine and automatic transmission. He smiled, thinking how often people "oohed" and "aahed" over his pickup, ignoring the Escalade right next to it.

"Here goes nothing," he muttered as he locked the truck. It was no secret that his father did not approve of his career choice. Buying property only to watch it appreciate did not constitute real work in John Stratton's mind. Nevertheless, Hal valued his father's business savvy and sought his advice on key decisions. In truth, these consultations had an ulterior motive. Not only did he want his father's advice, he wanted his father to be proud of him and see him as a good businessman.

That's the part that troubled Hal most. Just a couple of weeks ago his father had told him he was guilty of "brinksmanship" in his business. Hal brushed it off. *He doesn't understand deal-making.* But he knew the issue would come up again—no doubt today.

Hal entered the restaurant and headed to the back. His father was in their usual booth. A handsome man, white hair, startling blue eyes, and a trim build. The epitome of power and success.

"There you are," his father said as Hal approached. He rose and shook his son's hand. Hal thought it a rather formal custom for a father and son, but they'd been doing it for years.

"Hi, Dad. Sorry I'm late. Have you ordered?" Hal avoided eye contact.

"Nope. Waiting for you." John Stratton motioned the waitress, who immediately came over.

"The usual?" she asked.

John smiled at her. "Of course, Rose." He always ordered an omelet with ham, an English muffin, and a small tomato juice. Hal's staple was a bowl of oatmeal with wheat toast and orange juice. Not his favorite breakfast. He'd started the habit after his physician chastised him for a lifestyle with too much stress and a diet of too much salt and saturated fat.

"You look tired."

"I haven't been sleeping well." Hal cleared his throat. "I'm

31

afraid I've got some bad news."

John cocked his head. "The family okay?"

"They're fine." Hal picked up his napkin and carefully unfolded it. His hands were trembling. "It's Western. We had our monthly board meeting last Wednesday night. They voted to … to …" he finally blurted it out "… to remove me as president."

John Stratton's jaw dropped. "You've got to be putting me on. What happened?"

Hal shifted uneasily in his chair. "Charlie White happened. I told you about all our run-ins since he came onto the board."

"Yeah, so what happened?"

"Well, they were just a warm up. Wednesday night he mounted a full frontal assault." Hal scanned his father's face for even a hint of sympathy. "He always wanted me out," Hal continued earnestly.

John Stratton shook his head, and Hal could only imagine what he was thinking.

Intensity rising, Hal recounted the story of the meeting. "I was set up!" he insisted. "Charlie got the other board members on his side before the meeting even began. He challenged my decisions and continually interrupted every time I tried explaining my plans." Beads of sweat formed on his brow. "Charlie insisted the company was in serious trouble and I was to blame!"

John raised an eyebrow, suggesting that Hal lower his voice. Others were sitting nearby.

Hal leaned over the table. "The worst part is, he accused me of pocketing the company's money. Me! It's one thing to question my decisions. But stealing? I've never been so insulted in all my life."

"Here you go," the waitress said brightly and placed their plates on the table. When she saw their expressions, she beat a hasty retreat.

John shoved his plate aside. "Did I hear you correctly?" His tone was disapproving. "You've been *fired* for poor management and accused of *embezzlement*?"

"Not directly." Hal couldn't meet his father's eyes. "But I guess that's what it comes down to."

"How'd you ever let things get this bad?"

"I didn't." He spit the words out of his mouth. "That's the

thing. None of it is true."

John shook his head. "There has to be some reason for White to go after you this way."

"Why do you say that?" Hal's voice was tight and his face strained.

"Because you don't lose the support of your entire board overnight. This had to be going on for some time. At least since you brought White on board. Maybe even longer."

"Thanks, Dad. That's really supportive."

"I have to say it like I see it."

"You make it sound like there was a conspiracy to bring Charlie on board and use him to get rid of me." Hal looked at his father defiantly. "I don't buy it. My partners and I had a great relationship. Never once did any of them come to me to complain about how I managed the company. Never!"

John sat back, lips pursed. "Okay. But the point is, these things don't just come out of nowhere. Whether White played on your partners' misgivings or planted the seeds himself, I don't know. But *something* had to be going on."

"Well, I didn't see it."

"How can you plead total ignorance? You were president of the company, for crying out loud. It's your job to have your eyes open."

Hal clenched his fists under the table. "My eyes *were* open. I had no reason to doubt anyone's loyalty. There … were … no … signs."

"But why would you even call for a vote? Good grief, Hal. That was an incredibly reckless move on your part. You set yourself up."

"I was calling Charlie's bluff. I thought that when push came to shove, my partners would take my side."

John leaned forward and spoke in a low but authoritative voice. "There's your problem. You underestimated your opponent. I've seen lots of Charlie Whites in my day. They're cold-blooded. They know what they want, and they'll do anything to get it. If you're going to go up against them, you have to play by the same rules. You were naïve. You stepped right into his trap."

33

"I know. I know." Hal's mouth was dry. He took a gulp of water. "Charlie's more than cold-blooded, though. He's *crooked*. He had it out for me because he wants to control the company. It was an unabashed power grab."

"Why do you say that?" John frowned and shook his head. "Charlie White has lots of business interests, most of them bigger and more important than Western Realty. Why would he want to run your company?" John paused. "Maybe he just wanted you out of there."

The words stung. Why couldn't his father take his side? Give him a little support?

"I've done a great job running this company. I've turned it into a major real-estate business in only seven years. Why would anyone push me out with my track record?"

"The stakes are high, Hal. You're playing with *their* money."

"I'm not *playing*—"

"Okay. But you're taking *risks* with their money. They may have felt your gambles would cost them. I myself have thought you could be guilty of—"

"Brinksmanship? Yes, I know," Hal said loudly, not caring who was listening.

John crossed his arms. "What are you trying to prove anyway?"

"Prove?" He stood abruptly. "So this is the support I get from the great John Stratton." He tossed a ten-dollar bill on the table, next to his uneaten food, and hurried to the front door. His father called after him, but he didn't look back.

Seething, Hal pulled out of the parking space, squealing rubber, and sped past the front doors of the restaurant, ignoring his father's urgent wave. He roared south on Colorado Boulevard, then west on Highway 285. Heedless of traffic, he spewed out everything he not said to his father's face.

He drove sixty minutes, up into the canyon, approaching Bailey. He took an exit and pulled onto a side road, turned off the engine, and sat with his head on the steering wheel. Not only did he have to deal with being fired, he had to endure Kathy's displeasure … and now his father's criticism.

After several minutes, Hal looked at his watch. Kathy would be wondering where he was. He turned on his cell phone and saw three new messages. The first two from his father, both since he left the restaurant. He deleted them without listening.

The third was from Kathy. Nicole was spending the day at the mall with a friend; Derek and Susie had been invited to a water park. "I'll be gone most of the day, too," she said. "I saw the bill for the parts you bought yesterday. If you can spend money on that old beater, guess I can get the works at the spa."

He turned off the cell phone and threw it onto the seat. "Forget the lot of you!" he muttered. How had he been so naïve as to think his family would rally around him when he needed them? The only ones who'd expressed any *real* understanding were Janine and the old man in the mountains.

The thought of Donald Millhouse brought up a memory of his words. "I've been there, Hal. It was after many years of suffering that I finally understood I'd created my own misery."

Scratch you, Hal thought with disgust.

That left Janine. At least he could count on her.

Chapter 6

The Return Visit

Agitated and distraught, Hal slept fitfully over the next several nights. He would toss and turn and eventually get up to pace or turn on the television. Like a broken tape, his mind replayed the events of the board meeting. Exhausted and even more distressed, he would crawl into bed and fall asleep in the wee hours of the morning.

When he woke, the house would be again empty, the kids and Kathy off to their various schools. He'd make a simple breakfast, then go to his shop, where he'd sit on a stool and stare into space for a good part of the morning. The urgency to look for a new job nettled at him continually. But not yet. He needed to come to terms with being fired—but how?

On Wednesday, one week after being fired, Hal woke before the rest of the family. He had to go back to the office to gather his belongings and wrap up a few loose ends. He took his time getting ready so he'd look sharp and in control when he came face-to-face with the other board members.

Other than looking tired, he was pleased with what he saw when he checked himself in the mirror. He had dressed in khakis and a burgundy silk tee, topped with a tasteful plaid sports jacket in dark blue, light blue, and burgundy. Italian slip-ons finished the look. He noted with grim amusement that the outfit looked much like the kind of business casual his father often wore.

His father. The elder Stratton had called several times since Saturday, leaving messages on Hal's cell phone, and asking whoever answered the family phone to put Hal on. Hal had refused to take the calls. Kathy said John wanted to apologize, but Hal knew the kind of apology he would get from his father. *Sorry I upset you, son. But I'm worried about the way you're (blah, blah, blah). Your mother, too. I don't think you realize that you affect others when you (blah, blah, blah). We only want the best for you (blah, blah, blah), and if you'll just do it our way, you'll be so much better off!*

Well, John Stratton could shove his apology!

After one last look in the mirror, Hal went downstairs to eat a quick bowl of cereal before leaving. The more he thought about it, the better he felt about going to the office this morning. It was his way of saying he wasn't going to disappear quietly or let Charlie White's unfounded accusation linger in the air like a bad smell. Hal would push for that outside audit—the sooner, the better. Charlie White would soon be eating crow.

One other thing—Hal wouldn't help them wrap up loose business ends. *Let them find out what running Western is like.* Some of the people who did business with Western had worked only with him, and they wouldn't be pleased with his absence. He had the inside information and a rich network of personal and professional connections. Too bad. The board had made its decision, and they could live with its consequences.

He was rinsing the cereal bowl when Kathy came into the kitchen and gave him an appraising glance. "I take it you're going to the office?"

"About time, don't you think?"

To his surprise, Kathy stood on her tiptoes and kissed his cheek, lingering for a moment with her hand on his shoulder. "Good luck," she whispered affectionately.

Hal hugged her, breathing in the scent of her freshly shampooed hair. "Thanks. Kathy, I'm really ..."

She put her finger over his lips and smiled faintly. "I probably worry too much about the finances. Maybe we can talk about it tonight?"

"Maybe." He knew she was thinking of the twenty-four month, no-payment, no-interest option on her SUV, which was soon coming due. He'd expected that a commission on a piece of property would pay the whole amount. Not now.

Hal didn't like admitting it, but he was nervous when he started for the office. He'd made the drive six times a week over the past seven years—in rain, shine, or snow. The office was his second home, the place where he'd felt most truly himself. Only now, it had an entirely different feel. He was going into hostile territory.

He pulled into the parking lot and remembered the February day when he'd been the only one to brave the treacherous winter roads in a blizzard. He'd loved the solitary work and planning time that day in the office alone, the deep quiet with only an occasional ring of the phone and the sound of air blowing through the heating vent. The blanket of snow had muffled all sounds outside, and the silence deepened. He'd spent long minutes looking out the window at thick flakes piling onto the trees, the bushes, and the top of his Chevy. He'd actually been glad when he realized he was snowed in. He'd slept on the sofa in his large office, using his coat as a blanket.

Last Wednesday evoked the opposite mood. He'd prepared his presentation on the computer at home, and taken the disk to Kinko's for printing so no one would see the plan before he passed it out. Now he laughed at his secretive preparation. A lot of good it had done.

With a sigh, Hal picked up his briefcase and the flattened boxes he'd purchased at U-Haul a couple of days ago. What kind of greeting was he going to get?

"Hal!" Janine dashed around her desk with her arms open.

Hal set down the boxes and tightened his arms around her, faintly surprised by the attraction he felt. They'd carried on a light flirtation for years, but this was entirely different.

Janine stepped back, her cheeks flushed. She smoothed back an errant lock. "Sorry about that, boss. Just so glad to see you."

"The feeling's mutual." He looked toward the closed door of his office. "Has anyone asked to get into my files?"

Janine ducked her head with embarrassment. "Keith and Patricia, on Monday." She was close to tears. "I'm so sorry, Hal."

Though steamed, Hal knew the board had every right to the files. He controlled his voice. "It's okay, Janine. It's not your fault. None of this is."

"There's something else," she whispered. "Larry and Keith are both here. Keith told me to let them know the minute you came in ... and that I'm not to let you into your office unaccompanied."

He smirked. "Then you come with me."

She chuckled. "That's not what they meant, Hal. I wish I didn't have to, but ..."

"Do what you have to, Janine," he said flatly. "I understand. But I'm letting myself in."

He unlocked the door and walked into the stale air of the unused office. It wasn't really *his* office. It was the managing partner's office—and he wasn't the managing partner anymore. He briefly wondered who would be taking over that position. Not Charlie. He could control the company without taking on the job. Keith knew the business, but he lacked the persuasiveness necessary to influence people and close deals. Patricia was too unimaginative and prone to be bossy when she really intended to be assertive. Larry was the best choice, but he was far too conservative. The company would probably go backward under his leadership.

Hal turned on the computer and started assembling boxes. He was still a board member—at least until they bought him out. *If* they bought him out. He had every right to an office in the building and briefly considered moving his things into the small, unused office at the end of the hall. But the partners had made it clear they didn't want or need him.

He heard a noise behind him and turned to see Keith standing in the doorway. "What do you want?" Hal asked brusquely.

Keith rubbed his forehead. "I, uh ... I'm here to make sure you don't remove any files important to the business—for your protection and ours."

Hal stared at him. "You surprise me, Keith. We've known each other for years, but apparently that doesn't mean anything to you. May I remind you, I still own twenty percent of this company. Doing anything that would hurt it would be tantamount to shooting myself in the foot."

"Sorry, but I think it's best I stay. You haven't always been forthcoming with information."

"What are you talking about?"

Keith flushed. "Don't pretend you don't know. You love being the wheeler-dealer. You were always developing projects, then dropping them in our laps, expecting us to be grateful. Do you have any idea how much we hated it when you did that?"

Hal replied with insulting slowness. "Developing … projects … was … my … job. And don't you dare insult me by saying you don't trust me to gather my personal belongings."

Keith backed off a few steps. "Gather all you want, but I'm staying right here."

Seething, Hal cleared his desk and the bookshelves of his personal items, logged onto his computer, and put a memory stick into a USB port.

"Hold on!" Keith spoke in an uncharacteristically bold tone. "You can't do that. Electronic files are the property of the company."

"I have some personal files in this computer. Unless you think my love notes to my wife are crucial to the business."

Keith stepped back. "Go ahead, but I'll be watching."

Hal copied his files onto his memory drive, with Keith hovering behind him. When finished, he removed the stick from the port and put it in his briefcase. "I'm done here. Why don't we take a little walk down the hall?"

Hal entered Larry's office without knocking, Keith bobbing along in his wake.

Startled, Larry jumped up from behind his desk. "Hal! What are you doing here?"

"Taking care of business." Hal looked from Larry to Keith and back again. "Which one of you ten-pound weaklings decided I should be treated like a crook? The way you're acting, you'd think

I came to steal the silverware." He leaned over Larry's desk. "What in the world happened, Larry? You owe me an explanation."

Larry bristled. "You can't pretend you didn't get fair warning that things were going to change. We kept trying to get it through your thick head that we were concerned about the direction you were taking us. We told you straight out we didn't want to acquire any properties in the southwest part of the city, but you bullied us into giving you our support. And how about the money you sank into the McFee Ranch? That's expensive property that could set idle for a long time."

"Hah!" Hal scoffed. "I was prepared to give you the facts and figures supporting that purchase at the board meeting, but the great White shark kept interrupting." Hal held up his hand, to prevent Larry's response. "Yes, we might need to hold onto it four or five years, but at some point the price *will* go up, and we'll all be very rich. When you can pay for your daughter's Ivy League education out of pocket, you'll be thanking me for my foresight."

"Well," stammered Larry. "That's not how people around here see it. It's unwelcome debt that could strangle the life out of this company." Larry shook his head. "We started out here as a group of friends, Hal, but you squandered that friendship with your high-handed manner."

"That may be how *you* remember it, *old friend*, but I never heard any of you express serious concerns or question any of my decisions until you brought in Charlie White." Hal stepped closer to Larry. "He bamboozled all of you into thinking I was doing a poor job of running the company. The board meeting was nothing more than a power play, and none of you stood up to him. You threw me overboard just to please him."

Larry flushed. "You threw *yourself* overboard, *old friend*. You've acted like an ass ever since White showed up. And your habit of buying high-risk properties put the company in jeopardy."

Hal could scarcely believe what Larry was saying. "What about Charlie's accusation that I've been skimming?"

"We didn't know anything about that," Larry confessed, his anger giving way to unease.

"Maybe not," Hal chided, "but you let the accusation stand. By now, half the business community in Denver has heard about what happened." Hal paused as the truth of what he'd just said hit him. "You three could have stood up for me against White—but you didn't. And now my reputation is ruined. No matter that the audit will exonerate me completely."

Hal gave Larry and Keith a last scathing look, then left abruptly. No time for a rebuttal. There *was* no rebuttal. Once a reputation was ruined, even unjustified, it was ruined. Gossip about personal disasters spread quickly. The truth spread slowly, and doubt always lingered.

Hal headed back to his office for the boxes. Donna Chilstrom, whom he'd hired several years earlier as a bookkeeper, hailed him. "Hal? Hey, do you have a minute? Martha and Quentin are in my office. We'd like to talk to you if—"

"Hi, Donna. Sorry, but not now. It's not a good time." He felt guilty, but turned and walked away. He had to get out of the building, now.

He stacked his boxes on a dolly as quickly as possible. After transferring them to the pickup, he returned the dolly to the janitor's closet, then made a last stop in his office to make sure he hadn't left anything behind.

He was about to leave when he noticed the message light blinking on his phone. Curious, he picked it up. His father. He and Hal's mother, Virginia, would be *glad* to float Hal and Kathy a no-interest loan to cover the SUV payment and any other expenses.

Hal grabbed his briefcase furiously and stormed out of the office, slamming the door behind him. He ignored Janine, who stood when he walked through the lobby and out the front door into a bleak future.

Chapter 7

Resistance

Hal stood in his driveway staring at the boxes in the bed of his pickup. Tangible evidence of the end of his tenure at Western Realty. It was then he became aware that he'd been hoping, somewhere in the back of his mind, that his partners would have had a change of heart. Without Charlie around, maybe they would have been glad to see him. Even own up to their mistake. *Such an idiot to expect anything from them,* he thought.

Unable to muster a particle of energy, Hal went inside and downstairs to the rec room and lay on the couch. A couple of hours later, he woke to the sounds of the kids and Kathy in the kitchen. Groggily, he sat up, garnered his faculties, and made his way up the stairs and out to the driveway.

He hefted a couple of the boxes and carried them to the basement storage room. They were heavy, and the physical exertion got his heart pumping and blood flowing. It felt good to be doing something. *Anything.*

Moving too quickly on the last trip down, he missed the bottom step and landed hard on the basement floor, sending two boxes flying. He got up in a rage and kicked a half-full box, creating a bigger mess.

"Hal?" Kathy clattered down the stairs, eyes wide. "What's

43

going on? Are you okay? Can I give you a hand?"

"No!" He picked up the loose papers and tossed them willy-nilly back into the open boxes. Kathy heaved an audible sigh and went back upstairs.

After the boxes were stacked, Hal started up the stairs. Kathy stood at the top, her arms folded, tears in her eyes. Red blotched her cheeks. "I know this is terrible for you, Hal, but it's hard on me and the kids, too. We need you to—"

He stopped. "What? Pretend everything's fine? Like whatever I'm going through is okay as long as I shut up and don't let it affect you or the kids?"

"No, Hal." She hesitated. "But you're treating me like I'm your enemy. Half the time you bark at me. The other half you don't talk to me. I can't live this way."

"So you call my father and tell him I can't take care of my family? Thanks a lot."

"I—"

"I know all about it. He called while I was moving out of my office."

"I'm just trying to avoid getting into a bigger mess." She took a deep breath. "And you don't seem to care."

Hal leaned against the stairway wall. "What do you want from me, Kathy?"

Her look was stern. "I want you to stop acting like a baby. Grow up, Hal. And stop feeling sorry for yourself. You aren't the first person to lose his job, and you won't be the last."

"Grow up?" He could hardly believe it. "Stop feeling sorry for myself? You don't have a clue what's happened to me, Kathy," he added bitterly, "and apparently you have no interest in finding out." He charged up the stairs, brushing by her without a word. He backed out of the driveway too quickly, grinding gears, and took off down the road.

Late afternoon, Hal parked near a mountain creek, got out, and sat on a rock. He closed his eyes and focused on the soothing babble of the water. The sun warmed his face. Gradually, his breathing deepened and his shoulders relaxed.

He thought of staying the night in the mountains, but that would only make things worse. Still, he wasn't ready to go back home. He laughed aloud. There was someplace he could go. Donald Millhouse. He remembered the safety and acceptance he'd felt there, and suddenly he longed to experience it again. He didn't have the piece of paper with Donald's phone number, but he had an idea of the general direction. He was sure he could find the road again.

It took over an hour and several wrong turns, but Hal finally found the dirt road and, shortly thereafter, the fork in the road that led to Donald's cabin. On a fence post to the right was the mailbox with Millhouse handwritten unevenly in black letters. He drove up the single-lane road, surprised at his mounting excitement. But when he pulled to a stop in front of the cabin, he realized his hands were damp with nervous sweat. What if Donald wasn't here? What if he *was* here, but wasn't as accepting and easygoing as Hal remembered?

He was about to back out when Donald appeared on the porch, smiled, and waved. "Hal! Good to see you."

Hal climbed the steps self-consciously. "Came back for more of your coffee," he quipped.

Donald laughed and held the door open wide. He then filled two cups, and they settled into the large recliners in the great room.

As Hal sipped, he looked at the plaque on the fireplace mantel. "What's this *Hero's Choice* thing?" he asked.

Donald looked up and then back at Hal. "It means being willing to be responsible for ourselves, no matter what the situation. Accepting reality for what it is and seeing that we always have choices about how to respond."

"So why the *hero's* choice?"

"Because I've realized that the real heroes in life are people who are able to react to difficult situations in positive ways. It means giving up the impulse to act out our hurt and anger or fear in favor of choices consistent with our higher vision, what we really want for our life in the long run."

"Not as easy as it sounds," said Hal.

"Never said it was. In fact, it takes great courage. Private courage. The kind that comes from deep inside and isn't usually visible to others." Donald smiled wistfully. "You've only been here a few minutes, and I've already gone philosophical on you. Sorry."

"I asked. You answered." How strange that he felt more at home here than in his own house. "I guess that's what you were trying to tell me the other morning when I bailed out on you."

"Yup." Donald nodded.

"I can't say I've done very well since last week." He looked down, massaging the back of his neck. "In fact, just the opposite."

"I've been wondering about you," said Donald. "What's going on?"

With the pressured release of a clogged drain, Hal told Donald about the events since they'd last met. His agitation and inability to sleep. His encounter with his father and the return visit to the office earlier that day. He even told him about Kathy's "grow up" remark.

Donald listened intently. No judgment. No quick fixes. He encouraged Hal to share all his thoughts and feelings—the anger, blame, self-pity, powerlessness—until Hal ran out of steam. His voice lost its edge, and he began to speak in a calmer and quieter tone.

He looked at Donald sheepishly. "Why are you so willing to listen to me? We hardly know each other, and all I've done is dump on you. My own mother wouldn't listen the way you have. She'd tell me to stop whining and get a grip."

"Would that help?" Donald asked, his lips upturned and eyes sparkling.

"Not really."

"I may have something to offer that would."

Hal shook his head, not even trying to disguise his skepticism.

"I can see that even the mention of that puts you off. Can't say I blame you. I'd be a little cynical myself if I were up on a mountain at night with a crazy old coot."

Hal chuckled at Donald's self-reference.

Donald put his cup down and walked over to the fireplace. He looked pensively at the plaque and the photo of the woman and two children. "I wouldn't be here today if someone hadn't extended a hand when I needed help most." He turned back toward Hal, his eyes moist. "When I got back on my feet, I made a commitment I'd extend a hand to others."

"Paying it forward," said Hal.

Donald nodded. "Yes. And more than that. It's a calling, if you will. My purpose in life."

"Do it a lot?"

"Only when I have a feeling about someone. People at a cusp, at a point of choice. People who have the grit and courage to make big changes."

"I'm not at a cusp." Hal snickered. "It's more like I'm out on a limb, and somebody's sawing through it."

Donald laughed. "What are you going to do when the limb breaks? Will you be willing to call for help?"

"Guess that's what you're looking for? Someone who wants help?"

"That and someone who's willing to commit to the work." His eyes were locked on Hal. "Think you're up to it?"

Hal knew Donald wasn't trying to force him. It was an honest question. "What do I have to do?"

Donald walked back to his chair. "Make four commitments," he said matter-of-factly.

Hal's tone was guarded. "What sort of commitments?"

"Don't worry. I'm not going to ask you to sign over your life or give me your fortune," joked Donald. "The first commitment is to be honest with yourself. I can't help you if you aren't willing to look in the mirror and tell the whole truth about what you see—the good, the bad, and the ugly."

"That's a pretty tall order."

"But necessary. Without that, the rest of the commitments are meaningless."

Hal shifted nervously in his chair. "What's the next one?"

"The second commitment is to be accountable. You've got to give up blame and excuses. You have to see how you—and not circumstances, events, or other people—have created your difficulties."

"So what you're saying is everyone else gets off the hook, but I need therapy. Is that it?"

Donald chuckled. "Not at all, my friend. But the truth is you won't move forward until you're willing to trade stoking your anger and wallowing in self-pity for a willingness to be accountable."

Hal looked at the floor. "It's hard to know what that means." His curiosity was aroused. "So what's the next commitment?"

"The third commitment has to do with responsibility, being willing to choose a new path. If you don't like what's happening, you have to consciously make new choices about how to think, feel, and act."

"You make it sound so easy," protested Hal. "You can decide you're never going to do something again. Then you get in a situation and *bang*! Before you know it, you're right where you said you'd never be."

Donald was nodding. "Yep. That's what happens when we're trying to change a behavior pattern. But if you keep at it, you start to see a gap, a space where you can choose instead of react."

Hal looked around the great room. "Okay. What's the fourth commitment? Being willing to give up meat, sex, and booze?"

A gentle smile curled on Donald's lips. "The fourth commitment is the hardest for most people. It's to persist and have the patience to hang in there long enough to make steady progress. Change doesn't happen overnight."

Hal sat quietly, thinking about the four commitments and the magnitude of what Donald was asking. He blew out a long breath. Did he really want to be here? Or should he get out before he was in too deep?

But an instinct had drawn him here, the way it often drew him to the mountains. And now Donald Millhouse had put him on the spot. The four commitments made sense, theoretically. But living them?

"You don't ask much from a guy, do you? At least you don't require a pledge of undying allegiance."

"Only to your best self." Donald spoke positively. "So what do you think, Hal? Are you willing to live by these four commitments?"

"I don't know. You're asking a lot."

"Yes, I am. But what will happen if you don't? If you keep going down the path you're on now?"

A memory of Kathy's tear-stained face flashed through Hal's mind. He felt a pang of remorse, thinking of his kids at home, probably getting ready for bed by now, wondering about the whereabouts of their father. And he saw an image of himself working away on his car, alone and bitter, alienated from everyone in the world.

He looked at Donald, a kind man, offering him … a chance. "Okay. I'm willing to try."

Donald's laughter filled the room. He picked up a small pewter lighthouse from a nearby end table and placed it on the arm of Hal's chair. "I'm going to ask you to do something," he said. "I want you to *try* to pick up this lighthouse."

Hal reached for the lighthouse, but pulled back, a grin on his face. "You almost caught me, Donald. I know what you're up to. You're doing that bit from *Star Wars* where Yoda tells Luke Skywalker: 'Do or not do. There is no try.'"

"You got me," Donald said. "What Yoda wanted Skywalker to see was that when we say, 'I'll try,' it's like we're giving ourselves a ready-made excuse for not doing what we're agreeing to do. It's talking out both sides of our mouths. Commitment doesn't mean you won't have setbacks, make mistakes, and even fail sometimes. It *does* mean that you are honest in your intention to do everything possible to achieve a certain outcome."

"This isn't just a pleasant little conversation, is it?" Hal said pensively.

"No," Donald said. "Now, Hal, are you willing to take on those four commitments? And hold to them no matter what life throws at you?"

Despite apprehension, Hal nodded. "I am. But you can't help me get back what I want most right now, my position as president of Western Realty."

"True. But this is much bigger than Western Realty. It's

western *reality*, if you will."

Hal frowned, not understanding Donald's play on words. "What do you mean, western *reality*?"

"That's what we're dealing with here, Hal. Reality—the way things are, regardless of how you feel about them or want them to be. Reality is what's going on between you and your partners right now. Reality is that you are no longer president of the company, and your partners don't want you back." Donald leaned forward in his chair. "The question is, how are you going to deal with this reality?"

In spite of the four commitments, Hal felt like a bucket of ice water had been thrown in his face. "How am I *supposed* to deal with it!" he snapped. "Anyone in my shoes would be angry."

"I'm not minimizing what happened to you." Donald studied Hal. "But you have to make some choices here. Long-term, how do you want to deal with it? What meaning will you give it? How will you let it influence your future?" Donald's eyes were resolute. "Only *you* can decide these things. Most people don't even know they have choices, so they end up reacting in destructive ways." Donald sat back silently, resting his elbows on the arms of his chair and lightly touching the tips of the fingers of both hands together.

Hal could see that the older man was well aware of the impact of his words and was letting them settle in. "You're telling me I can *decide* how to react to this event, right? But to be honest, and you've asked me to be honest, I'm not sure I'm ready. Even though that's what you're trying to get me to do."

"I'm not trying to *get* you to do anything, Hal." Donald's words were emphatic. "This is *your* life, not mine. These are *your* choices. Your decisions are for you, not me. But I am trying to help you clearly see what's happening and accept that the choices you make now have far-reaching consequences."

Hal couldn't sit still. He stood and began pacing. "The truth is, Donald, I'm really pissed off. Those jerks completely screwed me over. I don't know if I can let that go—at least not until they acknowledge they were wrong." He stopped pacing to face Donald, square on.

Donald stood. "What will happen if you can't, or won't, let it go?"

"I don't know. But letting this go is like saying it doesn't matter, that it's no big deal. Well, it *does* matter. I put too much of my heart and soul into building that company to pretend it doesn't." He shook his head. "I can't do that."

"I *don't* want you to pretend it doesn't matter, Hal. But I *do* want you to see your part in what's happening."

Hal stared at Donald, shaking his head. "You've got it all wrong. I didn't want this to happen ... and I'm sure not going to forgive my partners and act like everything is all right. No way."

Donald walked to an end table and pulled a sheet of photocopied paper out of a drawer and handed it to him. "I made this up some years ago, based on my own experiences."

Hal took the paper and looked at the heading: THE THREE R'S. On top of the Four Commitments? He shook his head. This was simply too much.

Donald's look was soft. "Take it home. When you're ready, pull it out. Maybe it will be helpful."

Disappointed, Hal climbed into his pickup. He'd hoped to get some practical advice from the old man. No such luck. This concept of choices was too simplistic. It certainly wouldn't help him get his job back. Hal crumpled Donald's paper into his jacket pocket.

Too bad there are no real-life Yodas.

Chapter 8

Missing in Action

Kathy Stratton poured macaroni from a box into a pot of boiling water. Kraft mac and cheese with cut-up wieners, along with a fresh salad, which she insisted the kids eat, was a somewhat balanced meal. She turned down the heat on the gas stove and leaned against the counter, weary with guilt, worry, and anger. Hal was doing his disappearing act again. But then, she'd handled the confrontation on the stairs poorly by saying some pretty cutting things.

So much had changed since last Wednesday. She had always known Hal to be supremely confident, full of ideas, always looking toward the future. To him, life was a great adventure. That was part of what had drawn her to him when they first met, despite her need for a less exciting future and more secure present. Whatever happened at that board meeting had cut to the very heart of who Hal believed he was. His eagerness to meet the days and see what he could discover or create had been replaced by a dark cloud of anger, self-pity, and blame. And the cloud that followed him poisoned the air within the four walls of their home.

"Mom! The macaroni's boiling over!"

Susie's voice jolted Kathy into awareness. She reacted without thought, jerking the pot off the burner, sloshing water onto the stovetop. Seconds from breaking into sobs, she shook her head when Susie offered to clean up the mess. "I'll take care of it. You go see if your dad's come back and snuck into his shop." The moment Susie turned to go on the futile errand—Kathy knew Hal wasn't home—she grabbed a kitchen towel to muffle her anguished cries.

Susie returned with an impish grin and a light in her eyes. In an exaggerated motion, she placed her hands on her hips and said in her best *Gone with the Wind* Southern accent, "What*evah* are we goin' ta do wit dat man?"

Kathy couldn't help but laugh. Her youngest always seemed to feel it was her duty to bring lightness into every situation. But her smile faded when she heard a perfect imitation of her own words coming out of her daughter's mouth: "I guess he's doing his *disappearing act* again." Susie said it with a grin, but the look in her eyes betrayed an underlying disappointment and anxiety.

"I'm sure he's all right, sweetie," Kathy said. "Why don't you finish the mac and cheese while I make the salad."

When the food was ready, Kathy sent Susie to pry Derek away from his video game while she went up to get Nicole. It never worked to send one of the other kids to get Nicole; she would just yell at them to get out of her room.

Once at the table, they joined hands as usual, and Derek took his turn to bless the food. They ate in an uncharacteristic silence for several minutes. Before being fired, Hal had often missed eating dinner with the family, so his absence wasn't a new thing. However, now there was no job keeping him away, so his empty chair made them all anxious.

Derek, who seemed to bear the stress of the whole family, asked the question on everyone's mind, "Mom, is Dad going to be okay?"

Kathy laid down her fork. "I think so. Getting fired can be a terrible blow. Imagine how one of you would feel if your best friend rejected you or told lies behind your back."

Fourteen-year-old Nicole blinked several times, and Kathy knew she'd picked an example that hit home with her oldest child.

"Or if someone swiped a school or scout project you'd worked on for a long time," Kathy continued. "You wouldn't like that, would you?"

The three kids exchanged glances, but they didn't say anything.

"Well, that's how your dad feels," Kathy said. "He put his heart and soul into Western Realty. To lose it like this was a blow to his dreams. But he's a strong man." She wiped her mouth with a napkin. "Considering what he's dealing with, I think he's doing pretty well."

"Then where is he tonight?" Derek blurted out. "And why does he act like he's mad at us when he's home?"

Nicole jabbed Derek in the arm with her elbow. "He's not mad at us. If he's not here, it's because he's working, like he always does. Right, Mom?"

Kathy was touched by Nicole's defense of Hal. Of all the children, she was the most like him; an attack on him was an attack on her. "Could be," she answered noncommittally. "Wherever he is, I'm sure he's trying to figure things out."

"Are we going to have enough money?" Derek asked.

Before Kathy could answer, Nicole snapped, "Why do you always ask so many questions?"

Nicole sounded angry, but Kathy knew she was scared. They all were. They'd heard some of the arguments between her and Hal over finances. She reached out to Derek's arm. "We'll need to cut back on our spending for a while. Maybe you can all give me some suggestions for doing that?"

"Take away Nicole's cell phone and tell her she can't go shopping at the mall," he chided. "That'll save a lot."

"Mind your own business, twerp." Nicole's phone beeped, and she shoved back her chair. "It's Hanna." She dismissed herself and flounced up the stairs.

"It'll be all right," Susie said to Derek. "Daddy told me he can get anyone to agree to do anything. He's probably out making deals right now."

Despite her attempts to reassure them, it was clear to Kathy that the children weren't doing well. They were short-tempered and testy all evening, erupting into scuffles at the slightest provocation. When Nicole told Susie to stop trying to cheer everyone up or she would stuff a sock in her mouth, Kathy sent all of them to their rooms. Then she got ready for bed herself. She had a splitting headache and wanted nothing more than to sleep.

But she couldn't. Where was Hal?

She took some Advil and lay on top of the bedspread, listening for any sound of his return. All she heard was the muffled beat of Nicole's music.

It had taken Kathy a long time to realize that Hal went off by himself because he didn't like criticism. But there was another reason. He also liked to research and fully develop ideas on his own. They lived in this house because he'd decided he wanted to live in Littleton. One day five years ago, he'd come home to their three-bedroom rambler in Aurora to say he'd put money on the perfect house in Polo Reserve. Kathy had fallen in love with it at first sight, but she'd also felt left out of the process.

The Advil began to take effect, and Kathy drifted into a light sleep.

It was late when she heard someone moving downstairs. Surprised that she hadn't heard the distinctive sound of Hal's truck, she got up and walked quietly down the stairs and into the living room.

Derek was standing at the front window, leaning forward with hope as the headlights of a car came down the street. He then slumped with disappointment when it passed by. Kathy coughed to alert her son of her presence. "I guess you can't sleep, either," she said softly. He turned. She sat on the sofa and patted the cushion. "Worried about your dad?"

He nodded. "It's late." He leaned against her shoulder in a rare bid for comfort. She put her arm around him. Like his father, he held so much inside.

They talked about the weather. School. His scout troop. And finally about Hal. "Your dad's okay," Kathy said, pulling him tight.

"I just wish he'd come home."

"Me, too."

They were still sitting together when the phone rang. 11:15 p.m. Kathy's stomach flip-flopped. Hal? Was he coming home? Or was it the police? Had he been hurt? Killed?

Relief washed over her at the sound of Hal's voice.

"Mom?" Derek asked nervously.

"It's okay, Derek." She wiped away a tear. "You can go to bed now. He's on his way home."

Worry and guilt gave way to anger as Kathy waited for Hal to arrive home. *I've had it. Whatever is going on with you, Hal Stratton, you have no right to keep us up worrying.*

She was standing in the dark of the kitchen when he quietly opened the back door and stepped inside. She startled him when she spoke. "Finally decided to come home, did you?"

He flinched. "Kathy? You're still up?"

She kept her voice low so as not to wake the children, but it vibrated with anger. "Why didn't you tell me where you were going? The kids and I have been worried sick. Derek stayed up until you called, he was so distraught."

Hal tossed his keys on the countertop and turned on a light. "So you've had a hard time of it. So have I. You don't seem to care about that."

"I do too care! I wanted to talk to you when you came back with the boxes, but you got mad and yelled at me."

"Yeah? Well, I'd had an ugly go around with Keith and Larry. And then I got that voice mail from my father."

She sat on a chair at the kitchen table, but Hal remained standing. "Maybe I made a mistake in telling your parents about our finances. I'm sorry. But since they've offered, I think we should take the loan … and be grateful."

"No way."

"But we—"

"I'll get another job first."

"Really?"

"I won't let us go down the drain. You ought to know that after all these years. Why don't you trust me?"

She closed her eyes and drew in a breath. "I do, in my head. But you scare me sometimes. You always think things will work out, no matter what the facts are."

"That's comforting." Hal folded his arms across his chest. "Let's see. My wife thinks I don't have a grip on reality and that I should grow up and stop acting like a baby. That's the kind of support any guy would be glad to have."

"I didn't mean—"

"Sure you did."

Kathy threw her hands up in defeat. "It's impossible to please you, Hal. Okay, I blew it. But every time I try to talk to you, you take things wrong. Then you lash out at me. I don't know how to handle these feelings of yours."

"You don't *have* to handle my feelings, thank you very much." He continued in an imploring tone. "But a little compassion would be nice. It's not just that I've been forced out of Western. My reputation is ruined. My standing in the community. And you expect me to be Superman."

"Superman?" She laughed with an edge of hysteria. "Excuse me? But the last time I checked, Superman actually cared about people!"

Hal stared at her for a long moment. "You know what? I don't have to take this garbage from you." He headed to the door.

"Running away again?" she said sarcastically. "Twice in one day? That's a record, even for you."

"What do you want from me?" he shouted.

Any thought of speaking quietly to not awaken the children disappeared. "I'll tell you what I want," she shouted back. "I want a *partner*. A *friend*. A husband who *cares* about his family as much as he cares about himself!"

He turned away and she grabbed his arm. "Don't turn away from me! You need to hear this. You act like the kids and I don't even exist. And I don't mean just since you were fired. Your business has always been more important to you than us. And *I* won't live like this anymore. Do you understand? Those children upstairs are *your* children. And I'm your—"

He jerked his arm away. "Then why don't you try acting like one!"

"Where are you going?" Kathy cried, suddenly terrified he would leave. *Really* leave.

It was cold comfort that he stomped out of the kitchen and with a loud slam of the door headed down to the basement to sleep in the rec room.

Chapter 9

The Garage Mahal

I t took Hal a moment to remember why he was sleeping on the couch in the basement instead of in his comfortable bed. Hearing Kathy and the kids upstairs in the kitchen, getting ready for their day, he felt a sharp pang of loneliness, and he almost went up to be with them.

Instead, he stayed on the couch and ruminated about the roller-coaster ride of this past week. It was one thing to lose his position, status, income, and the support of partners he thought were his friends. But to have Kathy turn on him was more than he could stand. She had offended him to the core. No way was he going to pretend that life could go on as usual after that. Something—someone—had to change and, as far as he was concerned, that someone was Kathy.

When the upstairs noises ceased for the day, he rolled off the couch and made his way to the kitchen. Positioned prominently on the counter was a note. He reached for it eagerly—here was the apology, the offer of support he wanted from her. He read it through with anticipation. Then with disappointment. A third time with resentment.

Hal, I'm sorry about last night. I don't like it when we fight. I know that what is happening with Western Realty is

devastating and I want to be there for you, although I'm
sure it didn't seem that way.
    All my Love, Kathy

No kidding it didn't seem that way. The note fell far short of the apology she owed him. He tossed it aside, ate breakfast, wandered aimlessly around the house, then went back downstairs. He spent the rest of the day in a paralyzing lethargy, watching TV and sleeping in a numbing round that lasted until afternoon when, once again, the sounds of his children's voices floated down from the kitchen. Their lively conversation drew him up the stairs. He entered hesitantly, not sure how they would react to him.

Susie noticed him first. "Daddy!" She gave him a big hug. "We didn't know you were home."

"I was downstairs taking a nap. I haven't been sleeping well lately."

"That couch isn't very comfortable," Nicole said, letting him know she realized where he'd bunked last night.

"No kidding." He turned to Susie, who was standing in front of the gas stove. "What are you doing, Suz?"

She held up a fork with a marshmallow on the end. "Toasting marshmallows for s'mores. Want one?"

"You bet."

He watched with interest as Derek put a square of chocolate on a graham cracker. The toasted marshmallow came next, which Derek topped with another cracker.

"Looks like you guys have a system down," said Hal.

"Yeah. We do this all the time." Derek handed him a s'more.

Hal had no idea. What else didn't he know about his children? It was about time he found out. "How was school today?" he asked. The simple question opened the floodgates. Nicole proudly showed him the 95% on her science test. Derek gave a play-by-play run-through of the two goals he'd scored during PE. Susie recounted the fight she'd had with her best friend—they weren't eating lunch together anymore. Hal put his arm around her and gave her a little squeeze. "I'm sorry to hear that."

"Found a new job yet, Pops?" Nicole asked.

Hal smiled at her. He loved it when his kids called him Pops. And he felt better having his children around him, waiting for his answer. "It's a little early for that," he said. "I still have some things to take care of at Western. Yesterday, I went back to the office, packed up my desk, and moved everything back home."

"Yeah, Mom told us." Nicole shook her head. "That must have been hard."

"You could say that."

"What about last night?" Susie asked. "Mom hates it when you do your disappearing act."

Hal felt a flash of anger hearing his ten-year-old daughter echo his wife's complaint. He kept his voice even. "Listen, guys, there are times I need to be alone. It's when I do my best thinking. I haven't always let your mom know where I am and when I'll be home, but I'll do better from now on. I promise."

Susie patted him. "That's good, Daddy. Then Mom won't have to worry about you so much."

Hal saw in her eyes that she was talking about her own worry. He looked around and saw the same apprehension in Nicole and Derek. He'd been telling himself they were doing fine, that the turmoil he and Kathy were feeling didn't affect them. He was wrong.

They were still talking when Kathy came through the door. Hal could tell by her expression that she expected him to be eager to see her, to thank her for the note and offering of support. He noticed that his cool greeting made her smile fade and then disappear. He kept a distance while they fixed a quick dinner. Kathy picked at her food and then shoved her chair back. "I've got a headache. I'm going to bed." The kids watched her leave, their expressions, once again, unsettled.

"Are you mad at Mom?" Susie asked.

"We've got some things to work out, but we'll be okay," Hal said. "Don't worry."

He helped them clean up the kitchen and then watched Derek and Susie play a video game, but sensed they were uncomfortable with him looking over their shoulders. The ease they'd enjoyed earlier was gone.

Blast that Kathy, he thought as he went back to his basement lair. He flopped on the couch and started channel surfing, clicking from one program to another, not sure what he was looking for. He fell asleep with the clicker in his hand and the television blaring.

Hal breathed a sigh of relief when Monday finally rolled around. It hadn't been easy over the weekend spending time with the kids while avoiding Kathy. He certainly wasn't going to accept her limp apology.

After everyone left for the day, Hal went upstairs and found another note. For a moment he thought Kathy may have realized what he needed from her, but the note was about something altogether different. *Your father called to say he was sorry you weren't at breakfast Saturday. He really wants to hear from you. Call him!*

The last two words were underlined three times. Hal wadded the note and tossed it in the trash. If his father really wanted to talk to him, he'd have to apologize first. Grovel. Prostrate himself.

Hal grinned at the image he'd conjured up. He then added Charlie White and the rest of the board to the image and laughed. Then he added Kathy and Donald, the *supposed* mountain guru who'd said it was all his fault.

He ate a joyless breakfast and headed out to the Garage Mahal. Time to get serious about restoring the Coupe de Ville. He turned on all the lights and looked the place over with fresh eyes. As he started thinking about what he wanted to accomplish—restoring the Caddy to her former glory—his mood began to change.

His tools, hung in an orderly fashion or stored in a large, wheeled toolbox next to the vehicle, were calling him. His supplies were on the workbench. He took a moment to set out what he needed, his anticipation rising. It was a little odd, but in a way, he thought of his tools as his friends. They were always there, ready for him to take in hand. They made no judgments of him. They held no expectations. They performed as they were meant to perform. He could count on them. Maybe that was why he felt at ease out here; everything worked by principles that could be understood and explained. How different from the world of human beings.

Eager to begin, he walked around the antique Coupe de Ville, assessing the challenge ahead. He felt a rush of inspiration as he ran his fingers over the hood. He hurriedly donned his coveralls. First he would pull the engine and transmission. The "tranny" would go to a specialty shop, but he would rebuild the engine himself.

Using a hoist, he removed the engine. When he pulled it apart, he was pleased to find the crankshaft and cam and all the bearings in perfect condition. The cylinder walls would need a little work. The heads were pretty good, although he would need to send them in for a valve job so he could run the Caddy on unleaded gas. The carburetor was gummed up, but a twenty-four-hour soak in cleaner would work wonders. The radiator presented a bigger problem; the core would probably need to be replaced.

As he continued mentally cataloguing and coordinating all the jobs that would need to be done, he lost all sense of time. He was working on the underside of the car when he heard Susie.

"Daddy? *Pops!* You alive under there?"

For a moment, he felt a pinch of irritation at her intrusion into his world. The exhaust flange that he'd been struggling with for fifteen minutes was finally coming loose, and he didn't want to break his momentum.

"Watch where you're going," he called. "I've got parts laid out."

"I'm being careful." Susie was determinedly bright. "Whatcha doin' under there?"

"Rebuilding old Lucy. As long as I don't have an office to go to, might as well do something productive, right?"

"Lucy? I didn't know this old car had a name."

"She didn't until today. Like it?"

"Uh-huh. Hey, Pops, wanna come in and have a snack?"

"Sounds nice, but I'm really tied up here, Suz. Maybe later."

It was several minutes before he noticed she'd gone back to the house. He hadn't even rolled out from under the car to talk to her. But he was soon absorbed again in the work.

Hal got enormous satisfaction out of completing a physical task and doing it right. It didn't matter how many times he had to take something apart and put it back together. When it came together for the final time, and he knew it was right, and he knew no one in the world could have done a better job, the endorphins surged. The whole world could pass him by and he wouldn't even notice as he tightened the last bolt in a radiator or sanded a new paint job with 2000 grit sandpaper, then buffed it to a perfect finish. As the beer commercial said, it didn't get any better than that.

Kathy wouldn't understand, but working on the car was the best thing he could do to feel good about himself again. Okay, maybe he was guilty of avoidance. But he was baffled about Western Realty. He couldn't figure out what he'd done wrong or how to change the situation. Maybe while working with his hands, his subconscious mind would come up with a solution. Wouldn't be the first time.

Of course, he couldn't hide out under the car indefinitely. Kathy was continuing to pressure him to look at the finances. "I'll look at the ledger when I'm good and ready," he muttered.

"Whadja say?"

At the sound of Derek's voice, Hal jerked his head up in surprise, hitting it against metal, and grimaced in pain. "Nothing important. What do you need?"

"Nothing," Derek replied hesitantly. "Mom just sent me to tell you it's time for dinner."

Not out of *want to* but *have to,* Hal rolled out from under the Caddy. "Sorry I yelled at you, buddy, but I banged my head." He tried to smile while probing the swelling and checking for blood. None. "Guess I'll live."

"Dad? Could you teach me about cars? Like Gramps taught you?" Derek stood with his hands in his pockets. "I'd be really careful with your tools, and I wouldn't touch anything without permission."

"Well, Lucy's old and a bit touchy, son."

"What about when you work on the truck? You could show me what I need to know to get the merit badge for auto mechanics."

Hal caught the wistful tone of Derek's voice. "Sure, buddy. Sometime this week, okay?"

He removed his coveralls, washed up, then went into the house. Kathy had prepared a salad, meat lasagna, and garlic breadsticks. One of his favorite meals. A peace offering. Nevertheless, he hurried through dinner and excused himself back to the shop, where he worked on the Caddy until very late and again slept on the rec room couch.

It was the last week of August, and Hal put most of his energy into rebuilding the Caddy. Every so often he made dinner (hamburger or Tater Tot casserole), threw in a load of wash, or helped the kids with their homework. But those were exceptions. *Not much different than when I worked for Western,* he told himself. Being productive at *something* was the best thing he could be doing right now.

Indeed, every step forward gave Hal a deep sense of satisfaction. He replaced the smashed front fender with one he purchased from a junkyard in Nebraska. He pulled the rear end apart and replaced all the bearings and seals. He rebuilt the brake cylinders and installed new brake shoes, front and rear. He replaced all the springs and put new bushings in all of the shackles. He even found a great set of whitewalls on eBay. Thanks to the miracle of the Internet, he didn't even have to leave the house. Everything was delivered to the front door, leaving him time to work and think.

The week was going great until Kathy invited his parents for dinner—without telling him. She broke the news in the shop as they arrived. He couldn't even complain before he heard Susie calling excitedly, "Grandma! Grandpa!"

"Why did you invite them?" he hissed. "You know I don't want to talk to them." He didn't want to break for dinner, much less carry on a polite conversation with his parents.

"Because it's time to stop this, Hal." Kathy did nothing to hide her impatience. "You've ignored your parents long enough. And besides, the payment for the SUV is due, and we need help."

Hot with anger, he followed her to the kitchen. His mother, Virginia, was uncovering one of her famous carrot cakes. An upbeat John was shaking hands with Derek and asking him what merit badge he was working on.

"Dad's gonna help me with auto mechanics." Derek spoke with pride. "But not until this weekend. He's busy now working on Lucy."

"The Caddy," Hal answered John's questioning look.

He managed to put on a civil face during the meal, but was impatient to get back to work. When Virginia and Kathy cleared the table and began serving the cake, he made his escape. "Looks good, but I'm full," he said, patting his stomach. "I need to finish what I was working on."

"You know," John said, "that '59 Coupe is a classic. I always wanted to get my hands on one, but I never had the chance. Why don't you show me what you're doing?"

Hal led the way into the Garage Mahal and walked his father around Lucy. He pointed out what he'd done and explained what he planned to do next, hiding his nervousness that his father might criticize it as a less-than-perfect job.

John made a few comments, then asked, "Where's the tranny?"

"I sent it out."

"Good idea. That's a can of worms you don't need. I'm impressed. You're really making good progress."

Although he saw it as a peace offering more than a true compliment, Hal felt a swell of pride at his father's words. For the next several minutes, he pointed out some of the restoration problems and described his plans for handling them. Finally, the conversation wound down. Hal knew what was coming next and braced himself for it.

"Why haven't you returned my calls, son?"

"Sorry about that. This thing with Western has thrown me for a loop. I've been spending a lot of time out here, hoping to get some perspective and maybe come up with an idea about what to do next."

"I've had bouts of inspiration when working on a car," John said. "But I'd hoped we'd have breakfast last Saturday. That's the first time one of us has missed, except for when we've been out of town."

Hal was quiet in spite of the undisguised yearning in his father's voice.

John continued. "I've been thinking about what's going on at your company. I'd like to share some thoughts with you, if you don't mind."

"Like what?" Hal bristled and turned to work on the car.

"Have you thought of meeting separately with the partners? You might have more influence with them that way."

Gee, I would have never come up with that on my own. "It's too late for that," he answered sharply. "They're determined, and nothing's going to change their minds. Believe me, I know them well."

"It was just a thought. I'd like to help you, you know." John cleared his throat. "I guess Kathy told you about my offer to loan you some shekels to tide you over."

"Thanks, but I don't want your money, Dad. I'll figure something out. I'm not totally incompetent, you know."

John blinked. "I never thought you were." He turned and left the shop, and Hal soon heard the motor of his father's SUV spring to life.

A part of him chortled with glee at driving the great John Stratton off. But he also scolded himself for not accepting the olive branch his father had offered. He might have, had John not made it impossible by offering money.

Kathy came into the shop the moment his parents drove off. Hal grimaced the instant he saw her expression.

"Hal Stratton, I've had enough of your attitude. You've got a chip on your shoulder the size of Gibraltar. First, you insult me by not even acknowledging the note I wrote you. Then you disappear out here, leaving me and the kids wondering what's going on in that head of yours. Now you insult your parents by barely speaking to them tonight."

He rolled his eyes. "Here we go again."

"I know what you're thinking. It's just more of Kathy's complaints. But it's true! Before, your entire life was about Western Realty. Now it's this silly car. You might as well be gone, if this is how we're going to live."

"Is that what you want?" Hal slammed down the socket

wrench. "I'm not bringing home a paycheck, so I'm no use to you, is that it? If that's how you feel, then fine, I'm outta here."

"I don't want that!" Kathy pleaded. "I just want to feel like I'm part of your life."

"You could have fooled me. This 'silly car' is the only place I feel good about myself right now. I sure don't feel anything positive coming from you."

"What do you want from me? I told you I was sorry and wanted to support you, but you don't give me a chance. You're great at running a business, Hal, but you're also great at running away from our relationship. You've spent the entire week out here or downstairs—feeling sorry for yourself."

Hal winced. "Is that what you think? That I'm out here feeling sorry for myself? I'm trying to pull my life together, and you make a comment like that? Wow, you amaze me." He wiped the grease from his hands and headed for the door.

She cut off his path, her hands out in supplication. "I'm sorry, Hal. I'm sorry. I just hate seeing you so miserable. Yes, you got fired and that's unfortunate. But it's not the end of the world. Look around you. You've got a wife and children who love you. Your parents love you. You have good health and a sharp and inventive mind. Your life is not over yet."

In the deepest part of himself, Hal knew everything she said was true. He felt a sudden urge to pull her into his arms. In her eyes he saw a desperate need for reassurance and support. But his ego insisted on drawing a line. "If you hate to see me so miserable, then cut me some slack. Maybe I'm doing what I need to do to get back on my feet."

He pushed by, leaving her sputtering a reply to the walls of the shop. He considered jumping in his pickup, but loneliness trumped his desire for further vengeance. So he headed down, down, down to his makeshift bedroom in the basement.

Alone again. And just when he thought he was on the rebound.

He wanted to blame Kathy. But he recognized that she hadn't chosen his words or tied him to this couch. *I'm responsible,* he thought. *I made the choices that put me here.* He was astonished that such a thought had been coughed up by his own brain.

He dropped onto the couch, let out a moan, and pulled a pillow over his face.

Chapter 10
Solace

Doubt plagued Hal as he worked on the car the next few days. He no longer took pleasure watching his hands work. He didn't enjoy being alone and wondered why he was doing this anyway. What was the point? Did it make any difference?

So when he heard the satellite phone on the workbench ringing, he rolled out from under the Caddy and snatched it up with a breathless hello.

"Hal, is that you?"

"Janine?" He was glad to hear her voice. "Sorry I haven't returned your calls. I've been ..." He used Kathy's words. "hiding out."

Janine giggled. "I don't blame you, Hal." Her voice was warm and low. "But I've been worried. How are you doing?"

"A little stressed." He started pacing around the shop. "But overall, I'm fine." He hoped his words didn't sound forced.

"Well, I'm not." Her tone was emphatic. "You can't imagine how things have changed here. It's like a mausoleum. I *hate* coming to work."

Hal smiled at Jeanine's brashness. Or maybe knowing that things were not going well at Western.

"Sorry to hear that. Uh, Janine? What kind of scuttlebutt do you hear? No, forget that. I don't want to get you into trouble."

"Actually, that's why I called. I've been thinking a lot about what's happening here, and … Can we meet somewhere? I need to talk to you."

Hal stopped pacing. His heartbeat quickened. "Can't we talk by phone?"

"No. I need to see you. Will you meet me tomorrow at noon? How about PF Changs at Flatiron Crossing?"

Surprised, Hal didn't respond right away.

"Are you there?"

"Yeah."

"Well, what do you say?"

"I'm not so sure, Janine. It won't change anything."

"Just come. It'll be so good to see you."

"Okay."

Hal put the cordless handset back in its charger, feeling lighter. Thoughts of Janine filled his mind. They'd met when she responded to a newspaper ad for an executive secretary when he first started the company. Of the twenty people who applied for the job, she was one of the two best candidates. His partners couldn't decide, so they left the decision to him.

He felt a little embarrassed now, remembering that his decision had been made for less-than-noble reasons. Recently divorced and in her early thirties, Janine was a beautiful woman. She lit up the office during her interviews. He felt an instant attraction toward her.

Every once in a while, Hal had the impression that Janine wanted more from their relationship, but it was hard to know if it was merely her lighthearted personality. Focused on growing his business and committed to his family, he hadn't thought much about it.

Until now. Did she have some critical information to share with him about the business? Or was there another reason for the lunch date.

Hal felt energized the next morning as he got ready for the

lunch meeting with Janine. He looked forward to seeing her. It also felt good to have something to do other than hang around the house all day. The idea of getting out made him think that it might be time to make some phone calls, set up some appointments, see what possibilities were out there.

He dressed down, not wanting to give the meeting too much importance. As he negotiated the traffic, he wondered about Janine's choice of location—a corner of the city where the possibility of running into Western employees or personal acquaintances was remote.

Janine was just getting out of her car when he pulled into the restaurant parking lot. She waved and walked over.

"Good timing," she said.

"Hello, Janine." He was about to say, *You look great,* but settled for "It's good to see you."

When the hostess greeted them, Hal requested a booth, which was more private. They made small talk while they perused the menu. After they ordered their meals, Janine leaned forward. "First, I want to say for the record that I don't support the partners in their decision to fire you, Hal. But you knew that already, didn't you?"

"I hoped, after all our years together."

She nodded, the expression on her face one of sympathy and determination. "Here's how I see it. What was going on at the company was not your fault. You've always given us good, steady leadership. Maybe we were growing a little fast, but that's not a bad problem to have. It was amazing to me how you built that business from the ground up and made so many excellent investments."

"You're the only one who sees it that way. After the way I was treated the day I went back to get my belongings, it's pretty clear I'm persona non grata there."

Janine shook her head. "Not everyone feels that way. If you'd stopped to talk to Donna and the managers who were waiting to see you, you'd have found out. Charlie hasn't endeared himself to the rest of the staff. We think he and the board railroaded you."

Hal closed his eyes and put his head back. "That's good to

hear. You know, Janine, I've been racking my brain trying to figure out why the board members turned against me. You were there. What do you think happened? Was it my fault?"

She sat back in her seat as if trying to decide what to say.

Hal leaned forward. "Go ahead. Let me have it."

"You're a nice guy, Hal. Part of what I've always loved about you is your positive outlook." She ran a hand lightly through her hair. "You always think the best of people and give them the benefit of the doubt. Especially your friends. You weren't paying attention to the office gossip or the politicking at the water cooler."

He sat up. "I had better things to do."

"See what I mean?" she said, grinning. "Then there's that Charlie White. No way for you to go up against a buzz saw like him and win, especially when you didn't even realize what was happening. He got to the partners while you were out making deals. He intimidated them out of one side of his mouth and made promises out of the other." She looked down. "I partly blame myself for what happened that night. I should have warned you."

Hal shrugged. "It wouldn't have changed anything, Janine—I probably wouldn't have believed you anyway."

The food came and distracted them from the talk about Western Realty. Well into the meal, Janine said, "I heard Keith Mickelson talking to Marvin, our accountant, the other day about that audit."

Although her tone sounded deliberately bright, the word *audit* made Hal feel suddenly ill. "What did they say?"

"Marvin's really upset about it. He kept telling Keith that he'd gone over everything with a fine-toothed comb, and he swore there was nothing for an auditor to find."

Hal slumped with relief. "Thank goodness."

"You know what Keith said? 'Numbers don't always tell the truth.'" Janine paused. "Or was it, 'Numbers don't tell the *whole* truth'?"

The sick feeling returned. "I'm royally screwed," Hal said, dismay all over his face.

"Hal, it doesn't matter what Keith says. I'm sorry I even mentioned it. The important thing is that *Marvin* knows the financial history of the company better than anyone, and *he* says there's *nothing* to find." She reached across the table and gave his hand a reassuring squeeze.

Hal did his best to ignore the gesture. "What else is going on at Western? Might as well give it to me all at once."

Janine sighed. "I must get a dozen calls every day from people wanting to know if what they've heard is true."

"And that is?" He waited, then said, "Never mind. You don't have to say it."

Janine grimaced. "I'm so sorry, Hal. I wanted to cheer you up. Now I've made you feel even worse."

They sat in silence until the waitress took their plates away and topped their coffee cups.

"Thanks for bringing me up to date, Janine. I appreciate it." Hal's smile was strained. "But I'm also concerned for you. Meeting with me is risky. After all, Western is your employer."

"I don't care." Janine spoke nonchalantly. "If they fire me, they fire me. Anyway, how are they going to know we met? I've thought a lot about this, Hal—" she said, her eyes resolute, "—and I've come to the realization that I care more about what happens to you than that company."

Hal shifted awkwardly in his seat.

"You were the reason I loved working at Western." She blew at an errant lock of hair and shook her head. "In fact, I'm thinking of quitting."

"You can't do that. With you and me both gone, the whole place would collapse."

Janine hooted. "All the more reason to leave."

"Really, Janine. You can't be serious. You're such an asset to Western. You don't know how much you mean to everyone around there. You not only have exceptional technical skills, but..." He paused. How on earth had he gotten drawn into such a personal conversation? "...you're a delight to work with. Everyone loves you. You're upbeat and positive. It's *truly* a joy to be around you."

She reached across the table and took his hand, which had been tightly clasped around his water glass. The feeling was incredibly sensuous. She spoke softly. "Thanks, Hal. But it's not the same place anymore, and I don't feel the same commitment I used to. I guess I was surprised how much my love of the job had to do with you."

Hal blushed. "Thanks, Janine. You don't know how much your support means to me." He glanced around the restaurant. "You've probably got to get back. You've been gone a couple of hours now."

She looked him in the eyes. "I took the rest of the day off, so I'm not in a hurry. I came to support you." She stroked his hand and continued matter-of-factly, "I know how much the company meant to you. You had such high hopes for it. This has to be devastating."

"It has been tough," he admitted. "It came as a shock. I'm still trying to regain my balance. But life goes on."

She nodded. "Yes, it does. But you have to talk about it. You've got to get what happened out of your system if you're ever going to move on."

Hal smiled. "You sound like this guy I know. He says the same thing. But no one in my life is eager to listen to me complain and rehash events that are over and done with."

Janine leaned into the table. "I am. I'll listen. I know what you're going through. I watched it happen. Besides, we developed a good relationship at Western. I don't want to see it end because of this."

Hal motioned to the waitress. He gave her his credit card without asking to see the check. He signed the receipt, leaving an extra large tip. Then he and Janine stepped out into the midday sunlight.

"There's a park down the road a ways," she said. "You can tell me what you've been up to."

The invitation to talk and the encouragement in Janine's eyes were all Hal needed. Everything he'd gone through since the board meeting came rolling out. He told her about his night of despair and made a funny story out of his encounter with the mountain man-slash guru. Her sympathetic murmurs even had him disclosing his encounters with Kathy and his father and admitting his fears that he would never regain his status in the business community.

75

Janine actually *listened.*

Every once in a while she asked a question or made a comment, but mostly she let him talk. And talk. And talk. It felt good to pour out his feelings in this way. And have someone respond with something other than criticism. But there was something more. Opening up to Janine was a message to Kathy. Not that she'd ever know. But he knew. He was making a statement. If Kathy wouldn't listen, he'd find someone who would.

They'd been sitting side-by-side on the bench for a long time. Aware it was getting late, Hal said with a crooked smile, "Guess you didn't expect to get the whole sad story, did you?"

She put her arm through his and leaned against him. "I didn't mind. Actually, this has been the nicest afternoon I've had in a long time." She paused. "Hal? Do you need to get home, or would you like to come over for a drink and dinner?"

The words literally made him dizzy. Hal suddenly felt detached from his body and abuzz with thoughts and impulses. Never in his life had temptation announced itself so boldly ... or attractively. He looked into Janine's eyes and inviting smile. She had given him so much this afternoon. Acceptance. Support. Admiration. How could he say no?

But how could he say yes? What about his vows to Kathy? His commitment to his family? Hal was utterly speechless.

Janine rescued him. "Sorry, Hal. I shouldn't have asked." She sat up and crossed her hands in her lap. "It's late and you need to get home."

Hal took her hands and gave them a squeeze. "Thank you, Janine. I appreciate your support." He cleared his throat. "It's tempting, but ... I don't need any more complications in my life right now."

She laughed low and warm. "I certainly wouldn't want to be a complication."

They walked back to the restaurant parking lot in silence. He helped her into her car, then watched her drive away—more conflicted than ever in his life.

Chapter 11

Rebuffed

Hal walked into the kitchen. Kathy was standing at the stove, stirring what smelled like spaghetti sauce. She looked over, her face a mask, her eyes flat, not the dancing eyes that had captivated him when he first met her.

"You okay?" he asked.

She nodded.

"Where are the kids?"

She shrugged.

"Have you thought about what we might want to do over Labor Day weekend?"

She stopped stirring the sauce. "I have more important things on my mind than how to entertain the family."

Guilt averted a glib remark. He leaned into the center island, the way he used to back when they talked while cooking together. "I guess you mean the finances?"

"I've decided to accept your dad's offer of a loan."

Hal straightened up. "Wait a minute. I didn't agree to that."

"I didn't ask you to agree," she snapped. "The mortgage will take all of my next paycheck, and the SUV payment is staring us in the face. Unless you want me to sell the SUV?" She looked at him for the first time.

"We can't do that. It would leave you without a car."

"So? I can buy an old beater."

"When were you going to talk to me about this?"

"I already did," she said, stirring the pot more rapidly. "You made it perfectly clear you weren't interested."

"I'm interested now."

She glared at him. "I'm fixing dinner now."

A standoff. What a contrast with how he'd felt with Janine just an hour earlier. Her eyes full of promise, his imagination filled with possibilities. There was no way to describe what it meant to talk freely with someone who listened, validated his feelings, even the ugly ones, and still believed in him. If only Kathy would listen and give him some support instead of slamming him and putting him on the defensive every time they tried to talk.

"What about if we take the kids to play mini-golf," he suggested. "After dinner tonight. And then talk about finances after a good night's sleep." He took a couple steps toward her. "I know you're worried. I won't wiggle out of it, I promise."

Kathy's face scrunched up as she fought back tears. Hal reached out. She couldn't put her arms around him, but neither did she prevent him from embracing her. Hal drew her close, promising himself that he would spend more time with the family … and less time in the shop. They needed him. And he needed to avoid being alone with his thoughts and memory of his afternoon with Janine.

It wasn't until Labor Day Monday that Hal and Kathy finally sat down with the family ledger and checkbook. Kathy had created a flow chart and pie graph on the computer. When she began to go over her concerns, Hal felt as if he were a slow learner getting extra help after school. Before long, he felt their old push-pull pattern resurfacing.

"Putting the issue of the SUV aside," Kathy stated, "we need *this* much money every month to meet our obligations. My salary is only about a third of that. Bottom line, Hal, you need to get a job."

He tried not to show the irritation he felt. "I know. I know." He leaned back. She was right, of course, but her officious tone put him off. "Long-term, we'll be okay." He breathed a heavy sigh. "I've just got to figure out what to do in the meantime."

Kathy studied him before speaking. "It's hard for me to believe you're concerned about our finances when you spend so much time in the Garage Mahal."

"I *am* concerned," he protested. "It's just that ..." He hesitated, then finished in a rush of insight. "I guess I've been hoping my partners would come to their senses and realize they made a big mistake."

Kathy shook her head. "That's not going to happen. You've got to move on."

Move on. He flinched. It wasn't so easy to move on. Moving on was ... like admitting failure. That's what made it so hard to go out and look for another job. Plus the humiliation of crawling to other companies—mostly former competitors—after running his own company for seven years.

"I don't think you understand what 'moving on' means. It's so much easier said than done."

"Well, you'd better find a way, and soon, or I'm going to ask your dad for that loan."

Hal gritted his teeth. "I'll call some old contacts. I promise."

Tuesday morning, Hal got dressed as if going to work, brewed a pot of coffee, and sat at the desk on the main-floor study to devise a strategy for job-hunting. He'd always thought of himself as an idea man, but he soon found it wasn't easy to come up with a workable way to present himself to potential employers.

He considered several scenarios. They all boiled down to the same thing: *I've realized recently that the day-to-day managing of an office isn't for me. I want to focus on what I love most—buying and selling property.*

It sounded pretty lame. Anyone with any kind of connections to the world of property management would have heard about his ouster. They would know that anything he said was shorthand for *I need a job pronto.*

Okay, so the news would be out. However, he wasn't the only

businessman who had been forced out of a company, and he wouldn't be the last. There were lots of real-estate development companies in the Denver area, and many would be glad to employ someone with his level of experience and expertise. In fact, once the word got out that he was actively looking for work, he would be getting calls rather than making them.

"Yeah, it's time to get back in the ring," he said, doing an imitation of Mohammed Ali's "Float like a butterfly, sting like a bee."

Riding on his enthusiasm, he got out his Blackberry and looked up the names of several people he knew in the industry. Armed with a large mug of coffee and his cell phone, he made the first call. Not surprisingly, most of the general managers were not immediately available, so he left messages on voice mail or with administrative assistants.

He was still at it when Kathy got home from school. She stood in the doorway to his study. "How's it going?"

"Good. I'm plowing the field, so to speak. It'll take awhile to see results."

It was harder to stay positive the next day as the minutes and hours ticked by with no return calls. He had to remind himself that these were busy people. Late the following day, he decided to focus on the four people he knew best, whom he considered pretty good friends. He felt a wave of anxiety as he called them a second time. Again, the most he could do was leave a message requesting a callback.

His cell phone finally rang late Thursday. The caller ID told him it was Sam Richards, a well-connected, successful developer. Sam was to Suburban Real Estate Company what Hal had been to Western. Hal wiped his palms on his jeans and answered the phone. "Sam, thanks for calling back."

"No problem, Hal. How are you doing? Rough times over there at Western, huh?"

"The word's out, I take it. At least, Charlie White's version." Hal immediately grimaced, unsure of Sam and Charlie's relationship.

"You know how something like that spreads."

"Sam, I was wondering if we could have lunch someday, soon?" The silence on the other end of the line drew out long. "Sam? Are you still there?"

"Yeah. I'm just checking my schedule. Listen, what about next Tuesday? I'm tied up in the morning, but I could do a late lunch. How about one-thirty at the 3 Margaritas down on County Line Road?"

Hal hung up with relief. Finally a connection. But somehow it didn't feel right. Sam's detached manner was a marked departure from their past camaraderie. Had the gossip on the street raised Sam's suspicions about fiscal mismanagement? Hal couldn't rid himself of the feeling that he was in big trouble.

Tuesday morning couldn't come soon enough. Hal's nervousness and excitement about the lunch meeting with Sam had rubbed off on the family. Hal accepted their good wishes and Kathy's good luck kiss, gratefully.

He spent part of the morning in the Garage Mahal, letting the process of working with his hands calm him. Then he dressed in a nice sports coat and tie, which he hoped would project a professional and unruffled image. He was deeply embarrassed at having to meet with Sam under these circumstances, but hoped that Sam would realize being let go was just one of those things that happens in business politics and not a reflection of his ability ... or integrity. If word of the audit was also making the rounds, Hal was hopeful he could build his case by sharing his side of the story.

He arrived at the restaurant early, gave the hostess his name, and stepped back out into the pleasant September sunlight where he watched for Sam's arrival.

Sam eyed him with unabashed curiosity as he approached. "Hello, Hal. How have you been, all things considered?"

Hal exuded a willful confidence. "Not bad, actually. I'm cashing in on a little vacation time and working on a classic car I've been wanting to restore."

"Hey, that's great. What make and model is it?" Sam's enthusiasm sounded hollow.

"A fifty-nine Caddy Coupe de Ville."

"I remember that car. Isn't it the big one with the fins?"

After the requisite chitchat, Hal and Sam looked over their menus and ordered. Sam seemed friendly, not as guarded as yesterday on the phone. So, Hal decided to lay his cards on the table.

"Listen, Sam, I need to know what people are saying about me and Western. It's been like pulling teeth to get anyone to return my calls. It seems like the whole world is ignoring me."

Sam rubbed the back of his head. "It's not good. The truth is people are … well, wary of you right now."

Hal scowled. "Why? What are they saying?"

"Word is you were fired for some bad decisions, that you didn't do due diligence on some of your deals and ended up with a pile of bum properties."

"That's not the whole story, Sam," Hal objected. "Those are terrific apartments. We would be making money on them right now if Computrex hadn't taken its manufacturing south of the border. When that part of town booms again, we'll be in great shape. You know how it is."

Sam held up his hands. "Listen, Hal, I'm not here to argue with you about what went on at Western. You asked a question, and I gave you an answer. That's just what people are saying."

Hal regained his composure. "Sorry. This isn't your problem. I appreciate your candor."

The waiter brought their food. Both men moved their plates to the side, showing no interest in eating.

Hal folded his arms across his chest, eyes fixated on Sam. "What else are you hearing?"

Sam wrinkled his forehead. "I'm not sure it's my place to be talking to you like this. Maybe you need to go to your partners."

"I've been to them." Hal took a deep breath. "I apologize for sounding defensive. But I need answers, and you're the first person in the industry I've talked to." He uncrossed his arms and forced a smile. "I need to know, Sam, what else are people saying?"

Sam grunted. "Well, they say you bought some vacant land you couldn't afford. And …"

Hal bristled. "And what?"

"There's talk you were guilty of some kind of financial malfeasance."

"Jeez, I hope you don't believe that. It's not true. You and I go back a long way. Have I ever done anything to make you question my integrity?"

"Not that I know of personally." He hesitated. "I hate to say this, Hal, but sometimes, you know, greed does take over. I've seen it. People bite off more than they can chew, and they wind up in trouble."

"Are you suggesting that's what happened to me? It's not true, believe me. You know Charlie White. I'll tell you what happened. He intimidated my partners. He wants control of Western, and they were too cowardly to stand up to him."

Sam's face was emotionless. "It's not my place to say. I don't know what went on."

"How about this? Charlie called for an audit, and I swear on my life, it will exonerate me of any wrongdoing."

Sam nodded. "I'm glad to hear you say that. But the truth is, a lot of damage can be done between now and then. I hate to tell you this, but you're already damaged goods in this city. Don't be surprised if it takes quite awhile for you to bounce back, even if the audit clears you."

A combination of fury and dread washed over him. Hal took a couple of swallows of water. "Tell me this, Sam. Would *you* hire me?"

Sam fidgeted. "You want the nice answer, or the honest one?" He shook his head. "No, at least not right now. Does that mean I think you're guilty? No. But there's too much controversy swirling around you. It's not good for business." He sat back. "I hate to tell you this, but it's too late for damage control, my friend. You need damage *repair*."

Hal's chin dropped to his chest. A tense silence hung between them as Hal absorbed the implications of what Sam was telling him.

Finally, Sam spoke again. "Tell you what I *can* do. I need a manager for some apartment units. I could pay you a couple of thousand a month until you find something better. It's not what you want, but it's probably the best you can get right now."

"You're kidding, right?" Hal's voice was incredulous. "Manage a few apartments?"

"You might want to give it some thought." Sam signaled the waiter. "I don't know about you, but I'm going to pass on lunch."

Hal pulled out his wallet and offered Sam some cash, but Sam waved it off. The act was symbolic. Hal was officially second class.

Chapter 12

Near Miss

Hal got into his pickup, scarcely believing what he'd learned. He'd gone to the lunch meeting thinking he was moving forward. Hoping, in fact, that Sam might actually make him a good offer. Instead, he learned that the entire industry was talking about him as if he were a thief. How could he fight gossip and innuendo? The accusation alone was a reputation killer.

For the first time, real panic welled up in his chest. He needed to talk to someone—*now.* He looked at his watch. Kathy's classes were over for the day. He called her on his cell phone, hoping to air his worries. But all she wanted to know was if Sam had offered him a job.

"When are you going to start?" she asked excitedly. "How much is it a month? Hal, that's so great!"

"Not from where I sit." He regretted calling her.

"I know it's not what you want, sweetie, but it's not bad for a stopgap. Something to help us out while you're looking for something better."

"It may be a stopgap to you," he said, voice rising, "but it's a slap in the face to me. My services are worth far more money than that. Anyway, it's not just about the money. It's the principle."

"Principle, schminciple. I'm really frustrated. You call me at work to get my opinion, then shoot it down? I've got to get to a meeting."

Click. Dial tone.

"Nice!" he yelled as he drove down the highway. "I'm worthy of respect as long as I'm bringing home a fat paycheck. But the moment I run into tough times, *whammo*. What about the vows we took," he said bitterly, "for good times and bad times, richer or poorer, better or worse? Just filler, huh?"

Janine wouldn't react that way. He punched in the number for Western Realty but, with his thumb poised over the call button, changed his mind and tossed the cell phone onto the passenger seat and headed straight home.

In a foul mood, he grabbed a soda from the fridge and retreated to the Garage Mahal where Lucy, with her fancy chrome grill and extravagant tail fins, waited for him. At least here, any effort he put forth was worth something.

He picked up a piece of sandpaper and began working on the car's body. The more he worked on the Caddy, the more she seemed to be taking on a personality. She was a diva, this car. She deserved the best, and he was going to give it to her. He focused all his senses on the job at hand and slipped into a timeless state, sanding in a repetitive rhythm.

When the kids came home, each of them stopped by to say hi before going into the house. A short time later, he heard Kathy's SUV pull into the garage. He was surprised she didn't immediately burst into the shop and light into him for not accepting Sam's offer.

When Susie called him to dinner, he realized why. Kathy brought the subject up not more than a couple minutes into the meal. "Sam Richards offered your father a job. Isn't that nice?"

"Kathy." The fire in his voice got everyone's attention.

"Well, he did," she reiterated. "Only your father won't take it. Restoring his car is more important to him."

"I don't think we should get into this now." He gave her a look that neither she nor the kids could misinterpret. Then he explained to the children that yes, he had been offered a job, but it wasn't what he was looking for.

"Why can't you take it anyway, just for now?" Derek asked, pleading in his voice.

Hal shot a furious glance at Kathy, who smiled triumphantly. He remained civil during the meal, but as soon as he finished he excused himself and went back to the shop.

It wasn't long before Kathy followed him. With no warm-up she launched the first volley. "You need to take Sam's offer, Hal. I know it's not what you want, but we can't afford for you to be unemployed. It's as simple as that." She stood straight and tall, arms folded across her chest.

Hal groaned. "I *can't*. Don't you get it? Accepting that job would do me more harm than good in the long run. I'd be the laughing stock of the industry, labeled a has-been."

"But you've got to do something."

"I will. If nothing else, I can take out a loan and buy some property, then turn it around in the next few months. I have lots of options."

"Turn it around in the next few months?" Her tone was searing. "That's just more of your *deal-making*."

"You didn't complain when we were making money hand over fist," he said, matching her intensity. "I know it's a stretch for you, but you'll just have to trust me."

"Trust you?" She stomped a foot. "You're talking about gambling with your family's future."

"I would *not* be gambling! I know what I'm doing!"

"Well, *I* need to know what you're doing, too. If you have some kind of secret plan, you need to let me in on it. Otherwise, you need to accept this offer."

Ready to explode, Hal took a deep breath. "Well, you've made it perfectly clear how you feel, Kathy. Now leave me alone so I can think." He turned his back to her and began digging through his tool chest.

She didn't leave. "I'll be glad to leave you alone—as soon as you tell me *how* to pay the bills that are coming due. *I'm* the one who writes the checks around here. *I'm* the one who buys the groceries. *I'm* the one who has to answer the kids' questions. *I'm* the one who ..."

"Enough!"

In a fury, Hal picked up a wrench and hurled it. It sailed across the garage, flipping end over end. No sooner did it leave his hand than Hal noticed, with utter horror, the shop door angling open. The wrench struck the wall above the door with a jarring bam, then fell downward—just as Susie stepped under it.

"Watch out!" he bellowed. The wrench fell as if in slow motion and smacked his daughter on the shoulder. She cried out in pain and began sobbing.

Heart in his throat and the screams of his wife in his ears, Hal rushed to Susie's side and wrapped his arms around her. "Oh, Susie, I'm so sorry! It was an accident. I'm sorry. I didn't see you."

"Give her to me!" Kathy screeched, tugging Susie into her own arms.

Hal resisted her. Trembling, he pulled Susie's sleeve up to see the point of impact. It was angry red and already swelling. "Can you move your arm?" he asked.

She raised it, and, with great relief, he realized it wasn't broken. "I'm *so* sorry," he repeated as he pulled her close. He wiped her cheek and kissed her forehead. "I didn't see you coming, Susie. I'm so sorry. I'm so sorry."

"Wh … what hit me?" she asked, wailing.

It pained Hal deeply to admit what he had done. He wished he could reverse time and make a different choice. "I threw a wrench." At her look of horror, he added, "Not at *you*. At the wall. I didn't know you were there. I would *never* do anything to hurt you." Tears filled his eyes. "You know that, don't you?"

Before Susie could answer, Kathy tore her from his arms. "What's the matter with you? You're crazy! You could have killed her!"

Kathy's accusations frightened Susie, and she cried even harder.

"She's not hurt that badly, Kathy," Hal said. "Are you, honey?"

Susie shook her head, hiccupping as she gulped back sobs. "Why were you yelling and throwing things?"

Kathy gave Hal a withering look, but her voice was soothing when she answered Susie. "Your dad's upset, honey. This thing with Charlie White, and now Sam, has been hard on him." She stood and helped her daughter to her feet. "Come on, sweetie. Let's get some ice on that shoulder."

Hal started to follow, but Kathy turned on him with the ferocity of an animal protecting her young. "You stay here. You've done enough."

Shamefully, Hal watched his wife and daughter turn their backs on him and walk inside. Never had he felt so cut off. He wanted, desperately, to hide, disappear, to revoke his own birth. He wished for the earth to swallow him whole so he would never again face another human being. Overwhelmed by what he had done, he stood frozen as waves of grief and shame pulsed up from deep within him.

When he at last collected himself, he turned off the lights and slunk quietly into the house, then down the stairs to the basement. He sat in the darkness for a long time. He heard no sounds upstairs, and no one came asking about him.

Bereft, he thought of Janine's warm smile. He fumbled for his cell phone and started to dial. But an impression stopped him. Talking to Janine *would* make him feel better. But he also knew it would be superficial. It wouldn't change the reality of things. Who he was. The choices he was making. Choices that were boxing him in, hour by hour, day by day.

He put down the phone, thinking about how narrowly he'd escaped disaster. He could have struck Susie head-on, in the face … killed her.

He stared into the darkness. His life was spinning out of control … and everything he did was making it worse.

In the middle of the night, still awake, the image of the plaque on Donald Millhouse's fireplace mantel came, unbidden, into his mind. *The Hero's Choice.* At the time, the old man's words had sounded like psychobabble—reality, choices, responsibility—and he had dismissed them as simplistic.

He got up and began searching for the sheet of paper Donald had given him, and remembered it was in his jacket pocket. He retrieved it and smoothed out the crumpled page.

The Three R's

Reality + Responsibility = Results

Reality: What is, or the way things are. Reality exists independently of our opinions about it. Embrace it and find peace. Resist it and find pain.

Responsibility: The choices we make about how to think, feel, and act about reality. The quality of our life depends on our ability to make good choices that are consistent with our highest self-interest.

Results: The consequences or outcomes we get from the choices we make. Results are a function of the other two R's.

Reality + Responsibility = Results

Hal stared at the diagram. Reality, for him, was ugly—and only getting uglier. *Embrace that?* Donald had to be nuts. True, he didn't like his life right now. But a consequence of his choices? He didn't *choose* for his business partners to turn against him. He didn't *choose* to be fired. He didn't *choose* to have a critical father or an unsupportive wife.

He tossed the paper aside. A stupid riddle. How could he make sense of it?

But he did know one thing. He *had* chosen to pick up that wrench and throw it. The admission was sobering.

And he knew that he *needed* to talk to Donald Millhouse again. *Tomorrow.*

Exhausted, he curled up on the couch and pulled a blanket over his shoulders, a tiny whisper of hope in the back of his mind.

Chapter 13

Anguish

Numb with fear, Kathy hurried Susie out of the Garage Mahal and into the house. What was wrong with Hal? Was he losing his mind? He could have killed Susie! She gave her daughter some Extra Strength Tylenol and held an ice pack on the wounded shoulder, murmuring words of comfort. They didn't help. Just when she thought Susie had calmed down, she burst into tears again.

"It's your fault, Mom!" Nicole said snidely. "You're always fighting with Dad, and you never listen to him."

Derek said little. "Should I go see Dad, Mom?" His only words.

Kathy squelched her gut reaction. No need to add to her children's confusion and distress. "No, I think he wants to be alone."

By the time she finally got the three kids to bed—Susie in her bed so she could comfort and keep her eye on her—she couldn't sleep. She was so worked up, her thoughts kept spinning—at first with anger and disbelief and then with worry ... over money ... over Hal.

She finally drifted off, then woke with a pain behind her left eye and feeling nauseous. A migraine coming on. *Oh, great.* She took her prescription med, but one quick turn of the head sent her dashing to the bathroom.

She slept fitfully the rest of the night, and the alarm went off way too early. She showered, dressed, and realized she smelled coffee brewing. Frowning, she went to the kitchen and noticed a full coffeepot and a note from Hal.

"Right," she muttered cynically. But she wanted to believe.

Susie came down, her blond curls wild and pajamas rumpled. "Do I have to go to school today?" she whimpered.

"You're not feverish, are you?" Kathy felt her head.

"No. My shoulder hurts." She pulled her arm out of her PJ top.

The purple bruise on her shoulder joint was ugly, but not as bad as it could have been. "I'll give you some Tylenol, sweetie. You'll feel better by the time the bus comes."

"Mom, Daddy wasn't mad at me, was he?"

Kathy tipped Susie's chin up and looked into her eyes. "No, sweetie. Don't ever think that. Daddy loves you. We both do."

Susie looked toward the stairs. "Where is he?"

"He left early this morning. Why?"

"I want to tell him I'm okay."

Kathy bit back tears and hugged her daughter. "He'll be relieved to hear that."

Nicole and Derek came down to the kitchen. Their moods were somber and edgy during breakfast. Kathy did her best to reassure them, all the while moving slowly to keep from getting a full-fledged migraine. They were all so distressed that she hated sending them their separate ways, but what else could she do?

She gave Susie another encouraging hug. Then she reached for Derek, who let it in with stoic reserve. Nicole's disdainful look told Kathy a hug was not wanted.

At work, before third period, the vice principal of her middle school stopped her in the hall. "You look terrible, Kathy. Go home and take care of yourself. I'll make sure your classes are covered."

Kathy protested, but Juanita overruled her. "I know you pride yourself on never taking a sick day, but there's no point in slogging your way through."

Kathy nodded weakly. "You're right. Thanks."

As they walked together, Juanita asked, "Should I get a sub for tomorrow?"

"No. All I need are some meds and a good night's sleep."

Kathy put a few books and papers in her briefcase and stopped at a vending machine for a Coke, a real Coke, hoping the sugar and caffeine would help her make it home. *A good night's sleep? That's rich.* She hadn't had a good night's sleep since Hal was fired.

It seemed to take forever to get home. When she finally pulled into her side of the garage, she saw with relief that Hal's pickup was still gone. *Good.* Sure didn't want to face him right now. She'd never seen him behave this way before. So out of control. It was scary.

Her old fears roared to the surface. What if Hal couldn't get it together? Would they end up divorced? What about the kids? Where would they live? What about their after-school activities?

Kathy barely made it to the medicine cabinet. She swallowed another codeine, crept into bed, and cried herself to sleep.

Chapter 14

Moment of Decision

I t was very early when Hal quietly climbed the stairs to the master suite. Kathy was still asleep, her arm wrapped protectively around Susie. He quietly showered and dressed, then knelt by the bed. "Hang on, Kathy," he whispered, agonizing with regret and love. "Things will get better. I promise." He smoothed Susie's blond curls, which were damp from a restless night. "I'm so sorry," he whispered. "I'll never do anything like that again. I promise."

He smiled as he left the room. He'd just made a commitment. And it wasn't hard at all. It just took the right motivation. He looked in on Nicole, then Derek, his heart full of love for them. Whatever he'd lost, he was still a very rich man.

In the kitchen, he wrote a note to Kathy:

> *Dear Kathy. Just want you to know that I'm not doing my disappearing act. I'm going to see someone who can help me. I know I need it. Love, Hal*

He started the coffeemaker and placed the note in front of it where Kathy would be sure to see it. He was hungry, but didn't take the time for his usual bowl of cereal. He didn't want to talk to the family until after he'd seen Donald. He also didn't want to show up at the cabin hungry, so he stopped at the drive-through of the Golden Arches, ordered a sausage-and-egg sandwich, and wolfed it down. It would wreak havoc on his cholesterol.

He arrived at Donald's cabin near eight. He'd been practicing what he would say. Now he couldn't remember any of it—except the bare truth, that he needed help. It was a humbling admission for someone who'd always figured things out for himself, and gone to great lengths to avoid relying on others. Before he knocked on the handsome cedar door, he stifled the impulse to run. He knew he'd be running from himself.

He could hear Donald singing and paused to listen.

"Any fool can do it. There ain't nothin' to it. Einstein said we could never understand it all."

Grinning, Hal rapped three times.

A few moments later, Donald opened the door. "Look who's here! Restaurant's open, if you're looking for breakfast."

"Thanks, but I've already eaten."

"Well, come on in." Donald gestured broadly. "Can I offer you some juice? Or coffee? I just made a pot."

"Juice, I think."

"The juice de jour is sweetened cranberry. Keeps the kidney stones at bay, you know. Make yourself at home while I pour us a couple of tall ones."

"Thanks."

Hal stepped into the seating area. The morning sun gleamed on the honey-colored pealed-log walls. The room was even more beautiful than he remembered. A man's room, furnished simply, with good quality pieces. However, what summoned his attention was the plaque at the fireplace. *The Hero's Choice.*

Hal felt a sting of shame. His life was so out of control. Not heroic at all. With a sigh, he walked to the mantel and touched the plaque thoughtfully. Then he turned to the family photo beside it. Judging by the styles of hair and clothing, it had to be many decades old. A young woman with a toddler girl on her lap, a boy of three standing at her side, all captured in a moment of delight. All three were smiling at an unseen photographer. Donald, Hal guessed.

Donald came in from the kitchen with the glasses of juice. "Hal, I'd like to introduce you to my wife, Melanie, my daughter, Emma, and my son, Spencer." Donald introduced them as though they were standing right in front of him.

"Well, Melanie, Emma, and Spencer, I'm pleased to meet you." He turned to Donald, who read the question in his eyes.

Donald's voice softened, and he offered a sober smile. "They were killed in a car accident shortly after that picture was taken."

Hal caught his breath. He couldn't think of an appropriate response.

"It happened in the middle of a Chicago winter. Melanie was driving the kids to a doctor's appointment on some icy roads. A semi went into a skid and jackknifed. She was killed instantly. My children both died within twenty-four hours."

"I'm so sorry, Donald." Words were inadequate.

Donald put his glass on the coffee table and sat in one of the large leather recliners. He motioned for Hal to take the other. "No need to be sorry. My family has brought me great joy, Hal, not just in life but also in death. That's not how I felt at the time, of course." He had a distant look in his eyes. "It took me many years to accept their deaths and be able to think of them without pain. But I'm extremely grateful to have known each one of them, and they still live right here." He placed both hands over his heart.

Hal had promised himself as a boy never to shed tears in front of others. But the attitude of his new friend in the face of such a devastating loss pierced him deeply. The dam burst. His remorse from the events of the past several weeks burst out in deep sobs. He could not, and to his surprise, did not want to halt their flow.

Donald sat quietly, his simple presence offering silent support. He waited for the tears to subside and then handed Hal a tissue.

Gradually, Hal regained control. "I don't know what came over me. I can't imagine what it would be like to lose the ones you love the most." As he spoke, Hal realized how isolated he felt from Kathy and his children—and he was close to losing them.

"It almost destroyed me," Donald said impassively. "It was many years before I got over the blame and self-hatred. I very nearly didn't make it."

"Self-hatred?" Hal raised his eyebrows. "What did you have to hate yourself for?"

"For not recognizing what a gift I had in them—before it was too late. For having my priorities upside down, and not knowing how much I loved them until they were gone."

"But you did get over it." His face was somber. "How?"

"Well, there's a short version and a long version to that story. The short version is I learned about reality, responsibility, and results." He grinned.

"Ah. The three R's on that sheet of paper you gave me."

Donald nodded. "My thoughts weren't organized at the time. But there came a day when I started seeing how *I* was the cause of my own pain and suffering."

"How can you say that?" Hal asked incredulously. "You didn't choose what happened to your family. As for your pain and suffering, anyone would have been devastated by such a loss."

Donald rocked slowly in his recliner. "No question about that. Yet, some people find ways to handle loss with grace and courage."

Hal nodded slowly. "I know some people like that." He thought about his friend Rob, diagnosed the summer before with an advanced form of non-Hodgkins lymphoma. He thought about Preston, a former business colleague who'd lost a daughter in a horrible car accident. He remembered a recent conversation with a taxi driver from Afghanistan who told him about the ravages of war in his country. Hal felt a fresh surge of reverence for each of these people. At the time, he'd thought their equanimity was a form of resignation. *Maybe it was something more.*

"We all have challenges, every day," Donald continued. "Key Moments, I call them."

"What do you mean by *Key Moment*?"

"A moment of decision. A moment when we choose—consciously or not—how we'll handle what's happening. Some Key Moments are minor. Others mock us, challenge us to the core."

"Like …" Hal gestured toward the photo.

"Yes." He turned back toward Hal. "And like being fired from Western Realty. I guess that one has given you lots of opportunities to choose."

"Well, that's not the way I've seen it. I feel used, abused, and jerked around."

"One thing I've learned is that life isn't so much about what happens *out there* ..." Donald said, opening his arms to the room about him. "But what happens *in here*." He pressed both hands to his heart. "Experiencing life from *the inside out* is far more powerful than experiencing it from the outside in. That's what handling Key Moments is all about."

"Key Moments," Hal repeated, thinking about his life. Slowly, he told Donald about his confrontations with Kathy, and throwing the wrench. He hung his head. "I've never felt so low in all my life." He looked up at Donald. "What has become of me? I used to think of myself as master of the universe."

Donald nodded slowly. "Remember the last time you were here? I told you I was drawn to people on the cusp of change, people with the courage necessary to make big changes. Tell me, Hal. Why did you come back? Are you here because you want to feel better? Or because you're ready to look at yourself and make the changes that will make a difference?"

Hal didn't hesitate. "A few days ago I wasn't ready. But I am now."

Donald gave a thumbs up. "I'm glad. Do you remember the Four Commitments you made last time you were here?"

"Oh, oh," Hal said, slightly embarrassed. "I haven't even thought about them." He held up the fingers of his right hand and concentrated. "I might be able to dredge them up. Let me think. Honesty, that's the first one."

"Yes. Honesty takes courage. It's what brought you here this morning. Do you remember the next one?"

"Don't tell me." Hal closed his eyes. "Accountability. That's the second one. Boy, I remember not liking that one when you first told me about it."

"Why do you suppose that is?"

"You said something about giving up blame and excuses and

seeing our part in whatever's going on. Sorry, but I still feel justified in blaming the board for what they did, voting me out."

Donald nodded. "Pretty normal. Accountability is a bitter pill to swallow. But until you're willing to be honest and accountable, Hal, you're destined to repeat the same mistakes." Donald paused. "So what's number three?"

Hal leaned forward, elbows on his knees, chin in his hands. "Well, if the first one is honesty, then accountability... Ah, I remember, responsibility. Making new choices."

"Right." Donald high-fived in Hal's direction. "Once you *own* the way things are, you can begin to make new choices. How about the fourth?"

"That one I do remember." He shifted in his chair. "Persistence and patience. I'm definitely not good at that one. I'm not patient with others, and especially not with myself."

"You do seem to beat up on yourself when things don't work out the way you think they should. But give yourself credit. You're taking this on." He smiled. "You *will* have setbacks, of course. You're not perfect."

"I'm not?" Hal answered with mock surprise. "Too bad those commitments aren't like waving a magic wand. *Presto, chango,* and I drive down the mountain a new man."

Donald chuckled. "Sorry. It's a process. We have to be patient with ourselves and remind ourselves to stay on the path, even when we make mistakes." He stopped and turned so he was facing Hal directly. "And from what you told me, you blew it last night, big time."

Shame washed over Hal. He recalled the look on Susie's face the second the wrench hit her. "The worst part is I saw I was losing it with Kathy, but I couldn't stop myself. I was furious and I wanted her to know it."

"Let me be honest with you, Hal. You're putting all the blame on Kathy and waiting for *her* to change." Donald's expression was unwavering.

Hal spoke quickly. "If she hadn't been standing there arguing with me—" He stopped suddenly, stunned by how swiftly he'd reverted to his defensive mode. "Okay," he admitted, "I suppose I have been blaming her. But, man, whenever we talk, she has a way of hitting me where it hurts, and all I want from her is a little compassion and support. Is that too much to ask?"

Donald answered the question with a question. "What choices have you been making about how she's treating you?"

Hal frowned. "I've reacted to her, sure, but I don't think I've made any choices. I've just been feeling bad."

"Really?" Donald moved forward to the edge of his chair. "The truth is, Hal, you won't get beyond this Key Moment, or any such troubling reality, until you own up to your choices." He raised his eyebrows. "Are you ready to do that?"

Hal felt uneasy. He got up and walked to the picture window, staring with unseeing eyes at the landscape before him. *Huh,* he thought. *A Key Moment.* The decision he made now would set his course for the days ahead. Could he be honest? Was he willing to be accountable *and* responsible? To persist when the going got tough?

Many minutes passed before he turned back to Donald. "Okay, I'm ready. Now what?"

Chapter 15

A Change of Heart

Donald held out the virtually untouched glass of cranberry drink. "Come enjoy your juice."

Hal drained it in one gulp. Then he smiled. "Okay, let me have it."

"To start, take a look at the choices you've been making about how Kathy has been treating you."

Hal groaned. "Back to that? What about *Kathy's* choices? I'm not alone in this, you know."

Donald nodded. "That's true, but I'm not talking to Kathy. I'm talking to you. So, I'll ask it again. What choices have *you* been making about how Kathy has been treating you?"

Hal fidgeted in his chair. "I'm not sure how to answer that question."

"Try it this way. Think back to a particular event when Kathy said or did something that really bothered you."

"That's easy." He sat upright. "The day I moved my office back home, when she told me I'd been acting like a big baby and that I need to grow up and stop feeling sorry for myself." Even now, the words sent a flush of amber to his cheeks. "I can't tell you how that galled me. She was totally insensitive to how devastated I felt."

"Good example," said Donald. "Remember the three R's?"

Hal nodded. "Yeah. I found it last night and put it in my wallet."

Donald invited him to move from the great room to the kitchen table. He took out a new sheet of paper and sketched a diagram.

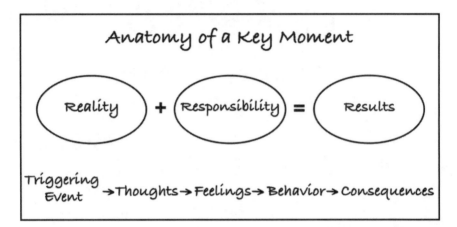

Donald motioned to him. "Pull your chair a little closer and let's talk some more about this concept of the Three R's to include what happens during a Key Moment." He pointed to the diagram. "A Key Moment begins with a triggering situation or event, usually an upsetting event that presents a challenge and demands a response. When this event occurs, you make choices about how you'll think, feel, and act. *Those* choices, not the event itself, determine the consequences or results you get."

Donald put down his pencil and pushed his chair back from the table so he was facing Hal. "So, think back to when Kathy made her comment. How did you choose to *feel*? How did you choose to *act*? What did you choose to *think* about what she said?"

"Well …" Embarrassed, Hal hesitated. "I guess I felt hurt."

Donald nodded. "Let me ask you to do something. From now on, use the words 'I chose' so you really own your experience. You *chose* to feel hurt. You see?"

Hal shook his head. "I don't see how I chose to feel hurt. It just happened."

"It seems that way, doesn't it? Our reactions during Key

Moments are so ingrained and automatic it doesn't seem like we choose them. But use the words anyway, even though you're not convinced." Donald leaned forward and spoke intently. "Think about what you felt and did after Kathy made her comment, and take responsibility for your reaction—by using the words 'I chose.'"

Hal sighed. "Okay. I *chose* to feel hurt … and resentful."

"Good." Donald sat back. "What other choices did you make?"

"I guess I chose to leave without saying goodbye or telling her where I was going." He sighed again.

"Hmm." Donald looked at Hal intently. "Let me ask you to do something else. "Take the 'I guesses' out of your statements. That'll help you be honest and clear, to really *own* your choices. Now, what else did you choose?"

Hal ran his fingers through his brown hair. Donald was leaving him no wiggle room, and was pushing him to face what was happening with Kathy in a new way. He thought of an old saying. *If you keep doing what you've been doing...* He soldiered on. "Okay, okay. I *chose* to punish her by brushing her off and not talking to her."

Donald nodded and smiled. "What else?"

Hal drew in a breath. "I *chose* to get in my truck and drive away."

"Anything else?"

He thought for a long time. "I *chose* to be defensive and argue when I came home late that night."

"That's it. You're starting to get the hang of it."

Unprompted, Hal continued. "I *chose* to sleep in the basement. I *chose* to avoid her by staying out in the garage and working on my car all the next week." He spit the next words out of his mouth, as if they were nasty. "And I *chose* to blame and resent her for the whole mess."

Donald reached over and gave Hal an encouraging pat on the back. "This kind of honesty is hard. You're doing great. Are you okay to go on?"

Hal nodded.

"Can you see the consequences of your choices?" he asked.

Hal dropped his head in silence. "They aren't pretty. Kathy and I both feel lousy. We don't talk or do things together. I'm sleeping in the basement. It seems like I'm on edge and reactive." He looked up, shaking his head. "It's gotta be taking a terrible toll on the kids."

"Sounds like it's been hard on all of you."

Hal nodded.

"I'd like you to consider something." Donald moved his chair a tiny bit closer. "You don't like how Kathy's treating you. But are you willing to see how *your* actions actually *provoke* her to act in the very ways you hate and even complain about?"

Hal raised his head. "No way. Aren't you taking this a little too far? The last thing I want is for her to be so insensitive and unsupportive."

"But think about it. You complain that she doesn't support you. Yet, you refuse to really listen and acknowledge the depth of *her* concerns. You get defensive and head for the hills, you move down to the basement, you hide out in your shop." He paused. "Can you see the effect of your actions on *her*?" Donald leaned forward to drive his point home. "You push her away. Then you claim she doesn't support *you*."

It was true. Hal saw with painful clarity the game he'd been playing with Kathy and what it had cost him. He'd rebuffed her many times, like when she'd asked him to work with her to create a financial plan. He'd *chosen* to be angry and defensive and build a case against her.

He then thought about all the ways Kathy did support him—working at a job she didn't love, paying the bills, running the household, being there for the kids, always asking him about his day. Even the note she'd left him the night he first moved to the basement.

"I've been busy looking for reasons to justify my resentment. Actually, there are lots of ways Kathy supports me." Hal's eyes glanced around the room. "But I haven't been willing to admit them."

Donald nodded. "Yes. It's not about what others do to us, Hal. It's about what we do to ourselves." His expression was warm and accepting. "You're the one who has made yourself unhappy and alienated from Kathy."

Hal closed his eyes and leaned back, blowing out an audible breath. He was quiet for a moment and then said, nodding, "I get it." He opened his eyes. "This is a lot to take in all at once, Donald. I'd love a little fresh air."

"How about a little walk?" Donald led the way to the door. They walked outside and down the path to the turnaround where they'd first met. Hal could see that Donald had a view of the turnaround where he'd parked that dark night. Suddenly, he had a moment of realization. "The first day we met, you didn't come down this path by chance, did you? You knew I was down here."

Donald nodded. "I saw you drive up that night. When you didn't leave the next morning, I thought I'd better check to see if you were okay."

Hal extended his hand. "Thanks, man."

They walked a further distance beyond the turnaround. Then Donald asked, "Ready to hear more about Key Moments?"

Hal grinned and quoted from *A Christmas Carol,* which his mother had always played on Christmas Eve. "'Lead on, Spirit. If you have aught to teach me, let me profit from it.'"

Donald laughed heartily. "Ebenezer Scrooge."

They returned to the cabin, and Donald made coffee. When they were seated at the table with their steaming mugs, Donald began. "We've been talking about how you chose to feel and act when Kathy made her comment. But the most *important* choices we make during a Key Moment have to do with our thoughts or the *meaning* we give events—the way we talk to ourselves about what's going on."

He invited Hal to look at the Key Moment diagram on the table in front of them. "See? How you feel and act flow from your *thoughts*." He gave him a minute to study the cause-effect nature depicted in the schematic.

"Okay, I see that."

"The reason we don't feel like we choose our reactions is because our thoughts are automatic. They're linked to beliefs that are often so deeply held that we aren't even aware of them."

105

"Okay," said Hal, nodding slowly.

Donald looked right at Hal. "So tell me about your thoughts. How did you interpret what Kathy said? What *meaning* did you give her comments that you should grow up and stop feeling sorry for yourself?"

Hal snorted. "That's easy. I guess ... Oops, I mean I *chose* to believe that all she cares about is my paycheck, that losing my dream doesn't matter to her."

Donald picked up a notebook. "Mind if I take notes? Only so you won't have to worry about remembering everything you're coming up with now."

Hal nodded and closed his eyes. "I *chose* to believe she's insensitive and doesn't care about what I'm going through. I *chose* to believe she thinks I'm a pain to be around, that I'm a whiner." He swallowed. "That I'm not much of a man."

Donald looked up from his notepad. "Anything else?"

Hal thought for a moment. "That's about it."

"That's quite a list. Can you see how *your* thinking about what Kathy said—your interpretations and the meaning you put on it—caused you to feel hurt and upset and to act the way you did?"

"Now that you put it that way ..." Hal had never examined his thoughts this way. He was astonished to realize he'd been reacting automatically and just assumed his point of view was the truth about the situation. No wonder he reacted to Kathy's words with little insight into why they disturbed him so.

Donald showed Hal the notebook in which he'd written his thoughts. "Choose the thought that's the most troubling to you," he suggested.

Hal rubbed his forehead. "I'd have to say it's my belief that Kathy is insensitive and doesn't care about how painful it was to be fired."

"Now take a moment to look at all the consequences of believing that thought." Donald paused to give Hal a moment to think. "Can you see how your thinking caused you to feel and to act?" he asked.

"Yeah, I'm beginning to." Then an uncomfortable thought intruded. "But what if it's true? What if she *doesn't* care that I was fired? She didn't like me getting into real estate in the first place. Maybe she's happy it didn't work out, and hopes I'll just get a *real* job."

Donald chortled. "That's certainly what you've been telling yourself, Hal. But in my experience, our negative beliefs distort the truth of a situation."

Hal cocked his head to the side. "I'm not sure what you mean."

"Well, we act as if our beliefs are the truth, the whole truth, and nothing but the truth—but they aren't. When we examine them carefully, we discover they are extremely flawed." Donald winked at Hal. "Let me share some common distortions in our beliefs. As we go over them, tell me which of them applies to your belief that Kathy is insensitive and uncaring about what's happened to you."

"Should I take notes?" Hal asked dryly.

Donald laughed. "For now, let's just chat. Probably the easiest distortion to understand is black-and-white thinking. This happens when we look at the world in *either/or* terms. Good/bad, ugly/beautiful, friend/enemy. We don't allow for anything in between." Donald paused, with a glint in his eye. "For example, sensitive or insensitive, supportive or unsupportive."

"Hey, hey. Let's not get personal." Hal smiled and stood. "I think I get what you're saying." He began pacing. "I've been telling myself Kathy doesn't care. Period. No gray. She just doesn't care. So I've felt justified in being angry at her and shutting her out." He stopped. "I can see now that things might look different if I allowed for the possibility that she *does* care … but is dealing with issues of her own. Is that what you mean?"

"Yeah." Donald nodded vigorously. "Let's look at another common distortion: *overgeneralizing*. This is when we see one event or a few events as the truth, and we only let in information that *confirms* that belief. We refuse to acknowledge any evidence to the contrary. Can you see how this type of distortion may have made you discount the supportive things Kathy has said and done?"

Hal frowned. "Okay, I can see how I've overgeneralized. She *has* said some things that I thought were unsupportive. And maybe they were. But, if I'm really honest with myself, I can also see ways she's tried to connect and be there for me. When I came upstairs the first morning after I slept in the basement, she'd left a nice note, telling me she felt bad for what I was going through, but I told myself it wasn't a true apology."

"I didn't know that."

"That's because I didn't tell you," Hal said, chagrined.

"Remember, Hal, that the mind sees only what it's looking for. If we go raspberry picking, raspberries are what we find. Perhaps you decided, even a long time ago, that Kathy doesn't support you. And all you have looked for—and found—has been evidence you were right. Any other evidence, you dismissed or didn't let in. You tossed it in the trash, kind of like that note."

Hal sat down again and rested his head in his hands. "I could have been nicer to her. Like leaving a message on her cell phone, saying thanks. Or being a little warmer when she came home that night."

"Courage, friend. All is not lost." Donald almost laughed. "What you're doing right now is indulging in *another* kind of distortion—*catastrophizing*. It's when we make an issue that is *this* big" he held his hands close together "into something *this* big." He flung his hands far apart in an exaggerated gesture that made Hal laugh. "You tossed away a note from Kathy. Now you're thinking you've tossed away your whole relationship."

"Guilty as charged." Hal held up his hands above his head. "I see how I did the same with her comment about me needing to grow up. It really upset me. I *let* it upset me," he amended.

"You're catching on, Hal. Ready for another pesky distortion?"

"Sure. Give it to me."

"*Mind-reading.* That's when we assume we know what others are thinking and feeling, but without checking it out. A friend fails to say hi, so we conclude he must be mad at us; but maybe he's having a bad day or is just caught up in his own thoughts. We really don't know what's going on in other people's heads without asking them. Does this apply to you and Kathy?"

Hal picked up the Key Moments diagram from the table and rolled it into a tube. He tapped it against the side of his chair. "She made her feelings pretty clear when she told me to grow up. I didn't read her mind about that." His voice was sharper than he intended.

"No, but you did interpret her words in a certain way, maybe in a different way than she intended." Donald gave Hal a moment to consider the idea. "Has Kathy actually *told* you she doesn't care? Is it possible she cares very much and still wants to tell you to stop feeling sorry for yourself?"

Hal sighed. "I suppose, but that doesn't seem very sensitive."

"Maybe not, but it was only *one* comment ... and you don't *really* know what was behind it without checking it out. Can you see any possibilities other than she doesn't love you or is insensitive to you?"

Hal grabbed a tissue from the box on the table and waved it in the air. "Okay, okay. I surrender. My thinking is a mess."

They both laughed.

Hal felt lighter. "What a different way of looking at what happened."

"If you're open and humble enough to see it," said Donald. Then he continued. "You know, there are *other* distortions that we haven't even talked about."

Hal rolled his eyes. "Save them for another Key Moment. If I'm ever dumb enough to have one with you around."

Donald laughed. "Fair enough." Then he looked intently at Hal. "Are you ready to move beyond the belief that Kathy is insensitive and doesn't care to a more helpful belief?"

Hal nodded. "Yeah, I'd like that."

"Then first, turn the belief around. Take the old belief, *Kathy is insensitive and doesn't care about what I'm going through,* and switch the subject and object so it's something *you* are doing to *Kathy,* rather than the other way around. Start the sentence with *I am ...*"

Hal sat up in his chair, anticipation rising. "Okay." He had to think for a moment. "*I* am insensitive and don't care about what *Kathy* is going through." Hal doubled over, burying his head in his hands. "It's true." He shook his head and looked at Donald. "I've been so wrapped up in myself, I haven't even thought about what she's going through." He bowed his head again, absorbing the impact of his realization.

"There's another step." Donald waited for Hal to look up before going on. "Turn the original statement around to its exact opposite. Instead of 'Kathy is *in*sensitive,' it would be—"

Hal nodded. "I know what you're asking. It would be 'Kathy *is* sensitive and *does* care about what I'm going through.'" The small change floored him. The effect on his clarity and feelings was stunning.

Donald looked at him intently. "What do you think, Hal? Could this possibly be true about Kathy?"

Hal nodded, too moved with emotion to speak.

Donald waited. "Now's your chance to choose a new and empowering belief about Kathy, to replace the old one. What would be a more honest and helpful belief? Brainstorm several."

Hal pondered. "I don't believe she's insensitive ..."

"Put that one in a positive way."

"Okay. Kathy is sensitive and she loves me a lot." Once Hal got started, a number of statements flooded his mind. "She supports me in a hundred ways. She wants me to do well. It matters to her that I was fired. She loves me deeply and cares about what happens to me." He looked up smiling.

"Great," Donald said. "Now choose the phrase you like best."

"That's easy. Kathy loves me deeply and cares about what happens to me."

"How would you feel if you acted from this belief?"

Hal's eyes moistened. "I would feel loved and cared for," he said softly. "I would be able to let go of my hurt and resentment. I would be less defensive ... and I wouldn't get offended so easily."

"How would this affect your behavior?"

"Well, I'd spend more time with her." He thought. "I'd ask her to tell me how *she's* doing ... and I'd really listen to what she says. I'd give her more hugs. I'd figure out ways to support *her,* like helping around the house more."

Donald's eyes were closed, his hands resting on his stomach. "What do you think would be the consequences of these new behaviors?"

Hal grinned. "Kathy and I would be close again. We would

work together to solve some of the problems we're facing." His eyes lit up. "The kids would feel safer, too, and less anxious about what's going on. We'd be more of a family, and I'd feel better about myself."

Donald opened his eyes and looked at Hal. "I'd say that's quite a change from how you were feeling before."

"No kidding."

"Okay, let's summarize. Your old belief was that Kathy is insensitive and doesn't care about how your loss devastated you. Your *new* belief is that Kathy loves you deeply and *does* care about what happens to you." Donald shifted in his chair so he was facing Hal. "So ... are you willing to integrate this new belief into your life now and act on it for the next month?"

A shiver went through him. Fear ... exhilaration? Maybe both. "Yes, I am," he declared soberly. He thought about his recent encounters with Kathy and the kids. He remembered the despair as he sat alone in the darkness last night after throwing the wrench. He looked right at Donald. "I'm starting to see how I've created my own misery." Making that statement gave him the first glimmer of hope he'd felt in weeks. "I don't know how to thank you, Donald."

Donald waved his finger back and forth. "Thank yourself. You did the work. Speaking of which ..." Donald took a sheet of paper out of a drawer and handed it to Hal. "Every good teacher assigns homework." He smiled.

"What is it?"

"Just something to help you work through your Key Moments." He grinned. "And the good news is, you're going to have *lots* of opportunities to practice."

Hal looked at the heading on the sheet of paper: *Stop – Look – Listen – Choose*. He smiled at Donald. "Sounds like instructions for a school kid learning to cross the street."

No longer hasty to dismiss Donald's homespun wisdom, he folded the paper carefully and tucked it into his back pocket, along with the Three R's and the Anatomy of a Key Moment. *Too bad they didn't teach kids Donald's insights when I was in elementary school,* thought Hal. *Might have made life a whole lot easier.*

Hal drove out of the mountains thinking about the hunting trip of his youth when he'd become lost in the new-fallen snow. Just as he was about to fire a few shots into the air, he heard the distant beep of a car horn, alerting him as to the direction and distance back to camp. There was a literal spinning sensation in his brain as the universe twisted back into shape and he recognized exactly where he was. *Hey, I've seen that tree! And that rock! They have a little snow on them, that's all.* He had tramped back to camp in less than five minutes.

That's the way I feel now, thought the adult Hal. It was as though the universe had twisted into shape. A measure of self-deception had been revealed. He felt as though he were back in the driver's seat of his life, having emerged from a heavy fog.

Chapter 16

A Beginning

Kathy woke to the sounds of activity and laughter in the kitchen. Laughter? She struggled to sit up, but the spinning room forced her back down. Then she heard the doorbell ring.

"Pizza's here!" Derek yelled.

More laughter and chatter, and the smell of cheese and tomato sauce wafted up the stairs, making her stomach do flip-flops. Fury added to her misery. How could they all be down there talking and laughing as if nothing was wrong? Maybe they were buying Hal's optimism— *Everything will be all right. Trust me. I love you guys more than anything in the world*—but *she* wasn't. She reached for the pills and water on the nightstand, swallowed another dose, and pulled the pillow over her head, blocking out the happy voices from downstairs.

She woke again, sometime later, to the thumping of music coming from Nicole's room. Tentatively, she rose up on one elbow. When the room didn't shift, she pulled herself up. *So far, so good.* She washed her face, got into her pajamas, and stood still a moment. Should she go downstairs, or back to bed? As much as she didn't want an encounter with anyone, she needed to get something in her stomach.

She made it to the kitchen and was heating water for a cup of strong tea when Hal quietly joined her.

"Got one of those headaches?" he asked. "The kids said you were already home and asleep when they got home from school."

Kathy nodded.

"Can I do anything for you?"

"No." She avoided eye contact. "I'm going to have some tea. Then I'm going back to bed. I need to be able to work tomorrow."

"Here. Sit down." He gently led her to a stool at the kitchen island. "Let me take care of that."

When the microwave beeped, he took the cup out and put the Sweet Dreams herbal tea bag in it. "I hope the kids and I didn't wake you. I kept telling them to quiet down. I know you need to sleep when you get a bad headache."

"It sounded like you were having a party. I'm not sure what you could possibly be celebrating after last night."

"We weren't celebrating anything, except maybe that we've come to an understanding." He clasped his hands together near his chest.

"That easy, was it?" she said. "What did you do? Tell them you were sorry and you'd do better next time?"

"No." She caught the shame in his eyes as he turned away. "The kids were pretty upset with me, and I don't blame them." He looked back at Kathy, his face grim. "It took some talking to get them to open up, and I think it's going to take some time to earn back their trust." He closed his eyes. "Kath, you were right about how worried the kids are. Once they started talking, I got a real earful." He shook his head. "Did you know they were afraid we'd have to move, start at a new school, and give up their lessons?"

"Yes. I tried to tell you before, but you wouldn't listen."

"I listened today. Maybe that's why they sounded happy during dinner. I think they feel like they have their dad back."

He removed the tea bag from the cup of hot water, pressed it dry, then placed the cup and saucer in front of her. "You look pretty wiped out, Kath. Why don't you call in and ask for a sub tomorrow? It might do you some good to have the day off." He paused. "Maybe we could talk, too."

Kathy glanced at him coldly. Why were the kids so willing to forgive him anything? "Whatever you have to say," she answered harshly, "you can say right now."

Hal pulled back, then nodded. "I'm really sorry for last night. It was stupid."

"That's a new strategy," she said. "I was expecting you to blame me, the kids, your father, the board, Charlie White. Maybe even God." She raised an eyebrow contemptuously.

Anger flashed in Hal's eyes, but then he calmed himself. "Yeah, I've been doing that a lot, haven't I? I'm ready to do something different now—if you'll give me another chance."

He looked so relaxed and positive that Kathy wondered if he'd been drinking. But she knew he never touched alcohol. Something was going on. This submissiveness was totally out of character. She sipped the hot tea and felt her body relax. "How did you explain to Susie about last night? Not only did you hit her, you scared her deeply."

"Susie knows I wasn't throwing the wrench at her." He paused as he looked at Kathy across the kitchen island, realizing that she wasn't only speaking of Susie. "I told her—actually, all of the kids—that I was a jerk, feeling like the whole world was against me. And I apologized to them for letting my emotions get out of control." His voice was solemn. "I promised that from now on I'll take responsibility for whatever's going on, and said they can count on me to act like an adult."

Kathy stared at him. Where was this coming from? "Did they believe you?" she asked.

He nodded. "I think so. They seemed relieved. Susie even gave me a hug."

"I'll bet that made you proud." She saw how her sarcasm erased the peaceful smile from his face. "You might be able to sweet-talk them, Hal Stratton, but not me. Unless I see some real proof, I'm not buying it."

He sighed and nodded. "I haven't been a very good husband lately. I know that. But I'm seeing things differently now. Will you please give me the chance to tell you about it?"

"I'm all ears."

"I know this seems abrupt, Kath—but I had the most extraordinary experience today. I was talking to this guy I met in the mountains—"

"This *guy?*"

"An old man named Donald Millhouse. He happened upon me the morning after I'd been fired. That's when I first met him."

"Right. After you had *Janine* tell me you wouldn't be home all night."

"I said I'm sorry about that, Kath. And I really am. I wasn't thinking about how it would be for you. I'm sorry."

She gazed at him with harsh skepticism. An apology. *Umph. Right.*

He sighed softly. "Anyway, Donald is a remarkable man. What he's been through makes my trouble seem small in comparison. He's been teaching me the lessons life has taught him—and it's been a real eye-opener ... and I'm beginning to see *my* part in what's happened."

"Has he told you to get a job?" she asked.

The excitement in his eyes faded. "Not in so many words. But," he added with a note of hope, "what I'm learning is going to open up a way for me—for *us*—to move forward. Like Scrooge said in *A Christmas Carol*." He stood with arms outstretched. "I'll honor Christmas—the past, the present, and the future. I will. I will."

She stared at him. "Are you out of your mind?"

"I'm just quoting Ebenezer," he explained. "The Spirits of Christmas changed *him* in one night." He laughed. "I'm a new man, Kathy. We'll be okay, I promise you."

"That was quite a speech. I'll give you that. But unless you can tell me you've got work, or you've decided to take your father's offer to give us a loan, I don't know what we have to talk about." She took another sip of tea.

"You're right about the job ... and the loan," he said, surprising her again. "We do need something to cover the car payment. Why don't you activate an advance on one of our credit cards? I know the interest rates are killers, but I'd rather pay them than owe my father money."

"Now, that sure sounds like taking responsibility to me," she said sharply. "Let's go even further into debt. And oh, yes, let's make sure we get an interest rate that will put us even further behind. What a great idea."

Hal held up both hands. He closed his eyes and spoke slowly, feeling his way through a new sense of inner guidance. "You're right, Kathy. The best place to get the money *is* from my father. I'm not going to let it mean I'm a failure for borrowing money from him." He opened his eyes. "I'll call him tomorrow morning. And I'll call Sam and take him up on his offer." He looked her squarely in the eyes and asked softly. "Would that help you feel better?"

His words shocked her, and she didn't know how to respond.

Hal stood up. "Now, let's get you to bed so you'll feel better tomorrow."

She let him help her up the stairs. She wanted to believe he had changed, but feared the old Hal would be back in the morning.

Chapter 17

Payoffs and Prices

The next morning, Wednesday, Hal was full of enthusiasm. He made coffee while Kathy got ready for school. Then he made toast and stirred up frozen orange juice. It was going to be a great day. He knew it!

Kathy looked pale but determined when she came into the kitchen. He handed her a cup of coffee and put a plate of toast on the table for her. "You sure you should be going to work?" he asked. "You look pretty shaky."

"Thanks for the concern, but I'm the one with a job," she said without looking at him.

"Kathy, didn't anything I said last night make a difference?" His tone begged for reassurance.

She sat on a stool and put her hand to her forehead. Even the sound of his voice was painful. "It all depends on what you do next."

"That's fair," he said, sitting next to her. "But will you at least give me the benefit of the doubt?"

She shook her head slightly. "I'm afraid to get my hopes up."

Hal realized he couldn't just talk himself out of his reactive behavior of the last several weeks. "Remember the man I told you about? Donald Millhouse."

She huffed. "Your mountain man guru? What about him?"

"He asked me to make some commitments." Hal ticked them off on his fingers one by one: "To be honest. To be accountable for the way things are. To be willing to make new choices. And to be patient, because real change takes time, and there are setbacks along the way." He sighed, feeling the truth of the last commitment all too clearly. "I'm not going to be perfect, Kathy, but I'm ..." he almost said *trying* "... committed."

"Interesting." She shoved her plate of uneaten toast to the middle of the island and stood to leave. She filled a thermos with coffee and put a protein bar in her purse, which she slung over her shoulder, then picked up her briefcase.

"Did you hear what I said?" he asked.

"I heard," she mumbled.

"Would you be willing to be patient with me?"

She looked at him through tired eyes. "Okay. But only for so long." She slipped out the door to the garage.

That went well, Hal thought. He was still wondering how he could get through to her when the kids started coming downstairs. They weren't the cheerful troopers he'd expected. They bickered with each other as they ate breakfast and then scrambled to gather schoolwork, lunches, and their bags for after-school sports. Was this the usual morning routine? Or were they still upset over his display of anger in the shop? Last night they had been full of hope, maybe a tenuous hope. It was a letdown.

Feeling the need for activity, he cleaned the kitchen, straightened the family room, and put in a load of laundry. The disappointing conversation with Kathy this morning kept intruding. He smiled slightly, thinking that Donald must have an idea of what he was going through. Why else would he have stressed patience and perseverance so much?

He went to his study to plan his calls to Sam and his father. But he couldn't stop thinking about Kathy. He desperately wanted to have a good conversation with her tonight and was alarmed by how easy it would be to get "hooked" into his old reactions. *First things first,* he told himself. His father and Sam would have to wait. He picked up the phone and dialed Donald.

119

Donald answered on the first ring, as if expecting his call. Hal gave him the rundown on what had happened last night and this morning. "I have a lot to make up for, and Kathy isn't going to let me off easy. Neither are Derek or Susie. Man, I can't believe how I've alienated my family these last several weeks, when I look back on it. What was I thinking? Why have I been acting this way?"

"Payoffs and prices," Donald responded, as if on cue.

Hal had thought his question rhetorical. "What?" he asked.

"You were getting something out of it. A payoff is a reward we get from our negative choices. You've been getting lots of payoffs from how you've been acting with Kathy."

"Well, that's good to know," laughed Hal. "Because it seems to me all I've been getting is turmoil and misery."

Donald chuckled. "Well, you get that, too. I call the negative consequences rip-offs." He continued. "The thing is, payoffs are immediate, and rip-offs are delayed, which makes it easy to slip into negative ways of reacting during our Key Moments. If we didn't get payoffs, we wouldn't handle these situations so poorly."

"Give me an example."

"Okay. What payoffs or rewards might someone get out of complaining?"

Hal smirked. "You're not talking about me, are you?"

"Oh, no," answered Donald. "This is purely hypothetical."

Hal leaned back in his chair and put his feet on his desk. "I guess a payoff is that it feels good to let off steam."

"Good example," said Donald. "Can you think of some more?"

"It feels good to get someone to take your side and agree with you." Hal concentrated. "It's easier than doing something about the problem … It's a way to blame someone else so you don't have to do anything about it."

"That's it," Donald interrupted. "Now, what are some rip-offs—or negative consequences—for complaining?"

Hal stared out his study window. "Well, it doesn't change anything. You feel stuck. Powerless. Like there's no hope, and nothing you do makes a difference."

"You've got the idea. Do you think you're ready to apply this notion of payoffs to what's been going on between you and Kathy?"

Hal took his feet off his desk and sat up. "Why not. I almost lost it a couple times with Kathy since I came home."

"Cut yourself some slack. Old habits are deeply ingrained. It doesn't take much to hit one of our hot buttons, and just like that, we're in an old pattern."

"That's the truth." Hal picked up a glass, pyramid-shaped paperweight from his desk.

"So, what payoffs do you get from being defensive around Kathy?" asked Donald.

"I get to leave." The words popped out of his mouth without thinking. "That's a big one for me. I don't like conflict."

"Any others?"

Hal rubbed his thumb over the smooth glass. "I can put all the blame on her ... I see myself as right, and her wrong. I guess that's a payoff. I mean, I *know* it is."

"Good example."

"It gives me a reason to be mad." Hal was glad he didn't have to look Donald in the eyes. "Being mad and offended gives me an excuse to avoid her and the kids."

"Yep."

"It's a way of punishing her. Wow, that's tough to admit. But I can see how I've been wanting to get even and make her feel bad ... and then hoping that she'd feel sorry for me and apologize." Hal laughed and then continued. "I hate to admit it, but I've also been getting some kind of pleasure out of licking my wounds and wallowing in self-pity."

Donald chuckled. "Lots of us do, Hal. Lots of us do."

Hal sighed heavily as he put the paperweight back on his desk. "I've never looked at it like this. I can see what you mean about payoffs."

"Can you see how being aware of your payoffs can help you avoid getting hooked into old patterns?" asked Donald.

"I can see that," Hal said thoughtfully.

"There's another reason we slip into being reactive," said Donald. "There's a price tag that comes with change, and sometimes we just aren't willing or ready to pay that price." He paused. "For example, what price would you pay to act from the new belief you came up with when you were here yesterday?"

"You mean, *Kathy loves me and cares about what happens to me*?" Hal considered the question. "I'd have to stop blaming her. I'd have to stop trying to make her feel sorry for me." He grimaced. "I'd have to stop feeling sorry for myself."

"Anything else?"

"Oh, boy." Hal chuckled self-consciously. "I'd have to stop walking out every time things get tense. I'd talk to her ... and really listen."

"Wouldn't that be something?"

"Easier said than done. Especially if she's blaming and accusing me."

"Yep. Anything else?"

Hal was drawing a blank.

"What about wanting Kathy to change, so you don't have to?"

Hal grinned and absently began moving file folders around on his desk. "You don't let me get away with anything, do you? I'd have to stop manipulating her. I'd have to admit I was wrong."

"So now you see why it's hard to change."

"Yeah. Payoffs and prices are very real."

"Like gravity," Donald said. "They pull us back to the old and familiar status quo—even when we want things to be different."

"I sure felt that with Kathy this morning."

"Going by how you feel right now, are the payoffs worth the long-term negative consequences in your relationships with Kathy and your kids?"

"Absolutely not," said Hal.

"Are you willing to pay a rather hefty price to make things different?"

Hal nodded, aware that Donald couldn't see him. "I am, but I've been in this pattern so long."

"Don't get caught up in thinking about the past," said Donald. "The key is to look ahead, at what you really want. You overcome bad behavior by creating a vision that is far more compelling than your payoffs." He paused. "In fact, I want you to do that right now.

Get a pencil and paper and start writing. I'll wait. Oh, and Hal, make sure to use positive statements: what you want, not what you don't want."

"Okay." With the receiver scrunched between his ear and shoulder, Hal grabbed a pad and pen and started writing: *Show Kathy I love her. Make time to talk. Not get defensive about money.* He looked at that last sentence. He crossed it out and rewrote it. *Listen to Kathy with an open mind and heart.* He continued writing his vision for Kathy and his kids until he could think of nothing more. He fidgeted with his pen a moment and then added *Move back to the bedroom.* He smiled. "I think I'm getting it, Donald. What's next?"

"Begin each day by thinking about what you want." And then Donald added, "You have to decide what matters more, Hal—your payoffs or your vision—because you'll be faced with that trade-off several times a day."

Hal sat at his desk, his scribbled list in front of him. His vision of what he wanted with his family. But if this was his vision, didn't it deserve to be presented in a fashion more suited to its importance? He booted up his computer and typed the words into a document, one sentence to each line, then played around with various fonts until he was satisfied with how it looked. Finally, he added a border and clicked "print." He taped the finished document where he could see it from his desk. The first time Hal Stratton had clarified what he wanted for himself and his family.

Chapter 18
Making Things Right

Time to get on with his day. He still had to place those calls to Sam and his father. But another thought deflected him from the task. The wrench episode and all the preoccupation with his family had eclipsed his concerns about Western Realty. He had no idea what had gone on there these last several days. He took a deep breath to calm himself—blowing out on a count of four as he dialed Janine's number.

Her assessment was blunt. "Things are really falling apart around here. Everyone depended on your enthusiasm, to say nothing of your ability to bring in new business. Despite the wretched rumor about why you were fired, lots of your old contacts don't want to talk to any of the other partners. They sure don't want to talk to Charlie. They want you."

"Hah!" Hal gave a victory punch. Served them right!

The silence on the other end of the line told him Janine didn't share his sentiment. "What?" he asked.

"I felt the same way," Janine continued slowly. "But then I got thinking that we all lose if we can't bring home some deals. The company badly needs cash flow."

His mood changed instantly. Hal gazed out the study window, thinking about Donald's words about the trade-off between payoffs and vision. It was tempting to gloat and let the partners flounder. But that was pretty shortsighted. He *did* care about the company. "You're right. Maybe I need to make some calls. Talk to some of my old contacts, encourage them to keep negotiating with the company even though I'm not there. I can refer them to one of the property managers, maybe Quentin. Anything else?"

Janine replied in a low tone. "The board is cooking up something. I don't know what. I think someone will be calling you soon to ask for a meeting."

"You think they're looking to buy me out?" His voice was animated.

"I don't think they're in the mood for that." Her tone was subdued.

"No, probably not. Hey, thanks for the heads-up." He paused. "Uh, you doing okay? I mean, the atmosphere being what it is around there and all."

She laughed. "Oh, I can handle it. But everyone I've talked to worries about the future of the company. And they all miss you." The other end of the line was quiet for a moment. "So do I." Then she added brightly, "But what can I say? Life goes on."

"That it does." Hal hung up feeling uneasy. The very thought of the temptation he'd felt during lunch a few weeks back ... and how close he'd come ... horrified him, especially in light of the vision statement he'd written for his family. The statement that now hung on the wall opposite where he sat.

Hal sat at his desk in the study, rolling a pen between his fingers. It was going to be tough making calls on behalf of the company without painting his partners as turncoats. But he had a responsibility for the business relationships he had carefully nurtured. Making the calls was the right thing to do. He picked up the phone and started dialing.

By mid-afternoon, Hal felt drained but satisfied. People were glad to hear from him and responded positively to his encouragement to follow up with Quentin. So he went out to the Garage Mahal to spend a little time with Lucy. He'd developed a real connection with the Caddy since giving her a name. She seemed to speak to him, letting him know how to solve some of the restoration problems he'd been working on. Actually, that was how she'd gotten her name. It had appeared in his mind while working on the car, as if the Caddy was letting him in on a secret.

He hadn't intended to sequester himself in the shop again, but when Derek appeared in the doorway to tell him dinner was ready, Hal realized he'd done it again. Dinner was stir-fry frozen vegetables with chicken, an easy meal for a tired woman after a long day. He kicked himself for not preparing the one thing he was good at, Tater Tot casserole. A hot meal would have let Kathy know he was thinking of her.

He approached her slowly. "How are you feeling? Headache gone?"

"Yes." She nodded as she emptied the contents of dinner from an electric frying pan into a serving dish. "Thank heaven for drugs." She looked at him. "Did you call your parents to arrange for the loan?"

"Darn!" Hal smacked his forehead. "I got so involved with making calls for Western that I forgot."

"Why am I not surprised?" she said, carrying the dish to the table.

"I wasn't frittering away my time, Kathy. Honest. I'll tell you what I did today during dinner."

She turned and stared at him, tears in her eyes. "I'm really not hungry. Why don't you and the kids eat. I'm going to put in a load of wash, and I've got a pile of tests to correct. If you want to help, you can do the dishes and make sure the kids do their homework." She turned abruptly and went upstairs.

Hal did as requested, without argument. He helped the kids clean up dinner, then stayed with them as they did their homework. The time couldn't pass quickly enough. Finally, he said goodnight to each of them and approached a closed bedroom door. He knocked lightly before entering.

Kathy was propped up on the bed, a pile of tests lying on the bedspread.

"Mind if I have a seat?" he asked, timidly.

She shrugged, making no move to put down the test she was correcting.

He sat on the love seat in the bay window facing the bed. As he opened his mouth to speak, he realized just how much humility was going to be required to accept personal responsibility. He would have to give up his pride, his need to "win." Abandon his self-justifying thoughts and the urge to defend his ego. Earlier in the day, this had seemed like an exciting idea, but at the moment, he felt vulnerable. He wanted to turn and walk away.

"I owe you a huge apology for not calling Sam and my father today."

Kathy rolled her eyes.

"I know you're mad at me, and I can't blame you." She continued looking down at her test. Several seconds passed before he spoke again. "Do you want me to leave?"

Kathy tossed the test from her lap onto the bed and glared. "I knew you wouldn't call your father. The moment I left this morning. Words! That's all they were."

"That was wrong of me, Kathy. I know that. I made a promise and didn't keep it."

"You and your phony promises. And now you think you can come in here and apologize to me and, presto, everything's supposed to be okay. Well it's not." Her expression was stern and angry.

Hal closed his eyes and nodded. He waited.

"You have no idea how concerned I am about our family." Kathy's voice blared. "We have about enough money in the bank to get us through the next month and that's it. And the worst part is that you don't even care. Every time I try to talk to you about it, you just blow me off."

Hal looked up. "I want you to know I *do* care. I care that we're almost out of money … and I care how worried you are." He studied her face carefully and continued, more slowly. "You must feel completely powerless. It's up to me to do something about our financial situation, and I don't seem to be taking it seriously."

"That's right." Kathy sniffed, grabbed a tissue from the bed stand, and dabbed her eyes. "I can't talk to you about it without you getting defensive or leaving."

"I see that." Hal regretted profoundly the way he'd been acting. "But I'm not leaving tonight … and I don't want to be defensive."

Neither spoke.

"I've been very insensitive to you, Kathy. I've been so wrapped up in myself that I haven't thought about how my being fired has affected you and the kids. I know you're really worried." He gave her a slight smile. "What would you like to see happen? What would feel good to you?"

"For you to get a job. Take the loan."

Hal sighed and then smiled. "You're right. I'll call my father tomorrow. And as far as the job goes, I really did start the process last week when I called all my contacts. But I have to tell you, it was devastating that no one called back except Sam. Then when he told me how badly my reputation was damaged, I was floored. The public humiliation is even worse than being fired."

Kathy drew her knees up and rested her arms on them.

"I know it looks like I'm not doing anything, but I don't want to take just any job. I want something I can put my heart into." Hal noticed Kathy stiffen. "But I don't want you to worry, either." His tone was upbeat. "In the meantime, I'll accept Sam's offer to manage some of his properties. It was generous of him to make the gesture ... And I *will* call my father."

Kathy lowered her head. Hal got off the love seat and sat on the edge of the bed. "Hey." He reached out and touched her lightly on the arm. "I know you won't believe me until it happens. But I want you to know I'm sincere."

She looked up with moist eyes. "I *want* to believe you."

He held out a hand. Kathy took it, and Hal pulled her into a warm embrace. After a minute he pulled back so he could look at her. "I'm also going to take the bull by the horns and find out if there's a way I can get some of our money out of the company."

"The mythical millions," she said sarcastically.

"What do you mean, mythical? The equity we have in Western puts us in a nice financial position."

"But I can't pay the bills with it. If it's not available for that, it might as well be mythical."

He grunted. "No wonder you think I'm taking our situation too lightly. Will it make you feel better to know I'm thinking of asking my partners to buy me out?" His voice was enthusiastic. "I'm willing to work out a deal that doesn't put too much strain on the business but gives us a steady flow of income. I can't see why they wouldn't accept my offer. They don't want me around; it seems like a win for all of us."

Kathy was quiet, leaning back against the headboard.

"What's the matter?" Hal asked.

"I'm just afraid ..."

"What?"

"Okay. I appreciate you listening to me tonight. And I love what you're telling me. But what about after you work out a deal with your partners or find a new job? You'll go right back to putting work first. That and your Caddy. What do you call it?"

"Lucy."

"Do you get what I'm saying?" She didn't wait for an answer. "I know finances have been my biggest concern. But it's more than that. You're not present," she continued. "That's how we experience you, the kids and I. Even when you're *physically* here, you don't interact with us like we're your first priority. Even before you were fired. You're in your own world."

Hal was quiet for a few minutes. Although a familiar refrain, it was the first time he let her words sink in. *Such a different perspective.* All he had seen was Kathy's insensitivity. Now he saw her frustration. Her fear. The loneliness beneath that. "What else?" he asked.

Her face was strained. "When things get tough, you run away."

"My disappearing act."

"Yes. You get in your truck and drive away without even telling me where you're going. I worry about you for hours. And it's not like you come home in a better mood. You're in worse shape than when you left. You send me all sorts of 'stay away' messages. If I try to talk, you get more upset. So I shut up to keep the peace, but inside I'm not happy. In fact, I'm downright miserable."

"Wow." Hal knew the truth of Kathy's words. "Is there more?"

"No." The edges of her lips curled upward. "Isn't that enough?"

Hal chuckled and took her hands. "I meant it when I said I was sorry, Kathy. I finally realize how difficult I've been to live with. I've been pushing you away and then punishing you for not being supportive." He laughed at the irony. "You don't deserve my anger. Thank you for all of your love and support."

Kathy brushed a tear from her cheek. "You mean it?" she asked softly.

"Yes, I do. I really do."

"Hal, don't get mad, okay? But I do have a question. I know being fired was hard, but why have you been taking it out on me?"

He took a deep breath. "Because I wasn't willing to take responsibility for my feelings and reactions. It was easier to take offense and misinterpret things you said to me."

"Like what?" She wiggled her hands free and folded them in her lap.

Hal wondered if he should answer. Why open up old wounds? Then he realized, if he wanted to keep from falling into old patterns, he needed to be more upfront. "Remember the day I moved my office back home?"

She rolled her eyes. "*Oh* yeah."

"You told me that 'lots of people lose their jobs' and that I should 'grow up and stop feeling sorry for myself.'" He looked down. "I took that comment very personally."

"That was mean of me. I'm sorry. I wish I could—" She stopped. "What is it, Hal?"

"Weird. I just had this memory."

Kathy put a hand on his knee. "What?"

"I'm about three or four, playing in the Petersons' yard when this older kid pushes me down. All the big kids start laughing at me, so I go running home, fast as I can, sobbing all the way. I open the patio door and run into the house looking for my mother. She's there in the living room, doing something—vacuuming, talking on the phone—I can't remember. I run up and grab her skirt, wailing like a banshee. She doesn't even look at me; she just sort of shoves me aside. 'Hal, stop being such a big baby. You're not hurt. Stop feeling sorry for yourself.'"

He closed his eyes, surprised by the ache of the memory. "I remember running down into the basement, as far away as I could get from her, or anyone else. I stuck a pillow over my face and cried until I finally fell asleep."

Kathy reached up and ran her fingers over his cheek.

"I feel silly even bringing it up." He placed a hand on his forehead, covering his face. "So many years ago. Not a big deal, for sure, given the scale of suffering in this world."

Kathy touched his hand lightly. "But it was a big deal to a four-year-old boy."

"I guess it was." He sat still for a minute. "I think I decided that very day that nobody cared, and I'd have to tough it out on my own."

Kathy stroked his hand.

"The thing is, it happened lots of other times," Hal continued. "When my best friend moved away in elementary school. When I didn't make the football team. When my girlfriend dumped me. It was like, 'Stop whining, you big baby. Get over it.'"

"And then I said the same thing the day you brought the boxes home." Kathy squeezed his hand. "I poked you where it really hurt."

He nodded. "Yeah. I didn't know this bothered me so much. No wonder I've always resented my mother." Hal looked in Kathy's eyes. "And you, sometimes. And I didn't even realize why. I'm sorry."

"Well, I'm sure I do my part," Kathy disclosed. "I have a fiery personality and get ticked off easily. But I wondered why you took those remarks so personally."

Hal laughed. "I've had to suffer dramatically to get you to see the wrong you've done to me. You know, so you'd feel guilty and treat me better."

Kathy laughed, too. "But it hasn't been working. I don't feel sorry for you. In fact, it ticks me off."

"So I keep upping the ante."

They laughed together.

"I've really gotten a lot of mileage out of past grievances," said Hal. "But, these last few days, I've caught onto the game I've been playing and what I've been getting out of it. And what it's cost me." He took Kathy's hands. "I want to change it. For our sake."

"Maybe I believe you." Kathy cocked her head playfully. "Is this something I need to thank your mountain man for?"

"Yeah." Hal nodded.

"Who is he? What's he been telling you?"

"You really want to know?"

"As long as there's no danger you'll ask me to run off with you and join a cult."

Hal chuckled. "No danger of that." He told her about Key Moments, responsibility and choices, distortions, and payoffs and prices. Hal and Kathy talked well into the night. Then he lay awake thinking, long after Kathy had fallen asleep. Astonished and grateful.

Chapter 19

Forward and Back

Hal woke early and felt great. He snuggled up to Kathy and put his arm around her waist, enjoying the warmth of her body against his. He kissed her cheek and rolled onto his back, thinking about the past few days.

His personal hell since being fired was not predestined after all. It was not a consequence of events—but of his choices. Wow. The realization was tremendously freeing. And here he was, back in his own bed, and immensely grateful for it.

When the alarm rang, he got up and pulled on a pair of sweats. Grinning, he bounded downstairs, started the coffee, and got out the cereal and orange juice. Kathy came downstairs equally cheerful. They chatted about possible plans for the upcoming weekend, and she kissed him as she got ready to leave. At the door she turned. "Good luck with your calls."

The calls! Sam and his father. Despite his earnest desire, Hal felt himself bristling. It took him a second to smile. "Yeah, I'll get at it as soon as the kids are gone."

She gave him an odd look, reading his thoughts.

"I'll call," he repeated. "I said I would."

After the kids were gone, Hal dressed for a business day. He felt he would handle the calls better if he were on the job. He was, in a way. But once at his desk, the good feelings dissipated. In their place, a noxious brew of resentment. He shouldn't have to ask his father for a loan. And it was humiliating that the only job open to him at the moment was far below his ability.

He paced the room, stewing and working up indignation. He ended up in the shop and, out of pure frustration, kicked Lucy's front tire. "Ouch! Oh. Oh." He immediately winced in pain and hobbled to his stool where he removed his shoe and inspected his throbbing big toe. It was turning black and blue. Closing his eyes, he cursed himself for being so reactive. He sat on the stool for a few minutes trying to relax as the pain slowly abated.

His action brought up a vivid memory of the night he'd thrown the wrench, and the terror of seeing it strike his daughter. The fact that he was capable of sliding back so quickly shocked him deeply.

"A Key Moment," he mused with sour humor. "Am I willing to take responsibility? Am I willing to make new choices?" He remembered the sheet of paper Donald had given him during their last visit. He went upstairs to the bedroom and searched for the pants he'd worn the last time up there. It was in the back pocket. Fortunately, Kathy hadn't laundered it. He sat on the love seat and read it, thinking about why it was so hard to make the phone calls to Sam and his father.

Step One. Hal thought about the path he was on and did not want to go where it led. He took a couple of deep breaths, stretched his neck, shoulders, and arms, and closed his eyes. He imagined himself on a rock near a mountain stream—and felt himself begin to relax and feel more calm. Encouraged, he read on.

Step Two. He wasn't used to such self-examination. What did he feel? Anger … resentment … embarrassment … and … even some inadequacy. Pretty grungy all of them.

Stop - Look - Listen - Choose

Step One: Stop

- Be aware of what is happening.
- Stop the negative flow of your thoughts and feelings.
- Do something to alter your physical and emotional state (breathe deeply, relax your shoulders, stand erect, think of a pleasant scene, etc.).

Step Two: Look

- Notice your feelings, without acting them out.
- Identify your thoughts. What are the distortions?
- How are you acting now? What are the likely consequences of that action?

Step Three: Listen to your inner voice

- What is your vision?
- What is most important to you in the long run?
- What outcomes do you want from this situation? For yourself? For others? For your relationships?

Step Four: Choose

- What choices can you make to have what you really want?
- What payoffs will you give up?
- What prices will you pay?
- What rewards will you gain?

He took some time to identify his thoughts. *Dad thinks he knows better than me ... Asking for a loan proves he was right ... Sam's job is beneath me ... Asking for help is a sign of weakness.* There were plenty of distortions. Black-and-white thinking. Catastrophizing. Mind-reading. Fortune-telling. Hal nodded to himself. They're all there.

He challenged his thoughts and looked at things more objectively. *Dad really does want to support me. He's been reaching out. He's critical of some things I've done, but not everything. Working for Sam is not my first choice, but it would be a good step to get back on track. Asking for help takes honesty and courage.* He nodded approvingly. That last thought, especially, brought him back to reality.

Step Three. The immediate answer was simple. He wanted things back the way they were. He shook his head and laughed at himself. No, that's not what he really wanted. *Constructive action, that's it.* Hal lit up with hope. He wanted to move forward. Bring financial stability to the family. And he wanted to be regarded as an honest and trustworthy man, despite the gossip going around. Emboldened and encouraged, Hal read step four.

Step Four. Hal ticked off the points. First, *choices.* He would call his father and Sam. And he would feel good about it and grateful for their help.

Next, *payoffs.* He'd watch his tendency to avoid sensitive situations and blame others.

Then *prices.* He'd take responsibility. Swallow his pride.

Finally, *rewards.* He'd actually be doing something instead of waiting. Kathy would feel more secure. That would improve their relationship and relieve some stress.

Feeling markedly more confident and centered, Hal folded the sheet of paper and placed it in his wallet. He rehearsed what he would say to his father, then picked up the phone beside the love seat and dialed.

But when his father answered, he blurted out the first thing that came to mind. "Hey, Dad, you know that loan you offered Kathy and me? I don't really think we need it, but it'd sure make Kathy feel a lot better if we had a bigger cushion in the bank." Even as

Hal spoke, he knew it wasn't fair, but he let the statement stand. "Are you still willing to make it?"

To Hal's surprise, his father sounded relieved. They talked for some time about the amount and the interest rate, which John didn't expect but Hal insisted on. "What about our usual Saturday breakfast tomorrow?" his father asked. "I'd sure like to get back to our tradition."

"Sorry. Tomorrow won't work. I've got a lot on my plate. Maybe next Saturday." Hal hung up feeling relieved that he'd finally made the call—but guilty about finagling his way out of breakfast.

Still, it was one down. Sam to go. When Sam came on the line, Hal said the same thing. "If that offer's still open, Sam, I'd like to take you up on it."

There was a slight hesitation. "I have to say I'm surprised to hear from you, Hal. But I think you're making the right choice. Come in this afternoon and I'll get you set up. Can you be here by three?"

"Sounds good."

"It won't take long. I'll give you all the information, then pretty much leave you to do the job on your own." Sam chuckled. "Shouldn't be a problem. You're used to being the Lone Ranger."

It wasn't the first time Hal had been called that. It felt like a backhanded compliment, as if the qualities of a Lone Ranger—independence, ability to make decisions and solve problems—had a downside. Well, he'd make sure Sam had nothing to complain about. He could do that job with one hand tied behind his back. Probably both hands.

With the rest of the day free, Hal went out to the shop. In the last three weeks, he'd stripped the Caddy down to the basics and was almost at the point where he could start rebuilding it. The job he needed to do first was paint the interior. He put on his overalls and went to work, feeling good about what he'd accomplished this morning and happy to immerse himself in a tangible project.

He stopped early enough to put away the supplies, clean the paint from his hands, and get ready for the meeting with Sam. He dressed with care. Chinos, a silk tee, and a jacket. It felt strange to be going to work as an employee. It had been seven years since he had been accountable to someone else. Well, he'd been accountable to his partners at Western, although now he was beginning to wonder. Perhaps he hadn't sufficiently appreciated that fact.

Sam's gray-haired and crisply efficient secretary greeted him formally, even coolly, as if Hal were a supplicant with hat in hand. But when she waved him into Sam's office, Sam greeted him warmly.

Sam had all the information ready, including property descriptions and issues particular to each, contact names, and phone numbers. Sam motioned Hal to follow him. "You'll be sharing an office with another manager, a young barn-burner named Ray Grijalva. Come on, I'll introduce you."

Sam stopped at the secretary's desk to get keys for the file cabinet that would be Hal's, then led Hal to an office where a dark-eyed young man was engrossed in paperwork. Hal smiled pleasantly as he shook Ray's hand, but irritation tightened in his neck. Not only was he working for someone else, he had to share an office, even though the office had a window, and each work area was well outfitted.

As Sam turned to leave, Hal followed him into the hall. In low tones, he said, "Thanks for taking a chance on me, Sam."

"I'm expecting to get more out of you than I would from two managers," Sam said with a grin. Then he sobered. "I think you made the right choice. Now it's up to you to prove I made the right decision in offering you the job."

After reviewing the information Sam left with him, Hal organized his files according to his preferred work style and familiarized himself with the computer applications the company used to track its properties. He made some phone calls and handled a few small issues. It felt good to be working.

Chapter 20

Derek

H al arrived home after six, eager to tell Kathy and the kids about his successful day. He smiled, thinking how they would swarm over him with excitement and relief. But walking into the house was like stepping into a whirlwind.

Nicole and Susie were in a shouting match over the disappearance of Nicole's favorite sweater. Derek was complaining about a history report due on Monday. "It's not fair, Mom! Miss Talbot dumped it on us with no warning. I have things I want to do this weekend."

Kathy stood her ground. "I'm sorry, but fair or unfair, school comes first, Derek. You have to get that report done."

"Hi, guys." Hal was the only family member in good spirits.

"There you are," Kathy said brusquely. "Where have you been? You have a voice mail from your mom. She's upset that you're not going to breakfast tomorrow with your father. You better call her."

"Oh brother." Hal turned toward his shop. Derek caught him at the door. "Dad?" he said in a wheedling tone. "Let me go to the movie tonight. I'll work on the report tomorrow. Please."

Hal attempted a stern look. "You've got a soccer game tomorrow."

"I'll start on it tomorrow afternoon. And I've got all day

Sunday."

"It takes longer than that to do a ten-page report, and you know it," Kathy chimed in from across the room.

"My teacher is so unfair!" Derek grumbled. "She gives us this big project to do by Monday, and now my weekend is ruined."

Hal tried to fix the situation by giving what he considered good fatherly advice. "Hey, it's only ruined if you think it's ruined, buddy. If you complain, you'll not only make yourself miserable but it'll take longer to get it done." He put on his best smile. "Just get to it and you'll be surprised how quickly you finish. You might even enjoy it." Hal nodded, his lips pressed firmly together.

His wise counsel didn't go over very well. "No, I won't!" Derek snarled. He started to stomp out of the room and happened upon the ubiquitous soccer ball, which he gave a good kick into the family room just as he started up the stairs.

"Don't pull that attitude on me, young man!" Hal shouted after him, unintended fierceness in his voice. "You get back here, you hear me?"

Derek slammed his bedroom door.

Hal stood at the bottom of the stairs wondering what to do. His typical response to defiance had been to go into his "command and control mode," bullying his kids into compliance and shutting down any further expression of negativity. He thought about the previous school year when Derek brought home a lousy report card. The best grade was a B-minus in geography; the other grades went down from there, including a D in Science and an F in English. Hal had reacted like his own father by berating him for his disgraceful performance, browbeating him about his study habits, life priorities, and lack of respect for his elders. When Derek had had enough, he'd thrown a paperweight across the room and smashed a hole in the wall. Hal really lit into him at that point, dictating all sorts of rules and punishments.

Derek's grades did improve somewhat, but he was also more withdrawn, avoided his dad, and rarely joined in family activities. His sullen disposition had lasted through the remainder of the school year and made everyone miserable.

I prevailed, thought Hal now, *but at what cost?*

Befuddled, he sat on the stairs as Kathy attempted to sort out the case of the missing sweater with Nicole and Susie. Hal realized that dealing with these Key Moments took a great deal of effort, restraint, and commitment—more than he was in the mood for at the moment. With a sigh, he retrieved the folded sheet with the *Stop - Look - Listen - Choose* steps and reviewed them for the second time that day.

He noticed something interesting as he examined his feelings and began challenging his thoughts. His feelings began to change from irritation to ... he had a hard time identifying it ... sadness. *That's interesting,* Hal thought. *Why am I sad?* It was hard to see Derek upset and struggling. That was a big part of it. But it was more than that. It was because ... he couldn't fix it. He *couldn't* make Derek's world better. The school assignment was something Derek had to learn to deal with. Hal needed to let go of his exaggerated sense of responsibility for his son. Derek would have to learn to handle his own challenges. And in that moment, his relationship with his son felt different.

Hal thought about what he wanted and remembered his new vision for his family. He wanted to be there for his son. He grunted. Exactly what he wanted from his own father. *I don't need him to tell me what to do. Just be there and support me. Wow. Maybe that's all Derek wants, too.*

He went upstairs and tapped a couple of times on the door.

"What do you want?" came the brusque reply.

"May I come in?"

"It's a free country."

Derek was lying on his bed, face down in a pillow. Hal sat on the edge of the bed. After a moment, he said quietly, "So this assignment has ruined your weekend, huh?"

Derek made an undecipherable noise.

"I want to apologize for how I acted, buddy. You didn't need me yelling at you or telling you that you were wrong."

Derek wiggled around a little on the bed, the best show of acceptance his wounded ego could muster.

Hal reached out and rubbed his back. "What did you have planned for this weekend, anyway?"

Derek rolled over on his side. "I wanted to go to Tony's house tonight to watch a movie. After soccer tomorrow, we were going to play basketball at the rec center."

Hal frowned. "And this homework really messed up your plans."

"Yeah." Derek's eyes darted about the room. "School's just started. No *other* class has a big report already. It's not fair."

Hal frowned and shook his head. "What a bummer."

Derek sat up and scooted back against the headboard. His expression was perplexed. Bewildered. Like—*Who are you? Not my dad, who likes to lecture. Who turned into the Terminator when I brought home one little F last year.* "I don't remember Miss Talbot telling us about this assignment at the start of school. I think she just snuck it in. She thinks her class is all that matters," he sniveled.

"And she doesn't realize there are other important things in life." Hal's bottom lip was sticking out ever so slightly.

"Yeah."

After a long silence, Hal asked, "What do you think will happen if you don't do the report?"

Derek snorted. "You and Mom would be mad at me. You'd ground me, like you did last year."

Relieved that Derek had gotten back to his energetic self by the end of the year, Hal countered. "I don't want to put you through that again. What other consequences can you think of?"

"I'll get an F on it." Derek fiddled with a button on his shirt.

"Is that what you want?"

"No. Not really." Derek looked at Hal and sighed. "There's no way to get out of it, is there?"

Hal didn't answer.

"I'll start working on it tonight. See how much I can get done."

"What are you going to write about?" Hal asked.

Derek pulled a crumpled piece of paper from his backpack, smoothed it out, and showed his dad a rough outline. His expression grew animated as he explained the assignment.

Hal smiled broadly. He reached over and squeezed Derek's arm. "Looks to me like you've got some good ideas. It'll take some work, but you can do it."

"Yeah." Derek grinned. "I'll call Tony and get at it." He turned on his computer and dug some books from his backpack.

Hal stood. "Need anything from me?"

"No. I'm good."

Hal left the room with a feeling of triumph. He'd *chosen* how to handle this Key Moment. He liked it.

Chapter 21

A Beautiful Day

Hal woke Saturday feeling edgy. It was now mid-September, and he'd missed several breakfasts with his father. His mother's message, which he'd listened to late last night, was blistering. What was the matter with him? Didn't he know how much his father worried about him? And missed their time together?

He rolled over with a groan. Why was it so much easier handling a Key Moment with Derek than his father? He thought of his father arriving at the Wellshire Inn, drinking refills of coffee and ordering a breakfast for one, and reluctantly admitted that he needed to show up if he was committed to being responsible.

He climbed out of bed, showered, and got dressed. But he didn't leave. He wasn't ready to sit across from his father and endure an onslaught of criticism. And he certainly wasn't about to let his mother bully him into it.

So when Kathy came down to drive Nicole and her friends to gymnastics, Hal offered to take Susie to her riding lesson; Derek's soccer practice at school was within walking distance.

Kathy gave him a quizzical glance, but accepted the offer. Susie jumped up and down with delight. "Will you stay and watch me?" she asked hopefully.

"Sure. It's about time I saw how you and Top Hat are doing." Top Hat, the bay gelding.

But all the time that Hal was watching Susie and Top Hat circle the rink, responding to the coaching of her instructor, he was uncomfortably aware of the choice he had made. Part of him stubbornly insisted that he didn't care. The other part knew it was a lie.

When they got home, Kathy was in the kitchen. "You've got a message from your dad," she said.

Hal waved in acknowledgement.

"Aren't you going to check it?"

"I know what it is."

They gathered for a lunch of turkey sandwiches and tomato soup, which Hal and Kathy made together. Hal spent some time with Derek, who was set up with sodas and snacks for a long stint at the computer. He came down the stairs and asked Kathy if there was anything she needed from him.

"Is Lucy calling your name?" She walked over and gave him a warm hug. "It's okay. I've got things to do."

Hal spent the afternoon under the car, declining a call from his father, saying his hands were greasy. "Tell him I'll call this evening." But when Derek asked for help again with the report, he conveniently forgot to call.

The next morning over coffee and the *Denver Post*, Kathy asked, "When are you going to call your mom and dad?"

"When I get done reading the paper," he said without looking up.

"I've heard that story a lot the last couple of days."

Hal clanked down his cup. "It's not your problem, okay?"

"Actually, it is." She matched his sharpness. "I'm the one who's been telling them you can't come to the phone, and you'll call back. I'm not going to do it anymore."

"So don't."

He held up the paper as a barrier between them. Kathy swatted at it in exasperation. "You need to go see your mountain guru again," she chided. "You're making a mess of your relationship with your parents. Maybe he can straighten you out."

Hal lowered the paper. He knew very well that Donald wouldn't let him get away with avoidance and crooked thinking. It was interesting that Kathy realized that, too. She really was listening when he talked about Donald. He stood and nodded. "Can you do without me?"

She gave him a questioning look. "You're going now? Don't you have to call?"

"No. He's always there."

"What if he isn't?"

Hal shrugged. "He will be."

Donald was splitting wood when Hal arrived. The older man's strength and agility amazed him.

"Hal!" Donald called. He leaned the ax against the chopping block and wiped the sweat from his brow. "Your timing couldn't be better. I was just wishing for an excuse to take a break."

Hal noticed how glad he was to see Donald. "You're looking at a working man. Thought I'd better take the opportunity to visit on my last free day."

"Come in. come in. Let's have something tall and cold, and you can tell me about it."

"It's just a stopgap job," Hal explained over the fruity blended drink as they sat together in the great room. "It relieves Kathy's worry about the money."

Donald's smile told Hal that his friend could see right through him. "How are you and Kathy doing?"

"Great." Hal told Donald about their talk. "For the first time I was able to listen without being defensive." He smiled and held up his fist in a sign of triumph. "These Key Moments of yours. It's amazing how often I notice them. The good news is, I'm learning to handle them. The bad news, I don't always make a better choice." He chuckled. "Must be doing something right, though. I'm not sleeping in the basement anymore."

Donald laughed. "That's good to hear. You won't always make positive choices, but stay committed and you'll get better at it … or at least better at cleaning up your messes." He grinned.

"I'm not doing so well with my folks. Giving in to them is like driving into a brick wall."

Donald nodded. "That's because so many of your hot buttons come from your childhood." His face grew more serious. "The trick is to be willing to realize that some of your interpretations may be wrong."

Hal nodded thoughtfully. "I suppose you're right. It's hard for me to see." He studied Donald's calm countenance. "I can't imagine you ever messing up the way I have. You seem to have everything figured out."

Donald's delighted laugh filled the room. "Don't put me on a pedestal, my friend. I'm just barely ahead of you on the learning curve." Then he turned sober. "I hope you can learn from my experiences and not have to go through so much pain yourself." He turned to the photo on the mantel, then took their glasses to the kitchen for refills.

Hal stood, intending to look at the magnificent view out Donald's picture window, but instead found himself drawn to the photo and the captivating expressions of the woman and children, looking at him with warm, loving smiles. Deeply moved, he touched the glass and felt a great sadness for Donald, who apparently had lived alone for the greatest part of his life.

Donald entered the room carrying their drinks on a tray, along with a plate of sliced golden delicious apples and cheeses. "Spending a little more time with my family, I see."

Hal drew back from the photo, embarrassed. His first impulse was to change the subject, but Donald's presence demanded honesty. "This photograph haunts me, Donald. I can't imagine how it must have been to lose your family."

Donald stood holding the tray and looking directly at Hal. "Worst moment of my life."

"How did you ever manage to find peace of mind after losing them? Your wife is beautiful, and your children look so bright and happy."

Donald set the tray down and joined Hal at the photo. "They gaze right at you, don't they? You can't look at this picture without feeling their spirit."

Hal looked into their faces. "Sorry to bring up painful

memories." He turned away from the photo.

"There are lessons in the painful experiences of our lives." Donald pointed to the recliner. "Come, sit, and have a snack. I'll tell you about it."

Hal took a seat in *his* recliner, as he'd come to think of it. He took an apple slice and wedge of pepper jack cheese. "You don't have to tell me the story, Donald. It isn't my business."

"But it is. At least in a way." He looked at Hal intently. "All of us have to make decisions about how we'll live, and that's what my story is about. In a sense, it's not just my story, it's everyone's story. Mine just happens to be a pretty dramatic version."

Donald took a few sips of his drink and then stood and walked over to the picture window. Hal's eyes followed him. He felt a surge of anxiety and anticipation. Did he really want to hear what Donald had to say?

Donald stared out the window, his gaze locked on a distant horizon. "It was a winter morning in Chicago. Both the kids were complaining of earaches, and Melanie was taking them to the pediatrician. We'd had a storm during the night, and the streets were snow-packed and icy. She'd grown up in the south and had never gotten comfortable driving in the snow, so she asked if I would take a half-day off and drive them."

He looked at Hal. "It seems a reasonable request, doesn't it? But back then my career was everything. People counted on me. I couldn't call in and cancel meetings just because my wife was afraid of a little snow and ice. Besides, we'd lived in Chicago a couple of years by then. So I gave her a quick kiss and said, 'Take your time. You'll be fine.'"

Donald was silent, apparently reliving what had happened. "It was midmorning when I got the call," he continued slowly. "I knew it was bad from the officer's tone of voice. A semi had jackknifed on the slick roads directly in front of Melanie. She ran head-on into the trailer, and then she was hit from behind. She was dead." He took a handkerchief out of his pocket and wiped a tear. "And my children were being rushed to the hospital. My schedule, the one I thought was sacred, went completely out of my mind. I drove madly to the hospital, grieving for Melanie and praying earnestly for Spencer and Emma.

"How my heart broke to see these two young children in intensive care, hooked up to tubes, surrounded by nurses and doctors working feverishly to save their lives. I could reach out and touch them, but couldn't pick them up or hold them." He dabbed his eyes again. "After hours of heroic effort, there was nothing left but to wait … Spencer died before the sun set that day. Emma passed away during the night."

Hal sat in silence, his head bowed.

"I was delirious with sorrow. I held myself together during the rituals that follow death. But later, when there was nothing to distract me from my grief and guilt, I went crazy." Donald smiled slightly. He walked back to his chair and sat down. "*Really crazy.* I started drinking, missing work, picking fights with both strangers and friends. I think I was hoping someone would put me out of my misery."

He looked down at his hands. "But nobody did. So I was left to my own destruction, and it was a long slide downward. I wanted nothing but oblivion through alcohol or death. Eventually I lost everything … and I mean *everything*. I lost my job and became a penniless, homeless drunk on the streets of Chicago." He looked at Hal. "That's what I was. No sense soft-peddling it. My family was gone, and my guilt was simply more than I could bear. My self-blame and hatred almost killed me."

Donald's voice quickened. "Of course, that's not the end of the story, or I wouldn't be here today. I remember the exact moment my life turned around."

"Please tell me." Hal was sitting on the edge of his seat.

"I had reached bottom, as they say. The darkest moment of my life. I made up my mind I couldn't live another day, and I didn't deserve to. So I came up with a plan. In the middle of winter, eight years to the day after my family's death, I went to the State Street Bridge in downtown Chicago to jump to my death onto the ice below."

Hal grimaced and shook his head.

"I was walking out onto the bridge when I saw an old man coming from the opposite direction. I kept my head down, but he stepped directly in front of me and said, 'Good morning, sir. Today is a beautiful day.' I stopped and looked at him. His face was nothing but scars from third-degree burns he must have suffered years earlier. He had no eyebrows or eyelashes. A horrific sight.

"Shocked, I brushed past him without a word and hurried to the center of the bridge, glancing around to make sure no one was watching. I wasn't seeking publicity and didn't want anyone to talk me out of it. To my surprise, the old man was still standing where I'd left him and watching me. He waved and smiled again.

"Despite his grotesque features, something in his smile reached out and touched me, and something broke loose inside. I slumped onto the bridge and began crying. I sobbed and sobbed and couldn't stop. I couldn't get the grotesqueness of the man's face out of my mind. I felt so much pity for him. And yet his smile. His kind words. The light in his eyes. At first I cried for him. Then for myself and the loss of my family. But at some point, I realized I was crying for all of us, for mankind, for the cruelty and difficulty of life.

"I lost all track of time. I have no idea how long I carried on. When I finally came to, I was sitting in the middle of the bridge sidewalk. And there was the man, sitting next to me, his hand resting lightly on my back. Without a word, he handed me a clean, neatly folded handkerchief. I looked into his face and, to my astonishment, he was no longer grotesque. He was beautiful, Hal. Radiant. All I saw was love and compassion.

"I don't know how to describe what happened next. It was like turning a kaleidoscope and seeing a whole new design fall into place. All of a sudden the world around me was miraculous: the blue sky, the sunlight, the pigeons strutting along the rail of the bridge, Lake Michigan and the skyline of the city shimmering in the distance. And, of course, the strange but glorious man sitting next to me, stroking the back of my head. In that moment, I said and meant it, 'You're right, sir. Today is a beautiful day.'"

Hal's voice was thick with emotion. "Thank goodness you didn't jump." He shuddered at the thought that Donald's life could have ended so many years ago.

"I learned many lessons that day, Hal. My world shifted. I'd been seeing what was wrong with life. But for the first time in eight years—maybe ever—I could see what was *right* with it and I felt an incredible gratitude. Gradually, I started to change and my life became joyful and abundant." He looked at Hal. "And I'm happy to say I've never gone back, at least not for long."

"I've never met anyone like you, Donald," Hal said, spellbound. "You've told me a heartbreaking story, yet your face radiates peace and joy. Is it real? Is it reserved for only a lucky few? Do you have to go through some kind of tragedy to get it? Is it something I can have in my life?"

Donald smiled. "Good questions." He didn't seem in a hurry to answer. "Yes, my joy is real. I love my life. And each day *is* beautiful." He paused. "You're probably right, though, that only a few people ever achieve this level of joy and effortless living." He spoke with a resolute tone. "But it's not because they're lucky, Hal. It's because of how they decide to live."

"But you didn't *decide*. It just *happened* to you," argued Hal.

"No, I *did* decide," Donald insisted. The decision rose from deep within my soul in a moment of agony and despair—but it was a decision, nonetheless. I could have jumped off that bridge that day."

Hal was quiet, trying to absorb what Donald was telling him. "Does a person have to go through pain and anguish to make such a decision?"

"Life is difficult. For everyone. We all have our share—sometimes more than our share—of suffering. We all face Key Moments when we have to decide how we'll step up to life."

"But my Key Moments are nothing compared to yours."

Donald shook his head. "There's no value comparing your problems to those of others. The crucible of your transformation is *your* reality, not anyone else's. What matters is not the reality of the situation but your choices."

Hal closed his eyes and sat back, interlocking the fingers of his hands and resting them in his lap. "What did you choose on the bridge that day, Donald?"

Donald smiled kindly. "I decided to stop fighting against life. Resenting it. Judging it. Comparing it to someone else's." He was quiet for a moment. "I decided to accept life on its own terms. To surrender, so to speak, to the will of the universe, to God. Until that moment, I hadn't realized the heavy burden of my resistance. When I surrendered, I was free to live in a new way, to enjoy the moment, and choose my experience and the meaning of my life."

Donald's words settled into Hal's mind and heart. He longed for such an experience, a change of heart and mind that would set him free. But Donald was an exceptional man. How could he himself ever attain such serenity?

Chapter 22

A New Way of Seeing

Hal was deep in thought when Donald stood and stretched. "I don't know about you, but I've been sitting way too long. I need to get the kinks out. You have time for a little hike? We could make some sandwiches and eat up on the ridge … Unless there's something you need to be doing with your family."

Hal stood. "Kathy's the one who suggested I come see you. She said I needed a tune-up from my 'mountain guru.'" He smiled.

Donald threw back his head in laughter. "Is that what she calls me? Sorry to disappoint her."

"But you are a bit … different from other men."

"Not that much, my friend. It's just the choices I've made."

Hal called Kathy while Donald put their lunch together. Still feeling deeply moved by Donald's story, he hung on her every word as she reported Derek's progress on his paper and discussed what their daughters were up to. She paused when Hal didn't speak. "You okay?"

"I love the sound of your voice." He spoke softly.

She giggled. "Ooh. Whatever your mountain guru does, I'm all for it."

After hanging up, Hal went out and grabbed his hiking boots and a hat from the survival box in his pickup. He took a deep breath of the pine-scented air. It was a great relief to leave the emotion-laden atmosphere of the cabin. He looked forward to doing something physical, to sort through his thoughts.

Donald set the pace as they started up a well-marked trail into a forest of ponderosa and lodgepole pines. They hiked for an hour and a half, speaking only to point out breathtaking vistas or loose rocks on the trail. By the time they came to the outcropping of rocks near the top of the ridge, Hal was breathing hard. He noticed with envy that Donald seemed less winded.

Donald sat on a large boulder and tipped his face toward the sun. "I come up here every few days, in the middle of winter on snowshoes." He breathed deeply of the pristine air. "The hike is great for my body, and the view does wonders for my spirit."

Hal found his own boulder to sit on. "I can see why."

The two men gazed out on the glorious panorama. The sky was a brilliant blue. In the distance, high mountain peaks were capped with early snow. Streams of white trailed off them due to stiff mountain winds, portending the winter to come. Below stretched a forested valley bisected by a river and dotted with meadows.

"You know what I love about being up here?" asked Donald. "Perspective. Looking out over this valley allows me to come from a bigger place. Somehow, I feel larger than the challenges of life."

To come from a bigger place. Hal savored the thought, considering the challenges of his life. He grinned. "That sounds like the introduction to another lesson."

Donald raised an eyebrow. "If you're up to it. I don't mean to dump too much on you all at once."

"No. I'm all ears. I've got some challenges coming up—talking to my father and taking the situation with Western by the horns. I need all the help I can get." He sat up cross-legged on the rock.

"Have you heard anything from your board?"

Hal shook his head. "No. But my administrative assistant—my *former* assistant, I should say—told me that something's brewing. I think I'll be hearing from them soon. If I don't, I'll call them and get something rolling. It's going to be interesting to see how it all goes down."

Donald nodded. "Whatever happens, remember, it's not the

facts that matter the most. It's our perspective." He gestured left to right, taking in the peaks of the magnificent Rockies. "View life from one perspective and arrive at one conclusion. View it from another, and the same facts seem altogether different."

He looked over at Hal. "Perspective was a lesson I learned on the bridge so many years ago. Of course, it was a long time before I could articulate it. None of the *facts* of my life changed that day. Reality was still what it was. What shifted was my perspective, how I viewed that reality."

Hal nodded spiritedly. "I believe you. I see what was going on between me and Kathy in a whole new way. I was miserable because of what I was doing to *her,* not the other way around."

"How do you think that fits in with dealing with your parents?" Donald asked. "And with your business partners?"

"You sure you weren't a drill sergeant before you retired?" Hal asked with a smile.

Donald smiled back and rustled through his daypack. He pulled out a couple of sandwiches, some dried fruit, and a couple bottles of Gatorade and set them on a flat rock. "Hungry?"

They ate in silence, enjoying their surroundings. Hal looked quietly at Donald. There was so much he *didn't* know about this man. And yet he felt he knew what was most important about him.

"I'm edging up there in years," Donald said, looking straight ahead, "so I've had plenty of time to give these things a lot of thought. And it seems to me we live from one of four attitudes or perspectives."

Hal finally asked, "Well, are you going to tell me?"

Donald grinned. "Just waiting to be asked. First is *survival*. From this perspective, life is a battleground. We don't like the way things are, yet we feel powerless to do anything about it. Our basic stance is reactive and self-protective. We feel like a pawn of events and circumstances, and try to make ourselves feel better by making excuses, blaming others, or escaping into drugs, or alcohol, or other addictive behaviors. Life is painful."

Hal nodded. "I've been there. In fact, I feel like I've been in survival mode since I was fired last month."

Donald looked at him, nodding. "A crisis does that to us. I lived there for many years after my family died—until the day on the bridge. After that, I realized no one could make my life better. It was up to me." He picked up a small rock and turned it over in his hand a few times. "I realized I had to start accepting responsibility for my life to get out of survival. Sometimes we need help to do that."

Hal knew exactly what he meant. Where would he be if Donald hadn't come along?

"So, what are the other three perspectives?" asked Hal.

Donald tossed the rock into the air a few times, catching it in his hand. "I call the second one *security*. This is how most people spend their lives. We're steady, dependable, and basically honorable in our approach to life. We want to be good parents, workers, citizens. To know the rules, how we fit in, where we belong. We like structure and routine. Our self-esteem has a lot to do with how we think others see us. We're governed by *shoulds* and *oughts*." He turned toward Hal. "Living in security is more about avoiding losing than about winning. We carve out a comfort zone to stave off failure, rejection, and discomfort. Life isn't exciting; it's safe. Or so we think."

"Hmm," said Hal. "I can see lots of family and some of my friends living that way. It's kinda tempting in some ways."

Donald nodded. "It's a decent way to live. The problem is it's only half a loaf. We don't take risks. We settle for less than our full potential."

"So what's next?" Hal asked.

"The *success* mode," replied Donald. "We meet life head-on, conquering challenges and taking advantage of opportunities. We're proactive and motivated, disciplined and goal- directed." Donald gave the rock he was holding a good chuck down the mountainside. It flew until it lost momentum, then dropped to the slope below. "We demand a lot from ourselves and, often, from those around us. We put out an image of having it all together and being in control. We don't like showing weakness. Life is good— but only when we perform well."

Hal chuckled. "You're talking about people who are attached to their Blackberries and cell phones. Movers and shakers."

"That's a good description. We push ourselves out of our

comfort zone and become active members of society. We trust our own authority and make things happen, rather than waiting for them to happen." Donald leaned back on his hands, raising his face to the sun.

Hal squirmed. "I got a good education, built a business, and married a good woman. We have three beautiful children. We live in a nice home in a good neighborhood. We've afforded just about anything we wanted. Until recently, I enjoyed a good reputation. But now I have a gnawing sense that there's more to life." He grinned. "Since meeting you."

Donald laughed. "Indeed. At some point, many people come to the realization that success doesn't automatically lead to happiness and fulfillment. In fact, their success begins to feel hollow."

Hal laid back on the rock, pulled his backpack under his head, and gazed at the blue sky. "Sounds like my high-school buddy, Duane. He was the most popular guy in my class. Voted Most Likely to Succeed. The whole thing. He went to a prestigious college, then Harvard Law School. Boy, did I envy the guy. It seemed like he got whatever he set his sights on. He even stole my high-school sweetheart." Hal laughed. "He graduated at the top of his class and was hired by a red-hot law firm and shot straight up their ladder. I even see his name in the paper, once in a while, because of the high-profile cases he works on."

He was quiet for a moment. "I ran into Duane not long ago, and we had dinner. I sat in awe as he described some of the cases he'd won. He told me about his Ferrari, his home in Hawaii, his travels. I was so envious I felt worse and worse as the night wore on. Then he told me he was on his third marriage and hardly had a relationship with his two kids. The sadness in Duane's voice made me look at *him*, not his watch or expensive suit. I noticed the strain in his face and the weariness in his eyes, and I suddenly felt sad for the guy." Hal was quiet again as he watched a hawk circle high above his head. "He'd missed out on a lot in his race to become rich and famous."

Donald nodded. "That brings up a distinction. There's success, or achieving a predetermined outcome. And there's fulfillment, the sense that life is full and meaningful. When success doesn't lead to fulfillment, most people redouble their efforts, believing that accomplishing even more will bring them their elusive prize. What they don't realize is that success and fulfillment are not the same thing."

Hal sat up. "Wow. I guess I've known that … but I see how much I've been caught up in the trappings of success." He rubbed his hand along the hard, coarse granite surface on which he was sitting. "But I hope we don't have to give up success to find fulfillment."

Donald tossed another small rock over the ridge. "Nope. In fact, most of us would have a hard time finding fulfillment if we didn't set goals and go after them. We have to get out there in the world and mix it up—but we also need to remember that success has to do only with outer, material things, and fulfillment has to do with our inner or spiritual world. We have to pay attention to both to be happy." He turned toward Hal. "The more important journey isn't the one out there. It's in here," he said, pointing to his chest.

"That brings up the fourth way of living," Donald added. "*Serenity.* I started to understand serenity that day on the bridge. The circumstances of my life didn't change immediately, but my perspective did. I saw myself and my life in a completely new and different way."

Hal thought back to his previous visits with Donald, and realized Donald's questions were also getting him to see his own life in a different way. "I don't think many people live in serenity. I don't know anyone who does … except you."

Donald laughed. "There you go again, trying to put me on some pedestal." His eyes twinkled.

Donald stood and immediately crouched to the ground. He turned toward Hal with a finger to his lips, indicating for him to remain quiet. Then he motioned for him to come toward him. Hal crept up alongside him, peeked over the hill, and saw a beautiful seven-point buck standing some 15 yards away. The animal stood erect and motionless, except for his ears twitching from side to side. He began moving forward, slowly, and then bounded down the mountainside in a graceful gait.

"Magnificent," Hal said.

"Sure was," said Donald. "It's not often you see one so close."

Hal stood for a few minutes trying to follow the deer through the trees below. Then he sat back down and asked, "How do you achieve serenity?"

"You don't really achieve it, like reaching a goal. It's something we create—and maintain—through our choices. The difference between you and me is that when I experience a Key Moment, I've practiced a lot, so I've learned to move through the perspectives quickly and back to serenity—where I *choose* to live."

"Okay, then, so what's it like *living* in serenity?" Hal asked.

Donald was quiet a moment. "Have you ever smelled a lilac blossom?"

Hal nodded. "Of course."

"Can you describe it to me?"

"Well, I'd say it's ..." Hal shook his head. "Sorry, no words do it justice."

Donald nodded. "Exactly. That's like trying to describe serenity. There are certain things we have to experience firsthand." He sat back down. "Think about a time when you had a *total* sense of peace and well-being; when life didn't need to be more, better, or different. It was perfect just as it was."

Hal took his time. "Just the other evening with Derek." He told Donald about his Key Moment, when he'd given up lecturing and just listened, and how great it felt.

"What was good about it?"

"We connected and felt closer than in a long time."

Donald nodded. "One characteristic of *serenity* is a sense of unity, oneness, love."

Hal thought. "Yeah. Normally, I have huge expectations and can be pretty critical when the kids don't act like I think they should. I think I personalize it. Proof I'm not a good parent. So I lecture and manipulate to get them to be different. But not that night. I let go of all my judgments, the need to fix him. I had no agenda, except to be there and support him."

"How were you able to do that?"

"Well ... I knew I was in a Key Moment. So I was more aware than usual and realized I could *choose* how to respond." He smiled.

"In fact, I used the sheet you gave me—the *Stop - Look - Listen - Choose* diagram."

"All right." Donald gave him a thumbs-up.

"I remember thinking I wanted to respond in a way that would be helpful to Derek. In a way that fit with my vision for my family."

"See, you know a lot about serenity," said Donald.

Hal nodded. "Wow. How about that."

"Notice how in serenity we're aware of what's going on within and around us. We're awake to our experience and not just going through the motions. That's why we can *choose* instead of just jerking the old knee."

"Yeah, I see that."

"What else did you notice that night?" asked Donald.

Hal smiled. Donald never made things easy, always asking questions that invited him to probe more deeply. He concentrated. "Nothing mattered except being with him. I was totally caught up in the moment. I wasn't aware of anyone or anything else."

"Athletes have a similar experience."

"Ah," said Hal. "They call it flow. Being in the zone."

"I like to think of it as living *here* and *now*." Donald punctuated those two words with downward gesture of his hand. "Most of us aren't grounded in the moment. We're holding onto the baggage from the past or feeling anxious about the future." He paused. "But when can a person make choices?"

Hal looked at Donald, who was waiting for an answer. "Now."

"And where can a person make choices?"

"Here." Hal chuckled.

Donald was grinning. "Seems simple. But all life happens 'here' and 'now.' Give your full attention to his moment and watch your life improve."

Hal nodded.

"What else did you learn during that conversation?"

"You mean there's more?"

Donald smiled. "Keep digging."

Hal studied him with puckered lips. Then he put his head down. "This is related to what I said before about giving up judgments. I realized the problem was Derek's, not mine. I recognized a boundary. I let him be responsible for himself."

"That was a gift, Hal."

Hal nodded. "For both of us."

"What do you think made it possible for you to do that?"

"Well, I was at peace in my own heart." He paused with an insight. "You know, what helped me get to that place was my honesty with Kathy. I'd stopped trying to manipulate her. I'd stopped blaming her ... I'd accepted my own responsibility, so I think I was able to let Derek own his."

Hal stood and walked over to the ridge, surveying the magnificent view lit by the slanting rays of the late afternoon sun. "One other thing happened that night."

Donald stood and walked over near Hal. "What was that?"

"When I left Derek's room, I went for a walk." Hal choked back emotion, wrestling with whether or not to continue. Donald was silent. "I uttered a prayer of gratitude for Derek and, most of all, for how I was feeling. So much of my life has felt like a battle. I've always felt ... well, unworthy. Like I had to prove myself." He looked at Donald. "But that night I felt at peace with myself and life. It was like maybe God and the universe were benevolent after all."

Wordlessly, Donald rested an arm on Hal's shoulder, and they shared a moment of unutterable sweetness. One that Hal knew he would remember forever.

Finally Donald said softly, "You asked me to describe serenity. How you're feeling right now, Hal, that's serenity."

Hal nodded. "How do I keep it?"

"You won't keep it."

Hal frowned.

"But you can get it back." Donald's eyes twinkled. "Learning to handle your Key Moments is a big step. Each time you make *the hero's choice* you move into serenity."

Hal nodded. "What else can I do?" he asked.

"Live from your heart not your head."

Hal was thinking about what that meant when Donald gave him a hefty pat on the back and made a sweeping gesture of the spectacle before them. "It's like climbing this mountain. Once you've been here, you can always remember what it's like … and how you got here."

Donald picked up his daypack. "Time to get back." He grinned. "Even Moses had to come down from the mountain."

Chapter *23*

Ambushed

I t was now Thursday, some four days after his last trip to see Donald. Hal was in his shop working on the Coupe de Ville. The work at Suburban took no more than three or four hours a day and so he'd often come home, change into his coveralls, and go to work. It felt good that the car was no longer an excuse to avoid his family. He could do some work for Suburban, spend some time with his family, and still work on the car.

The restoration was progressing nicely. Hal had finished the interior painting, so the engine could go back into place once it had been rebuilt. To his pleasant surprise, he'd found that the engine block was in excellent condition. Although the heads were in pretty good shape, he'd taken them to a shop to have the valves and valve guides replaced so he could run unleaded in the old engine. He decided to go the extra money for the three-face grind (a fact he hadn't yet told Kathy) for better sealing and power. He'd finally gotten the rebuilt transmission back from the tranny shop and had bolted it to the engine.

Today it was time to hone the cylinder walls. A few passes with the cylinder hone would be all it would take to complete the overhaul. Then it would be time to do his favorite part—restore the body. Hal loved this job, ever since the days of working in the

163

shop with his father. After putting on his coveralls, he filled an old paint can with kerosene and set the eggbeater-looking hone in it to soak. Then he put the hone into the cylinder and spun it with a drill while moving it smoothly up and down a few times—just enough to take off the glaze and the barest bit of wall. It was a little tricky, but when he tuned all his senses to the job, it seemed that the hones told him by their feel when it was time to stop.

Realizing that the family would be coming home before long, Hal put his tools away and cleaned up. He checked his cell phone and found Keith Mickelson had left a message—the call he'd been expecting. He dialed Keith's number and, when flipped to voice mail, left a message requesting a callback. He was tempted to call Keith at home, but he didn't want to appear overly anxious.

Hal distracted himself after dinner by doing some yard work in the cool twilight. Then he organized his workbench until time for bed. But his mind kept drifting back to the call. His irritation was proof that he wasn't over his resentment that his partners had betrayed him. What did they have in mind? How would he respond?

He laughed when he realized he was catastrophizing, letting his fear get the best of him. More than likely, things would work out. He would be cleared when the audit was completed, of that he had no doubt. Once the board learned that he had been falsely accused, quite possibly they would buy him out of the business, despite the influence of Charlie White.

And if they didn't? Hal committed to himself that he would not resort to anger, resentment, or revenge. He wanted to live in serenity. There was a lot to give up to live in serenity, he realized. No wonder Donald talked about it as making *the Hero's Choice*. It took enormous commitment and courage. Although not certain he was up to it, he knew it was the way he wanted to live.

He felt much better and even looked forward to talking to Keith the next day as he climbed into bed. And then Kathy reminded him that he had yet to make a call to his father.

The next morning, Hal called Suburban Real Estate to let them know he would be working from home today. He didn't want to be sitting across from his cubicle partner Ray when Keith called. He took care of some business on his landline, leaving the cell phone free, hoping the call would come soon so he wouldn't be sitting on the proverbial pins and needles all day.

It was close to 10:00 a.m. when his cell phone finally rang. Hal answered calmly, belying his anxiety. Keith got right to the purpose of his call. "I need to talk to you about something, Hal. Are you free for lunch?"

"Well, I've got a pretty full docket today." Hal smiled at his exaggeration. "But I can rearrange a few things to make time for you if it's important."

"Of … of course it's important," Keith retorted.

They arranged to meet at the Le Peep Restaurant at Quebec and County Line Road at noon, after which Keith hung up abruptly.

Keith's brusque manner made Hal wonder if he'd made a mistake in his slightly flip manner. He didn't want to chase that thought around, so he went into the shop and kept himself busy on the Caddy until time to dress for the meeting.

The first to arrive, Hal chose a table where he could keep an eye on the door. It wasn't long before Keith arrived and right behind him, Charlie White. Hal's heart skipped a beat. He'd imagined all sorts of scenarios taking place at Le Peep, but none included Charlie White, the man responsible for driving him out of Western Realty. He'd been prepared to extend an olive branch to Keith, but Charlie was another matter. Cold flooded his veins. Hal hated the man, everything about him, from his knowing sneer to his rolling swagger.

He wished fervently he could get away and considered getting up and walking out without a word to either of them. But then he garnered his faculties and decided to accept this reality. He would *choose* how to respond, and his choice would be to act cordial and cooperative. He felt a surge of strength as he realized that handling himself in a dignified manner with both these men would be a bigger personal victory than if he met with Keith alone.

Hal stood as they approached. Keith greeted Hal with a cool hello. Charlie said nothing. They pulled out chairs and sat without extending their hands. Hal handed them menus, which they set aside.

"Let's get down to business, Stratton," Charlie said coldly. "As Keith told you, we're here to—"

"Keith didn't tell me anything," Hal interrupted. "Only that he wanted to meet."

Charlie gave Keith a withering look, then turned back to Hal. "We're here to make you an offer, Stratton. We'll buy your equity in Western."

This was the last thing Hal had expected. But exactly what he wanted. He maintained a straight face and nodded.

"It's in your interest and ours," Charlie continued. "It would be nothing but an irritant for us to have to work together in the future. We buy you out and part company. It's a win for all of us."

Keith started to speak, but Charlie rode over him, eyes fixed on Hal. "What do you say?"

Hal took his time answering. Although he agreed with Charlie's assessment, he wouldn't have put it so bluntly. He was curious about the offer the partners were prepared to make. "I think you're right," Hal said calmly. "What's your proposal?"

Charlie leaned back, making himself comfortable. It seemed to Hal that his persona took up as much space as his actual physical stature. "As you know, Stratton, we believe the company has been seriously mismanaged under your direction, leaving it in a vulnerable situation. One in which it would be impossible to pay you full price for your equity."

"What are you suggesting?"

"We think it would be more than fair to buy you out at your original investment. You get a cash buyout and agree to walk away from Western Realty once and for all."

Hal was stunned. "My original investment? Are you completely insane, Charlie White? You're a thief!" The words flew out of Hal's mouth before he had time to think about them. But he didn't care. That was exactly how he felt.

"That's our offer," Charlie answered, unruffled.

Hal looked at Keith. They seemed united in the ridiculous. "You know that my original investment is a tiny fraction of what Western is worth today. I've given seven years of my life to putting together deals that have grown Western into a thriving business."

"It's not a thriving business anymore," Charlie said. "You've gotten us into serious debt."

"And, uh, you were well paid for your service as managing partner," Keith added. "You put some big deals together, that's true, but you got a hefty paycheck for doing so. You've already been compensated for building the company."

Shock gave way to anger that Hal could barely contain. "I can't believe you're saying that, Keith. You know some of the problems I had to work out to put those deals together. I spent hundreds of hours finding lenders. I fought battles with city and county governments, wrangled with contractors and builders. I personally guaranteed loans from banks, even went without paychecks. That offer is a slap in the face, and you know it. No deal."

"Get a hold of yourself, Stratton," Charlie said coldly. "You're creating a scene."

Hal looked around and saw several people staring, including the waitress, who was clearly distressed. Then he understood why Keith had invited him *here,* so things wouldn't get too nasty.

Charlie leaned over. "Now listen carefully, Stratton. You're a fool not to accept this deal. I've talked to all the partners, and we've agreed that if you don't accept it, we'll file a lawsuit against you for mismanagement of the company and breach of your fiduciary duty."

Hal felt as if he'd been slammed in the chest with a sledgehammer. He was barely aware that Charlie was still talking.

"Accept this deal, and we forget the lawsuit. Reject it, and we take you through the wringer." Charlie stood, forcing Hal to look up. "Your choice." He motioned Keith to follow and they walked toward the door.

Hal leapt up, bumping the table and spilling his glass of water. After regaining his composure, he approached the waitress and offered her a ten in consideration of the lunch they had never ordered. She graciously refused. He marched out of the restaurant feeling the gaze of others burning the back of his head.

He sat in his pickup, reeling from the shock. Lawsuit? Court?

Notices in the paper. *The gall of those two! How could Keith stoop so low?* The progress of the last few weeks, wiped away by one word. He was beginning to feel confident about an audit. But a lawsuit? Sometimes court proceedings were more about process than truth. And even a *not guilty* verdict would not wipe away the pretrial scuttlebutt and negative coverage in the business section of the paper. To put it bluntly, he was screwed.

He rested his head on the steering wheel. *Serenity? Ha!* The crazy musings of an old man. He was in a battle for his life, and all he could think about was how to survive.

A memory popped suddenly into his head. Hal had worked in a garage during his senior year of high school. He'd done some jobs for the owner free of charge, to prove he was an experienced mechanic. In a few months, he had acquired a reputation for service and attention to detail, and word-of-mouth brought a sizable number of new clients to the business.

Then one day, the owner shocked Hal by accusing him of stealing from the cash register at night. Hal pleaded his innocence, but the owner didn't believe him. Hal didn't tell him that the real thief was his own son, who would take money from the till and brag about it to his buddies. Hal stewed about whether to tell the owner the truth but decided that the matter was between him and his son. He couldn't work for a man who didn't trust him anyway. So, late one afternoon, he backed his jeep up to the garage, loaded his tools, and drove a half mile down the road to another garage. The owner had heard of Hal's reputation and hired him on the spot. Many customers followed him to the new place.

Sweet revenge. Even better, the previous owner came to apologize after learning it was his son who was dipping into the till. He even offered Hal his job back, but Hal didn't take it. A power trip for a seventeen-year-old. Wrongly accused, he'd gotten justice.

But this thing with Western Realty was far more dangerous and complicated. Charlie White was a Machiavellian businessman with lots of experience in getting what he wanted—by whatever means. If Charlie and the board were serious, he could be in real trouble. He could end up mired in legal action for who knew how long, with the outcome potentially ruinous.

Close to hyperventilating, he slowed his breathing. What were his options? Acceptance of the offer was out of the question.

He could call Charlie's bluff—that's what it had to be—and let it play out in court.

He could contact his attorney and file a countersuit. Would it be worth the cost? Much more than monetary.

He could ignore the whole thing and get into a new business entirely. That was an immediate no. This problem wouldn't go away by ignoring it—and he didn't want to do any other kind of work.

He could pack up his family, move to another city, start over. No. He would not turn tail and slink out of town.

Hal started the Chevy and pulled out of the parking lot. He didn't know how, but he knew one thing: he was going to fight this, all the way ... and he would survive.

But how? What to do next? He needed to talk to someone. Not his father. He would go off the deep end. Donald Millhouse? No, the mountain man wouldn't know about legal issues. Besides, how effective were high choices against down and dirty?

He drove to Suburban Real Estate. He doubted that Sam Richards was free ... but just in case.

"You look like crap, Stratton," Sam greeted him. "What's going on?"

Hal sat down. "You've taken a risk hiring me, Sam. I think that's because you believe I'm an honorable man."

"Why? What happened?"

"I got ambushed." Hal told Sam about the meeting, the outrageous offer, and the threat. "I didn't want you to hear about it from someone else, Sam. I wanted you to learn what was going on from me."

Sam tapped a pencil against his chin, a thoughtful look on his face. "So it's gone that far? Charlie wields a blunt instrument—and it is often effective."

"What do you mean?"

"This isn't the first time he's scared an opponent into giving him what he wants by threatening a lawsuit. What do you think you'll do?"

Talking to Sam helped him calm down. Hal could see his options more clearly. "Nothing, for now. This is a game of chicken, you know. Charlie's waiting for me to flinch. But I'll hold fast. And, in the meantime, I'd like to keep working for you."

"I've gotten some phone calls complimenting you, Hal. Well, complimenting *me* for being smart enough to hire you." He smiled. "It was a good move."

They parted with a handshake, and Hal felt immensely better. He was facing the fight of his life, but it helped to know he wasn't the first sucker Charlie had maneuvered into such a situation.

In a calmer state of mind, Hal thought again about Donald. What had Donald said? Something about moving from survival to serenity more quickly. In some ways, Hal wished he'd never met the man. It would be so much easier to launch a counterattack on his ex-partners and let the chips fall where they may. But he realized he'd learned too much to go back to who he was a month ago. His world was no longer flat. He'd seen the beautiful blue orb.

He was in the fight of his life, but he was past struggle and blame. To succeed against Charlie White, he would have to draw on a more productive way of thinking.

He *had* to talk to Donald.

Chapter 24

Owning Up

As Hal navigated the now-familiar route to Donald's cabin, he called home on his cell phone. Nicole answered.

"Where are you, Dad?"

"On my way to see a friend."

"Your mountain guru?"

He smiled. "Where'd you hear that?"

"Mom said he's like your personal coach or something. He's like the reason you've been acting so weird ... I mean *different* lately."

"Different good or different bad?"

"Good, for sure," she teased. "You're even fun to be around now."

"Well, that's high praise. Tell your mother I'll call when I'm on my way home."

The clearing around Donald's cabin was empty and quiet. Hal suddenly had the feeling that Donald was gone and he would have to negotiate his new Key Moment without coaching. But as he climbed out of his Chevy, Donald appeared on the porch.

For the first time since meeting Donald Millhouse, Hal felt uneasy about showing up unannounced, as if he had special claim to Donald's time and wisdom. He hesitated at the open door of his truck. But when Donald gave him a "come on in!" wave, he got out of his truck and climbed the porch steps. He felt the probing gaze of this large, elderly man and laughed uncomfortably. "I feel like you can see right through me, Donald. Like you know why I've come."

"I have no idea." Donald shook his head. "You're going to have to tell me."

They settled into the recliners in Donald's great room, and Hal told him about the visit with Keith and Charlie White. "I flipped right back into survival," Hal reported with dismay. "It was all anger, blame, and a desire for revenge. There was even a moment I thought—"

"That I'm a crazy old man who doesn't know anything about the complexities of modern life."

Hal lowered his head in embarrassment. "Something like that," he muttered.

"And that survival mode seems like the only mode tough enough to answer the current challenge."

"Yes," Hal admitted. "I'd *like* to operate from a bigger place, but it seems impossible ... and I'm not sure I can do it this time."

"What was your gut reaction to their offer?"

"Shock. Disbelief. Anger."

"The reason I ask, Hal, is that it's important to be honest about your gut-level reactions to the hard events of life. You're not a robot, you know. Sometimes strong emotion wells up, and the worst thing to do is to deny or suppress it or pretend you're above it. You have to *feel* your emotion before you can take responsibility and move beyond it."

Hal sat back and combed his hands through his brown hair. "Whew! That's good to hear. My feelings were so strong that I couldn't help but react."

"So, do you need to vent, or are you ready to move beyond your gut reaction and deal with this latest news?"

"I'm ready to deal with it," Hal muttered, wondering what he was in for.

"I'm going to ask you some questions." Donald leaned forward. "They won't be easy to answer. You might even feel defensive or irritated with me. But this is the hard medicine you need in order to deal with your partners from a position of strength. You ready?"

Hal nodded.

"Okay, then. First question: Are you willing to be accountable for being fired?"

Hal shook his head. "You're right. I don't like this line of questioning. Accountable for being fired?" he snapped. "Being fired was the last thing in the world I wanted. My partners hung me out to dry. That certainly wasn't my fault. I don't see what I could have done differently."

Donald did not change his demeanor. "I'm not saying it was your fault. Being accountable is not about fault or blame or who's right or wrong. But you *did* play a part in what happened. Being accountable is seeing and owning the choices *you* made that resulted in that reality."

Strong words, Hal thought. He stood and paced between the picture window and the fireplace. "I have to admit you're right," he muttered. "Okay, so I'm not a bystander. I *did* make choices." He slumped back into the recliner, put his head in his hands, and sighed. "To admit my part is like being back at the Wellshire Inn having just told my father I was fired. Instead of listening, he hurled questions that made me feel it was all my fault." Hal looked up. "When my father points out my mistakes, all I hear is that there's something *wrong* with me. I've always come up short in his eyes." Hal was staring blankly into space.

"What's going on?" asked Donald.

"This one time, Dad was underneath a car, working on a brake job. I was handing him tools. But when he asked for a brake spoon, I had no idea what he was talking about, so I handed him the nearest tool I could find. All of a sudden, he rolled out from under the car, shouting at me. 'Does this look like a brake spoon to you? What's wrong with you? Can't you do anything right? If this is your idea of helping, I'd rather work alone.'"

The sound of his father's voice echoed in Hal's mind. "Maybe that's why this talk about being accountable feels so threatening. It's like broadcasting my failure. It's like being that little boy in the garage being told that I'm totally inadequate and unworthy for doing something wrong."

"The old tapes of our parents' voices are a very powerful influence on how we see and react to life," said Donald.

Hal nodded. "No kidding."

"Remember our discussion about serenity?" Donald asked. "And living in the present?"

Hal looked at him. "Yeah."

"That's the key." Donald eyes were closed. "Our negative reactions are usually tied to our past. Living in serenity means responding to the present—what's happening *here* and *now*." He opened his eyes. "How can I help you stay present so you can be accountable today without mixing it up with the past?"

"Be patient with me. Help me see what I need to do—without criticizing or judging me." He forced a grin, hoping to cover up the inadequacy dredged up by the memory of working with his father. "Don't be like my father."

"You mean, don't be the way you *perceive* your father to be."

"I ... yes."

"Your memories of your father aren't the whole truth about who he is or was. And people do change." Donald looked right at Hal and spoke forcefully. "So, are you willing to move beyond the past meaning you've associated with owning up to the way things are?"

Hal nodded. "Keep going."

"Good." Donald stood. "How about a fire? It's getting a little chilly." He put some kindling and paper in the fireplace and lit it. They watched the flames grow stronger. "First fire this year," Donald said as he positioned small logs on the top, to allow airflow. "It's one of the reasons I enjoy the fall."

"If my kids were here, they'd want to make *s'mores*. Susie especially. She's the one who toasts the marshmallows." Hal smiled, thinking of his family.

Once the fire was going strong, Donald turned to Hal. "So, what decisions did you make that led to your getting fired? What did you do or not do?"

Hal stared into the fire. "I didn't block bringing Charlie onto the board. In fact, I could see some advantages in the beginning. Charlie has deep pockets and good connections, and I could see how he'd be an asset to the company. Even so, from the first time we met, we rubbed each other the wrong way. So I did have misgivings—and didn't say anything. I thought it would iron itself out."

"Let me see if I understand. You were part of the decision to bring Charlie on board. You had misgivings but ignored them."

"That's right."

"What else did you do or not do?"

"I didn't go out of my way to welcome him or build a relationship with him. Now that I think about it, I pretty much ignored him—which must have galled a man of his stature."

"Um." Donald pulled his recliner closer to the fireplace. Hal did the same. "What else did you do or not do?"

Hal sighed and shrugged. "This is tough."

Donald nodded. "Yes, it is. It takes courage to be accountable."

Hal nodded. "And humility—of which I am in short supply." He gazed into the flames. "I didn't pay attention to the warning signs when the tension was building among the partners. I could see Charlie causing a rift as early as June or July, but I assumed they'd never take his side. Stupid, stupid, stupid."

"Now who's judging?"

Hal gave a disparaging chuckle and pointed to his chest. "You want more?" he asked Donald. Without waiting for an answer, he continued. "I didn't talk to my partners, either, so I didn't know what they were thinking. We even had regular staff meetings, but it was business as usual. No one brought up the issues, and I didn't go to them, individually, to find out what they were thinking."

"Sounds like you did a lot of ignoring and sidestepping sensitive issues."

Hal rubbed his forehead. "I did."

"That seems to be a pattern, Hal—not just with your partners, but also with Kathy and your parents."

"I do, don't I?" He shook his head. "I guess pretending something isn't a big deal has been my way of avoiding a painful situation."

"That's a pretty big *aha*."

"It is." He stood and paced again. "I never saw it before." He stopped. "But it won't work to try sidestepping the lawsuit, although I told Sam, my new boss, earlier today that I thought I'd hold steady and see what Charlie does next."

"Holding steady isn't sidestepping if you do it consciously—as a choice, not a default mechanism." Donald paused and then asked, "What else did you do or not do?"

"I have a good nose for a good deal." He smiled. "When I find one, I don't lose time overanalyzing the pros and cons. I'm pretty quick to pull the trigger."

"Okay, how do you think that affected your partners?"

"By their recent feedback, I guess they thought I was too impulsive and my deals too risky." He shook his head and looked at Donald. "But I have to say that I made some really good deals." He began walking again. "I think my mistake was not keeping them in the loop, or giving them a chance to express their concerns."

He stopped in front of the picture window. "Wow. I never saw it like this before. I'm beginning to see why they weren't happy with my leadership."

"How does that feel?"

"Crappy, to be honest." Hal shuddered. "The partners were telling me to slow down. They said I was trying to make us grow too fast."

"What did you do when you heard that?"

"Ignored them. Defended myself." He laughed sardonically. "I thought most of my decisions were pretty good. I still do."

"But your team wasn't with you. They had major concerns, and they didn't think you were listening to them. So, is it really surprising that they took drastic action?"

Hal leaned against the windowsill and stared at the floor. "I can't believe I created this mess."

"Careful, Hal. It's easy, when you're owning up to your part, to go from blaming others to blaming yourself."

"Tell me about it. I'm pretty unhappy with myself right now," he mumbled.

"Bear in mind, being accountable isn't blaming—others or yourself. It's about telling the truth about how your choices contributed to things being the way they are. There's no judgment. Do you see the difference?"

"Yeah." Hal sighed heavily. "I need a break, Donald. Can we go outside and walk a bit?"

"You bet. Do you want me to come, or do you want to be alone?"

"Please come. I need to keep talking, but I need fresh air."

The September evening air was chilly. Hal zipped up his jacket as he looked up at the star-studded sky. "What a gorgeous night. I don't see this from the city, Donald."

"I'm sure you don't."

For a moment, Hal just stood there, in awe of the vast beauty of the starlit night. Then he said a silent prayer of thanks for being able to witness its grandeur. "It's a miracle, isn't it?"

They started down the lane and Donald asked, "Anything else you'd like to share about your responsibility in the Western situation?"

"You mean there's more?"

"I don't know," said Donald. "I'm just asking you to keep looking. Keep being honest."

Hal chuckled faintly. "I can't believe I asked for this. I must be nuts." He pondered the question again. *Was there anything else?* "I did make some mistakes in managing the business," he admitted.

"Like what?"

"Sometimes I was too eager to close a deal, and I let tenants in at too low a price ... And there was one time when I didn't blacktop one of our parking lots in an apartment complex. The tenants were all over us because of the potholes. Larry and Patricia told me we had to do something, but cash was tight and I wanted to wait until spring. That was a mistake. A tenant hit one of those holes, and it did major damage to his car. He sued us. It cost a bundle in legal fees and insurance. I guess I was responsible for that." Catching himself, Hal said, "Oops, forget the 'guess.'" He scratched his head. "But you know, Donald, those were mistakes in judgment, and awareness. A completely different category than

Charlie's insinuation that I pocketed extra money from the McFee deal. That's really been eating at me."

"Did you?" Donald asked.

Hal stopped in his tracks. How could his friend possibly believe he'd be capable of embezzlement? The very thought alarmed him. But another thought occurred to him. *Even if I had, Donald wouldn't judge me. He comes from a bigger place than that. He'd help me work my way through it.* "No, I didn't. I would never do that."

"I had to ask."

They started walking again, this time back toward the cabin. "But it worries me that they made the accusation," Hal said.

"You think they believe it?"

"I can't imagine why. In all the years we worked together, I never gave them any reason to question my character—unless Charlie believes it and convinced them."

"Have you asked them about it?"

"No," Hal answered sheepishly. In a flash of understanding, he laughed. "My getting fired—it's not about Charlie at all. It *is* about not talking to the others or involving them in what I was doing." He stopped and turned to Donald as he remembered a line from *Cool Hand Luke.* "What we have here is a failure to communicate."

Donald laughed. "That doesn't mean Charlie didn't play his part, though. The other board members, too. Everyone made choices."

"Thanks for saying that. I do believe Charlie has had an agenda all along to get rid of me."

"Maybe," Donald cautioned. "But you can't know unless you actually talk to him. Otherwise, you're just guessing about his motives. Instead of talking to your partners, you made up reasons, right or wrong, for their actions and then accepted them as the truth. We all tend to see our own motives as good and noble, and the motives of others as harmful and unjust."

Hal kicked at a rock. It skittered across the road and into a ditch.

"Tell me, Hal, how does it feel to own up to your accountability?" asked Donald.

"Like eating crow. I've been telling myself it was their fault so I wouldn't have to feel responsible—that is to say *blamed*—for what happened. Being accountable leaves me no place to hide." Hal stopped. "Funny thing is, it also feels good. Clean. Light. I'm not playing games with myself anymore. I've let go of some resentment and self-pity."

"That's heavy baggage, my friend."

"It sure is."

Donald reached out and touched Hal's shoulder. Hal stopped walking and turned toward him.

"You've crossed a threshold, Hal. Being accountable doesn't make everything all better. You still have plenty of challenges in the days ahead. But it does put you back in the driver's seat." He smiled and added, "Now it's up to you to decide on your next move. How are you going to respond to their ultimatum?"

"Hey, that's why I drove up here. I was hoping you'd tell me," Hal said with a grin.

Donald chuckled. "I'm sure you know by now that I don't give the answers."

Hal smiled his acknowledgement. "Well, I still have no idea what to do, but I feel a lot better. Stronger. More capable of making the right decision."

"Listen, Hal. It's been a long day. But if you can come back soon, there's something I want to show you. You and I need to take another hike."

"No problem. Let's see, today's Thursday. How about Monday morning?"

"I'll plan on it. And by the way, be sure to bring a jacket, backpack, and plenty of water. I'll provide the lunch to go."

With that, Donald held up his hand for a high five, which Hal delightedly delivered.

Chapter 25

Over Dinner

Kathy walked through the kitchen door and kicked off her shoes, ready for a short nap. Even on a good day, managing five classes of distracted eighth graders with little interest in math was exhausting. She'd run some errands on the way home: picked up dry cleaning, allergy prescriptions for Susie, and milk.

She called a greeting to let the kids know she was home. Susie answered with a yodel from her bedroom upstairs. Nicole hollered from the laundry room. "There's a message from Dad on the counter. He went to see that guy in the mountains."

"Did he say why?"

"No, but he'll call when he leaves for home."

Kathy tapped her fingers on the center island. What had prompted the visit? She stopped. Obviously, Keith had returned the call, and the conversation had not gone well. She circled the island. What had they talked about? She almost called Janine, to see if she knew anything, but decided against it. She didn't want to be a meddling wife, a boundary she had set for herself long ago.

She was too antsy to lie down, so she started fixing dinner. Chili and cheesy cornbread, a family favorite that she hadn't made since early spring. Before long, the kitchen was redolent with the

180

aromas of sautéed onion and chili spices.

She was folding the laundry after dinner when Hal finally called to say he was on the road.

"Nicole said you've been to see your mountain man."

"Yeah. I'll tell you when I get home."

"I'm supposed to wait an hour? What was it about?"

"Okay, Keith and Charlie White made an offer, but I'm not taking it. And they made a threat, which I'm not taking seriously."

"A threat?" she cried.

"It's okay," he said calmly. "I know what to do."

"Okay, okay." She took a deep breath. "So what is it?"

"A lawsuit."

She gasped. "A lawsuit!"

"It's a ploy. Don't worry, Kath. It's going to be okay."

Fear churned in Kathy's stomach after she got off the phone. She only half-listened as Derek prattled on about the high praise he got from Miss Talbot on his history paper. When Derek finally wound down, Kathy gave him a big hug. "You did great, honey. I'll bet you're glad you did the paper, even though you missed the movie."

"It's all cool," he said. "I was ticked when Dad came upstairs to talk to me, but he was different. I kinda liked it. And Tony's big brother is going to drive us tomorrow night … if it's okay with you?"

After what seemed like forever, Kathy heard the distinctive sound of the 1950 Chevy pickup coming down the street. She met him at the door. "I'm so glad you're home." She'd intended on dragging him into his office to pump information out of him, but something about his demeanor calmed her.

"I'll warm you some chili," she said. She heated it in the microwave, then set the bowl and a piece of cornbread on the table. "Want some milk?"

"Please."

She put the glass in front of him, then started unloading the dishwasher, trying to hide her anxiety. She didn't want to push him. It was nice to have him calm and … nonreactive. One by one, the kids came in to greet him. Although they acted unconcerned,

Kathy knew they were checking to make sure he was okay.

When Hal was done eating, Kathy rinsed the dishes and put them in the dishwasher. Then she leaned against the counter. "Okay, what happened? And I want the long version this time."

"I was pretty excited when Keith asked me to meet him for lunch. What he didn't tell me was that Charlie was coming, too." Kathy sank into a chair as Hal pushed his chair back from the table and gave her a blow-by-blow of the ambush and ultimatum.

"And I thought it wouldn't be long and they'd start making payments to buy you out. We could lose everything. You could go to jail." The color drained from Kathy's face.

"I'm not going to jail, Kath. I haven't done anything wrong."

"Innocent people go to jail all the time! You're too naive! If I get my hands on that Charlie White, and the board, I'll string them up by their curlies."

Hal burst out laughing, which made Kathy even angrier.

"It's not funny," she protested.

"It *is* funny. Here you are taking my side, giving me the sympathy I've craved all along, and I'm rejecting it. I think it's pretty funny."

Hal's mood didn't appease her. "Well, they're out to ruin you, Hal. And for no good reason." She launched into another tirade, berating everyone at Western, pacing the kitchen. The anger energized her. It was comforting in a way, not like the sinking feeling that accompanied her fear.

She was still going strong when Hal stood and blocked her path, bringing her to a stop. "This isn't doing you or me any good, Kath. I love hearing what you'd like to do to them, but you're really wasting your breath." He pulled her onto his lap, smoothed her hair, and kissed her cheek. "I understand you're upset," he whispered. "I was so furious today after that meeting. I fumed and plotted revenge for a good part of the afternoon. That's why I went to see Donald."

"So, what did he have to say this time?" she asked, with her arms wrapped loosely around his neck.

"He helped me be honest with myself. See my responsibility for what's going on." He was looking straight ahead. "I've never seen it before. Or maybe I pretended not to see it. I was too busy defending myself. But now I see my role in what's been happening." He looked up at her. "It's pretty sobering."

"Your role? Has something been going on you haven't told me about, Hal Stratton?"

"No, nothing like that. It's just that I've made deals on my own and refused to listen to my partners. You know. Thinking I knew best." He stroked her hair. "I alienated my partners by acting like the lone ranger."

Kathy leaned back and, for the first time, smiled. "And me Tonto. So, what else is new?"

Hal laughed. "You know more than anyone what my partners were going through."

Kathy listened intently as Hal told her about his meeting with Donald. When he finally paused, she said, "This is truly weird. I don't know what to think. I see you changing and I think I like it. But it's also scary to me."

"What do you mean?"

"It's flippo-chango. For weeks I listened to you rant about how you were betrayed. Now you say it's all your fault. Why? What's changed?"

He smiled and wrapped his arms more tightly around her. "It's a new way of looking at things for me, too. I'd convinced myself that I was right and they were wrong. I was so upset about being fired that all I could do was blame. But looking back, I was wrong, too. In fact, the lion's share of the responsibility rests right here."

She got off his lap and moved to a chair opposite him. "But what about Charlie's agenda? You said he wanted to get rid of you from the beginning."

He nodded. "I still think that's true … but now I see why. My partners couldn't talk to me, so they brought him in to stand up to me."

She shook her head. "You should be furious that they went behind your back."

"I was. This morning. Before I saw Donald. But I couldn't stay furious after I saw my role. I didn't listen to my partners, and so they got frustrated and reacted the best way they knew how."

"Okay, I get it. The same thing you did with me. But I still think they were cowards for not talking to you and letting you know what they were up to."

"And I was arrogant for not being open and listening." Hal surprised even himself by his remark.

Kathy shook her head. "What about the offer? It's one thing to accept your responsibility. But Charlie White's offer was an insult, and he expected you to reject it. He was planning all along to threaten you with a lawsuit."

"I know."

"He's driving us into a corner, Hal. What are you going to do? It scares me. I don't want to have to go to court."

Hal got up and pulled Kathy to her feet. He put his arms around her. "There are other options, Kathy. I just need to figure out what they are."

She pulled away. "You mean you and Donald didn't come up with a plan?"

"No."

"Why not?"

It was a good question. "Because more important than what's happening 'out there' is what's happening 'in here,'" he said, pointing to his chest. "The whole purpose of the meeting today was to help me get right on the inside. Then I can decide what to do on the outside."

She leaned against him. "But I still don't see how you can be so calm. Aren't you worried?"

"Yeah." He took both of her hands and looked deeply into her eyes. "But whatever comes, I can handle it now. We'll be okay, I promise."

"I hope you're not trying to appease me, Hal Stratton. You've got to be more worried than you're letting on." She looked at him, trying to decide whether to tell him something or not.

"What?" he asked.

"Uh ... you're not going to like this. It happened before I knew you'd had such a bad day. Otherwise I wouldn't have." She took a deep breath, then blurted it out. "I invited your parents to dinner tomorrow. I'm sorry." She stuck out her bottom lip. "I shouldn't have without asking you."

"It's okay, Kath. I've been avoiding them for weeks now. It's time." He got a glass out of the cupboard and poured some water from the refrigerator. "Donald is helping me see my patterns—in all parts of my life. This thing with my parents falls under sidestepping." He'd said the right words, but she could tell he was still resisting.

"I can call them and put it off," she offered.

"No. Let's get it over with." He took a drink of water. "When do you want me home?"

She brightened. "Five would be good, if you can. We'll eat at six."

He put his arms around her. "Five it is. And I'll be on my good behavior."

Dinner was ready and on the table when John and Virginia Stratton arrived. Kathy greeted them warmly and sent them to the family room with Susie for entertainment. Bubbly and always full of stories about school and the riding arena, Susie was delighted. Derek kept an eye on the breadsticks for his mom to make sure they didn't burn, and Nicole filled the water glasses on the dining-room table.

Kathy glanced at the kitchen clock. It was after five, and Hal wasn't home yet. "Blast!" she muttered. Where the heck was he? She stalled, providing chips and salsa, and suggested that Derek tell his grandparents about his school report. Finally, she said, "I guess Hal's held up. Let's start without him." As she motioned them to the dining room, John Stratton gave her shoulder a squeeze, as if to say, *Good try.*

The kids were on their best behavior; they knew how particular their grandmother was about table manners. Table conversations, too, for that matter. Food was passed in the proper direction, breadsticks and salt politely requested. Susie kept the conversation going, with some help from Derek. But when Virginia Stratton asked Nicole about her gymnastics, Nicole communicated the barest minimum. She was irritated at having to eat with the family; she would rather be in her room text-messaging her long list of friends.

"I'm sorry Hal isn't here," Kathy apologized. "He said he would be home by five. Guess he got hung up with something at work."

"Well, thank goodness he's working," said Virginia. "It's important for his self-esteem. Work means a lot to a man."

"Hear, hear," John said, then changed the subject. "This lasagna is fantastic, Kathy."

Hal finally appeared after they'd finished the meal and were back in the family room. Despite his apologies and reasons for being late, Kathy was furious, but she restrained herself. His parents were polite and gracious. "I had a problem with one of Sam's properties," Hal explained, putting enough humor and drama into his lively recital to make it a good story.

Later, the kids gravitated to the television and the adults to the living room. Hal thanked his father for the loan, but his words were stiff, looking for the right words and not finding them. When they left, he gave his father's hand a perfunctory shake and his mother a social hug.

So much for The Donald Effect, Kathy thought glumly.

Chapter 26

From the Heart

Hal loved this time of year in the mountains. Swaths of brilliant yellow quaking aspen and orange scrub oak contrasted with the dark green of the pine forest.

But he was disgusted at his behavior a couple nights back when his parents came to dinner. The thing that got to him most was realizing how he'd played a game of pretense, keeping himself artificially busy in order to justify not getting home when he said he would.

Kathy had lit into him after his parents left. "What's more important, your hurt feelings over something that happened thirty-five years ago, or your mother and father? What if something happened and they weren't here anymore? Would you be pleased with your behavior?"

Without knowing it, she'd said the perfect words to remind him of Donald's loss, which made him painfully aware of how ridiculous his behavior had been. The funny thing was, he still felt justified in holding himself aloof from his mother and father. It wasn't as though they were overflowing with unconditional love.

Donald was waiting on the porch when Hal pulled up. He handed Hal a sack lunch, while shrugging into his own daypack.

"Where are we going?"

"You'll see."

They started out on a familiar trail, but after several minutes turned onto a less-worn path. Donald stopped at a meadow, pulled off his daypack, and took a long drink from his water bottle.

Hal did the same and asked again, "Where are we headed?"

"Right here." When Hal frowned, Donald added, "Look around."

Bemused, Hal scanned the surroundings. They were on a gentle, sloping hill amidst tall grass and scattered small pines. A lovely spot, but unremarkable. Then he noticed a rough-cut stone several feet in front of him. "A cemetery? Way out here? You brought me to a cemetery?"

"I stumbled onto it a few years back. It's one of my favorite spots on the mountain."

Intrigued, Hal wandered around, making a halfhearted examination of the stones. Most dated back to the late 1800s. Some still had legible inscriptions. Others were so worn they were indecipherable. He read the names out loud. Who were these people? What had their lives been like?

"Remember during our last visit in the mountains when you asked what you could do to live from serenity?" Donald asked.

Hal thought for a moment. "Yes."

Donald nodded. "A key is to quiet your mind and listen to your heart." He paused. "Today's an opportunity to listen to your heart and decide what's really important to you. No better place to do that than a cemetery—"

"—because it's a reminder that someday I'll be joining these souls?"

Donald nodded. "We know we're going to die. But if we truly pondered what that means, we would change the way we live."

Donald's words struck a deep chord and brought to mind Hal's friend Rob, who'd recently been diagnosed with an advanced form of non-Hodgkin's lymphoma. Rob had lost eighty-three pounds, endured five blood transfusions, suffered two rounds of chemotherapy, and undergone a bone-marrow transplant that brought him to within inches of death. Against all odds, he had survived and one day told Hal, "I don't know how long I have to live. It's not a matter of *if* my cancer returns, but *when*. But I wouldn't change this experience with cancer for anything in the world."

"You're *glad* you got cancer?" Hal had asked in disbelief.

"Yes," Rob had answered with a beatific smile. "It's given me a new perspective on life. I love every minute of every day. I love my wife and kids more than I ever thought possible. I get tremendous enjoyment out of the smallest things, the song of a bird, a Dairy Queen ice cream cone. I wouldn't trade the way I experience life now for another thirty years above ground."

Hal had choked down his emotions, not only amazed at Rob's attitude but, to his surprise, even envious of his friend's transformation. Now, as he looked around the old cemetery, he wondered how his own life would change if he were facing imminent death. How would his perspective and priorities change? What would he do that he wasn't already doing?

He raised his eyebrows and grinned slightly. Smart of Donald to bring him here. He noticed Donald lying on his back in the meadow, gazing up into the blue sky and cumulous clouds. "Okay," Hal asked, "so how do I do it? Live from my heart?"

With his eyes closed in the gentle light, and tranquility on his face, Donald answered, "By reflection and stillness." He sat up. "Take some time today to quiet your mind. Feel and listen to your deep intuition. Inside you already know who you are and what your life is about. Ask yourself some questions. What is your purpose? Why do you exist? How do you want to live? What do you want to stand for? What are the qualities and principles by which you'll govern your life?"

Hal stroked his chin. "Those are big questions."

"They are. Most people don't take time to think about them. We're born, go to school, get a job, get married, buy a house, raise children, retire, then die. But we don't think about *why* ... until life is nearly over. It's too easy to get caught up in the mechanics of living without answering the big questions life poses."

Donald stood and stretched effortlessly, a few mountain butterflies dancing around him. "I'm going to leave you alone for a while now. Think about two things: endings and beginnings. Think about how you want to be remembered—by your loved ones and by the world. Endings. Then think about what you would like your purpose to be, starting today. Beginnings."

Donald picked up his daypack. "I'll be back at the cabin. Take your time. Come back whenever you're ready." He turned decisively and headed back down the trail and into the woods.

Wary, Hal stood alone amidst the gravestones, reading the inscriptions and wondering about the lives of the people who had settled these mountains and passed away so many years ago.

After a while, he sat on a large granite rock at the edge of the cemetery, his mind ricocheting from one thought to another until, gradually, it became quieter and calmer. He began to notice the sights and sounds of nature: the cloudy sky with patches of blue, birds circling high above, a stream flowing in the distance.

What is my life about? Why do I exist? From where he was sitting, he could see a tombstone:

Here lies
Jacob Scovil
b. August 28, 1851
d. July 31, 1906
A person who never quit.

Who was Jacob Scovil? What had he done to merit such an epitaph? It also got him wondering about himself, how he would be remembered. *Hal, a person who…* He thought about how he'd *like* people to finish that sentence.

Then a less pleasant thought intruded. How would they finish it *today?* He thought about Kathy. She'd say something like: *Hal, a man wrapped up in himself, who put his business ahead of his family, who didn't listen, disappeared when there was something unpleasant to deal with.* He felt a tug of grief. She'd given him this feedback often throughout the years. But he'd deflected it by arguing and turning it back on her.

But surely she'd have something nice to say, he thought. *A hard worker, a good provider.* A rush of sadness flooded him as he came up short trying to think of anything more. At least about the "old" Hal.

His thoughts went to his father and their ill-fated breakfast a month back. No doubt, John would say that Hal was defensive, that he didn't listen, took offense way too easily. *And he'd be right,* Hal admitted. He wondered why he felt so insecure. Why he was afraid of feedback. The thought certainly didn't match up with who he wanted to be.

How would his business partners finish his epitaph? *It wouldn't be pretty,* he told himself. *Hal is arrogant. He wants to make all the decisions. He doesn't value his partners.*

The realizations stung. *But surely, if I died today, people would put a positive spin on things,* he reassured himself. The thought didn't bring much consolation. He didn't want people to just *say* nice things. He wanted them to believe them.

Like Ebenezer Scrooge, facing the ghost of the future, he hoped he still had time to change his epitaph. In the background, he could almost hear a clanking of chains.

He was beginning to get stiff and uncomfortable from sitting on the rock. He was also hungry. He stood, stretched, and walked around a bit, then took out the lunch Donald had fixed. A sandwich of cheese and meat, a small bag of carrots and snap peas, another of almonds, and an apple. Donald's thoughtfulness touched him. He never would have thought of making someone's lunch.

After eating, he put on the daypack and started hiking up an incline of rocks and brush. He found a game trail. Up, up, up, not sure where it would take him. The exertion felt good, the rhythm of his breathing, the beating of his heart. At last he noticed he was approaching a summit. The incline leveled off, and he could see more sky than mountain. To his delight, it was the same mountaintop he and Donald had climbed the day they'd had the conversation about perspective and the four ways of looking at life.

He found the same outcropping of rocks, plunked himself down, took a big swig of water, and gazed out over the valley and mountain ranges in the distance. He was grateful to be here again and, for the better part of thirty minutes, took in the view.

Gradually, Hal's thoughts drifted back to his epitaph. What would people say? How would they finish the phrase, *Hal Stratton, a person who...* More importantly, how did he *want* them to finish it? If he came from a bigger place, his higher self?

He closed his eyes. A scene began to form in his mind. At first, faint. Gradually it became clear. He was an old man with wrinkled skin and age spots on his hands, lying in a bedroom full of flowers and sympathy cards. Family and friends gathered around him. Kathy and the kids, grown up now. His brother and two sisters. A few close friends. Even his business partners, Larry, Keith, and Patricia. Noticeably absent were his parents, who would have been long departed. Hal felt a sting of pain. He had taken their presence for granted, as if he would always have them for another day.

Then he realized he wasn't looking at himself as the old man. He *was* the old man. He felt the sheets beneath his fragile body, a pillow beneath his head. And something else, the light touches of his loved ones around him. Suddenly, he was overwhelmed with a feeling he had never experienced. He felt loved. Not just a little, but wholly and completely. He'd never felt so safe, so ... worthy in all his life.

Then, one by one, they began whispering their appreciation for his life.

"You, Hal, are a person who trusts the goodness and abundance of life."

"You make others feel good about themselves."

"You handle the challenges of life without breaking a sweat... You hold your head high in the face of adversity... You give service unselfishly... You see the hand of God in all things... You never complain... You put a positive spin on situations and events... You trust your inner voice... You challenge everyone to be their best... You seek the opinions of others... You climb a mountain because it is there... You bring people with you... You accept mistakes... You never judge..."

Tears ran down Hal's cheeks as the outpouring of love, affirmation, and support went on and on. Each phrase bubbled up from deep within his being. Some of the sentiments arose slowly. Others more quickly. Many of them surprised him. But all were real, and in the depths of his heart, he knew they expressed the person he desired to be.

He opened his eyes and slowly looked up, not wanting to unravel the blanket of love enveloping him. He thought about perspective. Serenity. What it would be like to surrender his ego and live from his heart. Mostly, he thought about the people in his life and how much they meant to him.

He reached for his daypack, took out his notebook and pen, and began writing.

September 25
I, Hal Stratton:
Trust the goodness and abundance of life.
See the hand of God in all things.
Act boldly...

On and on. His thoughts flowed easily and clearly as he listed qualities of being. He read it aloud. It felt good. More than that, it felt *right*. With a thrill of excitement, he realized—this was not just the man he *wanted* to be. This was who he already was deep inside, his core self.

The sun was low in the sky. He took one last look at the panorama, stood, and began the descent, contemplating the new course of his life. He would make mistakes, sure, but his guiding principles would always call him back on course, demanding that he make choices consistent with what was deepest within him.

Light of foot and light of heart, he bounded up the steps of Donald's cabin. Donald opened the door, and for a moment, Hal felt his probing gaze. Hal put his arms around his friend and gave him a long embrace. "God spoke to me today," he whispered.

"What did he say?"

Hal swallowed hard and stepped back to look into Donald's radiant face. "He said, *I love you.* Me!" Hal whispered. A sob pulsed up from deep within and morphed into a chuckle and then laughter. "It's the first time God ever talked to me," he said in a hushed tone.

"Maybe it's the first time you listened," said Donald.

Hal smiled. "You're right." He put his hand on Donald's shoulder. "Thanks, my friend, for everything."

Chapter 27

Choosing Sides

A few days after his trip to the cemetery, Kathy informed Hal he had a message from Western Realty. Anxiety turned into curiosity when he learned it was from Donna, the company's bookkeeper.

"Hal! Thanks for getting back to me," said Donna. "I called to see if you would join me for dinner. Well, not just me, but a number of us."

"What's the occasion?" Hal asked, uncertain what to expect, but trying to remain optimistic.

"Most of us worked with you for a lot of years, and we didn't get a chance to say goodbye. We hoped to see you the day you picked up your things."

"Sorry I didn't make time for you that day. It was thoughtless of me."

"You had other things on your mind," she said politely.

Hal was hesitant. "Sure, I'd love to see all of you, but do you think it's a good idea? I don't want to do anything that might jeopardize your jobs."

"Oh, we're not worried about that," she said cheerfully. "We just want to say a proper goodbye."

"Do the partners know?" he asked.

"No. This is just between us."

"When were you thinking?"

"Tomorrow night at Bennigans, over on Wadsworth and 285."

Good choice, Hal thought. *Discreet.* "Okay if I bring Kathy?"

"Of course."

Hal realized he should have asked Kathy first. He sought her out. "Will that work for you? I'd really like you there."

She smiled brilliantly. "I wouldn't miss it for anything."

When Hal and Kathy arrived at the restaurant, the hostess led them toward an alcove. The entire staff, including Janine, were already seated at a long table. They all stood and began applauding.

Hal was glad Kathy was with him to share the outpouring of affection. He took her hand as he greeted each of those present. He hoped Janine would see Kathy's presence as a statement. He had brought his wife because he loved her.

The conversation at dinner was lighthearted. It wasn't until dessert that Donna stood and called the group to attention. "We got talking as a staff, and none of us felt good that we didn't get to say a proper goodbye, Hal. You are, after all, the person who hired us. You were our boss for a long time, and we really appreciate you."

"Thank you," Hal said. "I'm surprised, and touched."

"It's the least we could do," said Quentin, the property manager to whom Hal had referred some of his clients. "We should have done it sooner. We were shocked to learn you were fired. None of us saw it coming. We still don't understand it. The partners haven't given us a good explanation." He held his hands up and shook his head.

"They felt they had their reasons," Hal said.

"They sure haven't communicated them to us," said Martha, another property manager. "In fact, we think you were scapegoated, Hal. The only thing we can figure out is that Charlie White doesn't like you and wants control of the company."

Not so long ago, their words of validation would have inflamed his vengeance. It was different now. He was merely grateful for their kindness.

"Actually, some of us have been thinking about leaving," said Adam, another property manager. "We're not so sure we want to be associated with the new management. Besides, we wouldn't have trouble finding new jobs."

Hal raised his eyebrows. "I don't want you to do anything rash. That's a bit extreme, isn't it?"

Adam shook his head. "We knew we were going through a rough patch before you left, but we were confident you would get us through it. We're not confident with Keith as the managing partner. He doesn't have your drive or imagination. As far as I'm concerned, he's Charlie's puppet."

Hal felt a stab of concern as he watched all of them nod in agreement. He was sure they didn't know about the lawsuit and didn't want them caught in the middle. "Your support means a lot to me. I've had many of the same feelings. But now I've experienced a change in perspective that you might find surprising." He looked around the table. "I'd like to share it with you, if I may."

Hal felt Kathy's reaction, her eyes pleading with him to be careful. He understood the concern. He didn't want to say anything that could be used against him personally if the lawsuit went forward. Yet he had crossed a threshold from self-deceit to honesty and felt compelled to continue.

He drew in a deep breath. "I want you to know that I understand *why* I was fired. I didn't get it for a while, but now I do. Looking back, I see lots of things I did that caused the partners to distrust me." Hal could hardly believe he was saying this. "For one thing, I was trying to get us to grow too fast."

"We knew we were growing fast." Janine came to his defense. "But it was your boldness that built this company. You made a few mistakes, but overall, Hal, you had a great track record, and we trusted you." The tension around the table ebbed a bit as the others nodded their agreement.

"Thanks," he said to the group in general. "But I made other mistakes, too. The biggest one was keeping my partners in the dark on some of the deals I was making. I didn't do it deliberately. It was just my style. Fact is, I'm not a strong collaborator. I think the partners got tired of that."

He could tell by the puzzled and astonished looks that he was making them uncomfortable.

"Why did they bring in Charlie White?" Donna asked. "Everything was okay until he showed up. That's how we see it, anyway."

Michael piggybacked on her comment. "To tell you the truth, none of us like him. He's aloof and arrogant. He hasn't taken the time to get to know any of us. The way we see it, he just came to—"

"Get rid of me?" Hal finished the statement. "You all need to know that I was involved in the decision to bring Charlie on board. We sought him out for his reputation and financial strength."

"But you didn't really want him," Michael insisted. "It was the others."

Hal pointed to his chest. "Believe me, I was as much a part of the decision as anyone." He surprised himself by adding, "I don't know Charlie's motives. Part of the problem is he and I never had that discussion." He took a sip of water. "I have a request. Don't blame the partners for what happened. I believe they tried to make a sound decision and do what is right for the company. They need your support."

Hal felt as though he'd burst a bubble. No one said a word for what seemed an eternity. Then Janine broke the awkward moment by standing. "We have a couple of things for you, Hal." She smiled at him as if they were the only two people in the room. "Tokens of our appreciation."

She handed him a card on which each person had written thoughtful words. Hal read them, one by one, and thanked each person. Then she handed him a beautifully wrapped gift. "Go ahead. Open it now."

It was a gorgeous coffee-table photo book of classic cars, along with a gift certificate from a specialty auto-parts store. "This is great!" Hal's voice was husky with emotion. "Who came up with this?"

Quentin raised his hand. "You told me about Lucy when you called to ask me about taking on some of your contacts. I figured this was a no-brainer for a car buff."

"You couldn't have come up with a more appreciated gift. I'll put it to good use." Hal handed the book to Kathy, who also raved about it.

Slowly, people said their goodbyes to Hal and Kathy and wished them the best. Hal could tell they were disappointed by his speech; they had expected him to tear into Charlie and the board, an activity some of them would have been happy to join in.

As Hal and Kathy drove home, they talked about the wonderful evening, the support, the nice sentiments. And to think that only days earlier he'd felt like a pariah, a castaway. Hal shook his head, haunted by the thought he could be so wrong in his assumptions.

Chapter 28

Partner Meeting

After the Friday night dinner with his former employees, it was clear to Hal that he needed to go on the offensive regarding the offer to buy him out at his original investment. The ball was in his court. It was up to him to take the next step. Monday morning, he called Keith. "I need to give you an answer to your offer. I want to be on the agenda for the October board meeting."

Keith sounded wary. "How about a lunch or breakfast meeting?"

"No," he said emphatically. "This concerns everyone, not just you and Charlie. I'm also not willing to meet in a public setting. We need to have an honest discussion, free from distractions. I propose we meet in the conference room at Western and settle this matter."

"I'll have to talk to the others," Keith answered hesitantly.

Translation: you have to talk to Charlie, Hal thought. He almost commented, but let it go. He wanted to find a solution, not antagonize.

The next day, he got an email from Keith letting him know he was on the agenda for the next partners' meeting, scheduled for the second Wednesday in October, just over a week away. Hal told his family about the meeting over dinner that evening. "I'm going to beard the lion in his den," he said.

"What does that mean?" asked Susie.

"It means he's going to take on Charlie White," said Kathy, looking straight at her husband.

Hal noticed a look of alarm on his children's faces. In the days after his firing, he'd used a lot of choice words to describe Charlie and how he felt about the man. The thought of him confronting Charlie worried them.

"We're not going to get into a wrestling match," he joked, "not even a shouting match. We have some issues to work out, but I think we can do it in a reasonable fashion." He stayed close to them that evening, reassuring them. It occurred to him as he gave them hugs and kisses at bedtime that he'd been reassuring Kathy and himself as well.

Bouts of anxiety welled up in Hal during the next few days. They surprised him. He'd thought he was making such great strides under Donald's tutelage. But his body seemed to have a mind of its own. He found he could handle his feelings by going to a quiet place, usually his study, where he could meditate. He'd visualize himself in the grove of his youth or up on that rocky promontory where Donald had taken him. He thought, often, about the epitaph he'd written the previous week, looking for guidance as to how he should approach the board meeting.

One sleepless night, he remembered that Donald had asked him to think about *two* things that day in the cemetery: endings and beginnings. He'd accomplished the endings part when he wrote his guiding principles. But he had yet to address beginnings.

He padded down the stairs and retrieved the journal he'd taken with him to the mountains. Then he made hot chocolate, which he took to his office. Seated at his desk, he opened the journal to an empty page and wrote:

My Personal Purpose / Why I Exist

He laughed. People would think him grandiose. But here he was contemplating one of life's big *whys:* Why was he on planet earth? Was there something he was supposed to accomplish?

He considered what he'd accomplished so far in his life. Achieving success had been his purpose. He enjoyed doing and accomplishing. He liked figuring things out, solving problems, making things happen, getting things done. He thought about his strengths. His interests.

But if he'd learned anything from Donald, it was to go deeper. So he asked himself, what would he do if he had only six months to live? Or if money was not an object? What difference had his life made? He didn't get very far with that question, so he reversed it. What would be missing in the world if he had never been born? What contribution did he want to make?

In the quiet of the night, he wrote down ideas, fragments of thoughts, everything that came to mind. He quietly went upstairs and slipped into bed, skooching spoon-style next to Kathy. It didn't bother him that he hadn't completed his work on beginnings. Coming up with a statement of purpose didn't need to be forced. It would come. He knew that.

The day of the board meeting, Hal woke before 4:30 a.m. With nervous anticipation for the 7:00 p.m. meeting, he put on coffee and wandered out to the Garage Mahal, where he spent some time thinking through the meeting to come. Around 5:30, he went back upstairs to see if Kathy was awake. "Morning, Mrs. Van Winkle." He kissed her forehead.

"Morning," she murmured. "You're up early. Worried?"

"A little. I have no idea how they'll feel about me being at the meeting or how they'll react to my response to their proposal. But mostly, I'm excited. I've waited too long for this meeting, and I can't wait to get it rolling."

Kathy sat up. "What about Charlie? Won't he make trouble."

Hal smiled. "I'd expect no less from the dear man."

She looked apprehensive. "How will you deal with it?"

"By staying focused on my principles. And on everything I've learned from Donald about choices and perspective. As Donald says, it's not what others do to us, it's what we do to ourselves. No one in that meeting can harm me except myself."

Kathy's look softened. "My, my. Philosophy at this hour of the morning."

He sat down next to her on the bed. "I know it sounds rather out there, but, Kath, I'm clear about the outcomes I want and the role I want to play. How well I keep to that will be the ultimate measure of my success tonight."

She kissed his cheek. "I'll be thinking about you all day, sending you my love."

When she and the kids had left for the day, Hal headed out to the Garage Mahal again. There was nothing pressing with Suburban Real Estate, so he enjoyed a day with Lucy. He was beginning to see the car as a metaphor. He had stripped it down to the frame and was now rebuilding her, nut by nut, bolt by bolt. Sort of like his life. As he'd completed each automotive step, he felt a thrill of accomplishment, the same way he felt each time he made *The Hero's Choice.* He was a work in progress, just like his car.

He put on his coveralls and laid out the items he would need to put another coat of black paint on the underside of the car. Then he got to work. Now that he had clarified his thinking by talking to Kathy, he could let go of his worry about the board meeting. Instead, he focused on the purpose statement he was trying to craft. That felt more productive than obsessing over something he couldn't control.

As always, he was so absorbed in his work that he was surprised when he heard Nicole calling him from the house. "Pops. You here?" A moment later, he heard her come into the shop. "Hey, Pops. What are you doing under the car?"

He rolled out from under it, waving his brush. "Painting."

"I thought you'd be getting ready for tonight?"

"I am," he replied with a grin. "Working on the car is how I solve problems. How was your day?"

"Okay. Uh, this guy I know at school wants to come see Lucy. Would it be okay if I bring him over sometime?"

"Sure. Just let me know ahead of time, to make sure I'm here in case he has questions."

"Great." Her bright smile told him she was interested in the young man. "Well," she said, "I'll let you get back to what you were doing."

"No need. It's time for me to start cleaning up."

He was cleaning the paint brush when Derek came in and walked around the car, running his hand along it as Hal had so often done. When he came to a fresh patch of tan goop on the front fender, he stopped. "What's *that?*"

"Body filler. You use it to patch up holes. Once it's set, I'll sand and prime it. After the final paint job, you won't even know it's there."

"Cool."

Hal took off his coveralls and washed up at the shop sink. Susie joined them all in the kitchen, and they sat around the table, chatting and enjoying Oreo cookies and milk. Listening to them talk was a delight.

They were still at the table when Kathy came home. "Oh, good. You're all here." She placed a small paper sack in front of Hal. "Something you might want to take with you tonight. Go ahead, open it."

He made a show of peeking. "What could this be?" He slipped a hard object out of the sack into his palm.

"It's a worry stone." Kathy smiled. "You keep it in your pocket, and whenever you're tense or worried, you rub your thumb over that slight depression. And, look, it's shaped like a heart, so you know you always have our love with you."

The family ate dinner around 4:30 so Hal could shower and get ready for the meeting. He wanted extra time to prepare himself mentally and emotionally. He was dressed and ready by 5:30, so he went to his study. He closed his eyes and tuned into the rhythm of his breathing. As he did, he realized that his mild nervousness was actually eagerness, excitement. With a smile, he turned his attention to the board meeting, reflecting on the outcomes he desired and the role he wanted to play. Most importantly, he confirmed his intention that the meeting would be beneficial for all concerned.

At 6:25, he wandered out to the garage and slid his hand over the body patches on the Coupe de Ville, walking around the car.

"It's going to look just like the one in the book," came a voice

203

from the shadows.

"Derek? What are you doing out here?"

"It's really a cool car, Dad. Hey, good luck with your meeting."

"Thanks, son."

Hal walked into the Western Realty lobby shortly before seven. Janine looked up from her computer, relief obvious in her expression. "There you are. I was getting nervous waiting for you." She drew in a quick breath and let out an audible sigh. "Are you ready for this?"

"As ready as I can be. Are they already in the conference room?"

"I think they're in Charlie's office. Guess he's holding a pre-game strategy review." Her mouth was set in a stern line.

"Hey, it'll be all right."

Hal sat in the reception area, and Janine picked up the phone to notify the group of his arrival. Before long, Keith came out to meet him. He looked at Hal and quickly glanced away. "Uh, we'll start in a few minutes. You can go in if you like."

Hal picked up his briefcase and walked down the hall to the conference room, willing himself to remain calm and centered. He placed his briefcase on the table, then wandered around the room waiting for the others to come in.

A few minutes later, all four board members entered at the same time. *Strength in numbers,* Hal thought. He put out his hand and greeted each of them by name. The response was tepid, all offering a quick glance, then looking away. *Guilt, contempt, or fear?* Only Charlie looked directly at him, and squeezed his hand as if to establish his superiority.

Keith took Hal's former place at the head of the table. Charlie sat at Keith's right. "Let's get started," Charlie said.

Keith picked up the agenda, then put it back down. "Let's forget the minutes for now. Hal, we decided to let you go first so you can leave. You don't need to be here for the whole meeting."

Hal wanted to remind Keith and the rest of the board that he was still a partner in the company and a member of the board, that he possessed exactly the same authority and voting privileges as the rest of them. But what was the point? That would be inconsistent with his intent and desired outcomes.

"Keith and I presented you with an option a couple of weeks back," Charlie said. "Everyone in this room was party to drawing it up. We'd like to know your response."

Hal looked around the room. The only encouraging glance came from Janine. "I'd like to begin by acknowledging that this is an awkward moment for all of us," he said. "You probably dreaded my coming here tonight. I've certainly felt my share of anxiety and apprehension. I want you to know I don't intend to make this difficult. I don't hold any animosity or grudges toward any of you. My intention is to work things out in a way that's best for all of us."

"Enough of the speech-making, Stratton," said Charlie. "That's not why we're here. What's your answer to our offer?"

Hal looked Charlie squarely in the eye. "I mean no one ill intent, Charlie, including you. The last thing I want tonight is to get into a power struggle. But I will speak frankly. I started this company. I served as the managing partner for seven years. I brought each of you into the business, and I'm an *equal* partner at this table. I've earned the right to share a few words with you before I answer."

Charlie's expression showed how rare it was for him to be challenged. "Well, make it quick. You're wasting our time."

Hal knew he was walking a tightrope. He didn't want to start a fight. Neither did he want to allow Charlie to dictate the terms of this meeting. Or more importantly, the future of Western Realty.

"The night you fired me," Hal said, "was the darkest night of my life. I plunged into a bitterness and despair I've never known before. It hasn't been an easy journey to pull myself out of it. But once I stopped defending myself and blaming all of you, I realized there were good reasons I lost your support. I'd like to try to understand those reasons more fully."

The partners glanced at each other and shifted uneasily in their seats.

"We're not here to rehash why you were fired," Charlie said.

"That's water long under the bridge."

"I disagree," Hal stated, his voice unyielding. "We've never had an honest discussion about why I was fired. In fact, we've never had an honest discussion about *anything,* and I think that may be part of the reason I was fired. I made a huge mistake in my leadership with Western. I was arrogant and insulated. I loved making deals and thought I could do everything on my own. All of you had concerns about some of the decisions I was making, but I ignored you, and that's no way to run a business."

Charlie huffed. "Sounds to me like you're campaigning to get your position back. I can tell you right now it isn't going to happen."

"Wrong, Charlie. I understand your decision to fire me, and I intend to live with it. But I don't want us, as directors of Western Realty, to go on making the same mistakes. The future of this company depends on being honest and frank with each other. I regret that, as your president, I failed you by not making that possible." He looked at the other board members. "Am I right?"

"It doesn't matter." Charlie's tone was agitated. "Now let's move—"

Patricia interrupted him. "No, it does matter. You're right, Hal. That *was* a primary reason why we were willing to take the vote against you. In fact, it was the most frequent topic of conversation among the three of us—Keith, Larry, and me—over the last several months. We complained to each other many times that you didn't value our input. We resented the fact that you wanted to make all the decisions on your own."

Larry looked at Keith, and Keith looked at Charlie. Before Charlie had a chance to say anything, Hal asked, "What were the consequences of my not listening to the three of you?"

"You're asking us?" Larry said.

Hal nodded.

"We got into some bad deals, like the McFee Ranch," Larry answered. "The three of us didn't believe we had the cash flow to justify purchasing that property, but you went ahead anyway."

"And the Queen Anne Apartments," Keith added. "I tried to warn you, Hal, that it would be hard to fill them, but you were so sure you knew what you were doing."

Without further prompting, the partners talked about a few other questionable deals. He listened, amazed that he didn't feel the need to jump in and justify his decisions. Instead, he allowed them to do something he wished he'd done months earlier.

"Okay, okay," Charlie interrupted brusquely. "I think we all agree that Hal made some bad business deals and that's why he was fired. Can we please move on?"

"Hold on a minute," Hal said, looking directly at Charlie. "If you'd really listened to what was just said, Charlie, you'd realize these folks didn't vote to get rid of me because of my business deals. They voted me out because I didn't listen or communicate with them. That's why it's so important that we do so now."

Hal and Charlie stared at each other, tension building.

Larry shoved his chair back. "How about a short break? We still have a sizable agenda ahead of us."

The room emptied quickly. Only Hal and Janine were left sitting at the conference table. She burst out laughing. "That was amazing, Hal. They had no idea what you were up to." She turned serious. "I can't believe the change in them, the way you got them to open up."

"Thanks, but it's something that should have happened a long time ago."

She smiled and reached out to touch his hand, but Hal drew it back. It was a sharp gesture, the effect of which he saw in her eyes. "Sorry, Janine. I appreciate our friendship very much, but that's all it is. I'm sorry for giving you the impression that it could be something more."

She shrugged off the hurt with a crooked smile. "Can't blame a girl for trying." Then she turned all business. "I like what you're doing with the staff."

"Thanks," Hal said, letting the word do double duty, thanking her for both her compliment and willingness to respect his boundary. "But the night isn't over." He excused himself and walked down the hall toward the men's room. He passed Larry's office. The door was closed, but he heard muffled voices within. For a moment, he wanted to listen. *No,* he stopped himself. *That's their business, not mine.* He continued down the hall. By the time he came back to the conference room, the entire group had reassembled.

"Okay, Stratton," Charlie said authoritatively. "Enough of your pontificating. Give us your response to our offer."

"I'm prepared to discuss it now," Hal said. "Would you mind reviewing the terms, just so we're all on the same page?"

Charlie heaved an irritated sigh. "We've talked it over, and we believe that, given the problems the company is facing—problems caused mostly by your decisions—buying you out at your original investment is the best we can offer."

Hal let the words hang in the air, hoping they would sound as ridiculous to the partners as they did to him. If he could just get one of them on his side, it would make all the difference. But they all avoided any eye contact with him. Even Janine kept her eyes on her notepad.

Hal took a deep breath. "I was appalled when you made me that offer. I'm still appalled. Your price is way too low, given what I've done for this company and the long-term value of the properties we own."

Keith's frustration was clear. "We can't do any better than that right now, Hal. You of all people should know that."

Hal smiled at Keith. "I understand. That's why I'm willing to make the terms workable for you—if you give me a better deal. But I won't accept the one on the table."

They all looked at Charlie. "Why should we pay you more?" he barked.

"I don't agree with the assertion that I got the company into a mess." Hal couldn't believe how calm he felt. "The value of the properties we own is extremely high, and the long-term picture is very bright."

Charlie slammed the conference table. "Don't you listen, Stratton? I told you that we'd sue you for mismanagement if you don't accept our terms."

Hal ignored Charlie's bullying and turned to the others. "Do you three believe I mismanaged the company? If so, tell me how."

"Hold it," Charlie said, bounding out of his chair. "We're not going to lay out the claims of the lawsuit. You've refused our offer, so I guess we'll see you in court."

Hal felt his face heat up, but his voice was resolute. "I've made mistakes, and I'm willing to acknowledge them. But I will *not* concede that I ever did anything unethical or illegal or even close to egregious enough to warrant a lawsuit." He gave Charlie White a challenging stare. "And that includes supposedly pocketing money from the loan I took out to buy the McFee Ranch. That's a dangerous and ridiculous claim on your part, Charlie, and one you will regret."

He turned to the other three. "I hate to see us spend money fighting each other in court, instead of moving this company forward. But I'm willing, and prepared, to take that step."

"We know where we stand now," Charlie said, standing aggressively. "It's time for us to get on to other business. You're free to leave."

Hal cleared his throat. "I'm still a partner in this company, Charlie. I have as much right to be here as any of you. But it's not my purpose to provoke or antagonize. I'm willing to leave, if that's what you all would like."

"No question about it." Charlie White looked nervous and uncharacteristically flustered.

Hal picked up his briefcase. He started to leave but turned back. "I owe a great deal to each of you, Keith, Larry, Patricia. Western Realty wouldn't be what it is if not for your willingness to invest in it and your trust in my ability to run it. The last seven years have been the best of my career, and I'm proud and grateful for what we created here." He turned and headed to the door.

"Thanks, Hal," Larry called out.

Hal turned to acknowledge his thanks and saw something in the faces of his three friends.

The evening was a victory for his new way of being.

Chapter 29

Reassuring Kathy

K athy hurried to Hal's side the moment he arrived home from the board meeting. "How'd it go? Did they drop the ridiculous lawsuit?"

"Great … and nope." He dropped his briefcase by the door, filled a glass with water, and gulped it down. Turning, he saw Kathy's white face.

"What are we going to do?"

"I'm not sure. No doubt I'll need some professional advice." He looked around. "Where are the kids?"

"I sent them to bed, at least to their rooms. I wanted to be able to talk."

They sat on the family room sofa as Hal recounted the events of the evening. Kathy listened, playing nervously with her wedding band. "I'm so sorry your partners didn't budge. This idea of a lawsuit really worries me."

Hal caught himself about to give his usual response—to dismiss her concerns and offer blanket reassurances. Instead he waited.

She started to tear up. "I hate the thought of you going against your old friends. The time and energy it will cost us, the expense of hiring an attorney. And what if we lose? I believe in you, Hal, but you have to admit losing is a possibility."

"Yes, it is."

"Why don't we just settle with them? Accept the terms of their offer."

"I can't do that, Kathy." Hal stood and walked to the other side of the room and leaned against a window ledge. "I honestly believe their terms are unreasonable."

"Maybe so, but is it worth a fight? A lawsuit leaves people so bitter and angry. Is money worth so much acrimony? And I'm worried about how you'll feel if ..."

Hal stopped her abruptly. "Listen, Kath. I'm not going to be bitter no matter what happens. If I've learned anything these last weeks, it's that my happiness is not dependent on events. That's living from the outside-in. Believe me, I'll be okay, win or lose."

She looked up at him, supplication in her voice. "Then I don't get it. Why not accept their terms?"

"For one thing, their offer discounts the huge contribution I made to the company over the last seven years. I'm not willing to walk away from that. But there are other reasons."

"Like what?"

"My good name. The fact that I was fired is public knowledge. People in the business community are watching to see how this plays out. I have a responsibility to defend myself. It's a matter of honor."

"That sounds like pride and stubbornness to me." There was an edge to her voice.

"I see how it can look that way. You think I'm doing this because I don't want to give in or let Charlie win."

"Yes. And it's not worth it if it destroys our family." Her look was sullen.

"I agree. But I'm not playing a game to placate my ego. I know the idea of being sued is terrifying, but, Kathy, I actually feel good about what happened at the meeting tonight. I didn't feel the need to defend my point of view or to prove myself right or anyone else wrong. There's a big difference between pride and self-respect, and I'm finally learning what that difference is."

She sat quietly, her hands folded in her lap. "So you did what you said you'd do this morning?"

"Yes. Exactly." Hal rejoined her on the couch. "There's something else at work here, Kath. All my life, I've run away from difficult conversations. I've done it with you and my father. I did it with my partners. I did it the night I was fired." He paused. "I'm beginning to understand why," he said, thinking of his memories of his parents. "But I'm unwilling to continue. I want to get issues on the table and work them out."

"But people don't work out issues by going to court, Hal. That's where they go when they *can't* work them out."

He laughed. "I'd love nothing more than to work this out. I tried to get us to that point tonight, but my efforts were too little, too late. And I don't have anyone to blame but myself."

He then frowned. "I see now that the problem was not the direction of the company, or the decisions we were making, as much as our failure to talk openly with each other. What my partners don't understand is how, by bringing Charlie on board, they've got more of the same. Only he doesn't avoid, he dominates and intimidates. They've gone from the frying pan into the fire. They haven't come close to solving the reason they wanted to get rid of me."

"That doesn't sound so good."

"It's not. That's one of the reasons I kept pushing the dialogue tonight."

She shook her head. "I don't see how you can be so calm about this."

"Would it make you feel better if I ranted and raved?" he deadpanned.

She laughed. "It might. Ranting and raving I understand."

He smiled and took her hand. "Listen, Kath. They may never change. They might follow through on the lawsuit. I might never set foot in my office building again. I might lose my equity. And it would be okay, because tonight, I lived my principles."

Chapter *30*

The Defendant

The next night, Hal and Kathy were getting ready for bed when the doorbell rang. "Who could that be at this hour?" she asked.

Hal sighed. "I think I know." Trying to calm himself, he threw on a robe, went downstairs, and opened the front door. A stranger stood before him holding a manila envelope. "Hal Stratton?"

Hal braced himself. "That's me."

"You've been served." The man shoved the envelope into Hal's hand.

Hal's first impulse was to yell, *Hey, wait a minute! You can't just dump this on me and walk away. Who do you think you are?* He was deeply disappointed. He'd hoped last night's meeting would have influenced the partners to drop the suit.

"Who is it?" Kathy asked from the top of the stairs.

He held up the envelope. "The lawsuit."

She turned ashen. "So much for your principles."

"What does that mean?"

"Last night you felt good because you had lived your principles." Her tone was caustic. "Big deal. It didn't save us from a lawsuit." She whirled around and headed back into the bedroom.

Anger flashed through Hal. He tossed the envelope onto a

kitchen counter and headed for the Garage Mahal. But he stopped. *Stop - Look - Listen - Choose.* He'd told Kathy he needed to stand up to his challenges, and here he was, on the verge of running away again—from Kathy and the papers that posed such a threat. And from his own fears, if he was honest with himself. The effects of a lawsuit could be far-reaching.

He went to his office and got the copy of his guiding principles from his briefcase. He leaned back in his chair and read them over and over again. Then he closed his eyes to recapture the way he'd felt during that moment of serenity the day he'd first written them.

As his emotional state changed, his mind began to clear. Kathy wasn't insensitive or unsupportive. She was scared. And being served papers didn't invalidate the words he'd spoken at last night's board meeting. He had been authentic and honest, and he had not attempted to manipulate the others into getting what he wanted. He'd known the lawsuit was possible, even probable. So receiving the papers wasn't really a surprise. Nor was it a catastrophe. He would handle it.

He went up to the bedroom. Kathy was lying face down on the bed, crying. He sat next to her and tenderly stroked her back. She rolled over and looked up at him through tearful eyes. "I'm sorry. I didn't mean that. It's just that I'm really scared."

He took her hand and kissed it. "I know. It's okay." He understood how his high-stakes game of buying and selling properties felt the same to her as when her father had risked their survival on his next drink. And now there was the lawsuit.

"I've made life pretty hard for you all these years." His eyes were moist. "And I'm sorry, Kathy, that I've been so insensitive to you." He took a deep breath. "But I do need to fight this lawsuit. It's the right thing to do. Not just for me, but our family."

"I know. I told you I would support you all the way, and I will. I'm sorry for letting my fears get the better of me." She smiled weakly and touched his cheek. "Maybe I should read those principles of yours. Get my head screwed on straight."

The following Monday, mid-October, Hal was sitting in the office of Mitchell Cross, his personal attorney, waiting for him to finish reading the details of the lawsuit. One who never put on a pound no matter what he ate, Mitchell radiated nervous energy. His fingers were long and thin, and the cut of his fine hair resulted in a dramatic flop over one eyebrow.

After perusing the papers, Mitchell leaned back in his executive chair. "The board has filed five claims against you, related to usurpation of corporate authority, breach of fiduciary duty, and negligence. Those are pretty serious charges, Hal. What's your response?"

"Want the R version or the PG-13 version?" Hal tried to laugh, but his mouth was too dry.

For two hours, Hal and Mitchell discussed the charges, the financial state of the company, the rationale behind Hal's purchase of the various properties, and the decision to bring Charlie White on board.

Mitchell exploded when Hal told him about the recent partner meeting and how he'd owned up to his responsibility for being fired and alienating his partners. "You said all that at the meeting with your partners? Are you nuts? You just handed them their case."

Hal looked intently at Mitchell. "My statements weren't about building a case or winning a lawsuit. They were about opening an honest dialogue with my partners. Probably for the first time."

"I'm touched," said Mitchell, tossing his pen onto the desk. "They're sure to bring up that point in court. It was your responsibility as managing partner to communicate with your board of directors. The fact that you didn't—and have admitted it—plays perfectly into their claims that you overextended your authority and made bad decisions."

Hal held up his hands in a gesture of surrender. "I know. From your point of view, it was stupid. From mine, it was long overdue. I was hoping my partners would see it that way, too, and that we'd begin to really communicate with each other."

"And?"

"I don't know. Charlie kept cutting me off, saying it didn't matter. But there was a moment when Patricia acknowledged what I was saying, and Keith and Larry agreed that communication had been their biggest concern about me." Hal looked at Mitchell with a patient smile. "I don't know if this will make sense to you, but I had to let them know that I understood why they fired me. Not just for their sakes, but for my own. I needed to stop deceiving myself and get honest and accountable to move forward with my life."

Mitchell stood and walked to the window. "That's all well and good. But ultimately, this suit isn't going to come down to how much you talked with your partners. It's going to come down to their claim of a breach of fiduciary duty. They charge that you made some poor decisions. That you didn't do due diligence before you purchased ..." He picked up the document and thumbed through a few pages. "... the McFee Ranch and the Queen Anne Apartments. And those decisions put the company in financial jeopardy. These are serious claims, Hal. What do you say to that?"

"I can defend those decisions, especially the ranch. It's true that it left us financially strapped in the short run. But it's equally true that we bought that property for twenty cents on the dollar. In five years, it will bring in a lot of money, and my partners will be singing my praises."

"Well, you're going to have to offer more than your crystal ball in a court of law. What about the apartments?"

"A bad purchase in retrospect, one I wouldn't do over again. The real-estate development business is risky by nature, Mitch. Every company has property that doesn't bring in as much money as expected. You know that."

"Are your partners going to claim that you didn't consult them on this deal?"

"Probably, but it's not entirely true. They knew when negotiations were in progress, but they never questioned me about the details, so I took their silence as approval."

"That's pretty thin."

"I know," Hal acknowledged. "But there is some really good news in reading the suit."

"Do tell."

Hal sat on the edge of his seat. "Charlie accused me of going south with some of the company's money, and he said he was having an outside audit of the books to prove it."

"And?"

Hal held up a hand and shrugged his shoulders. "There's nothing to the charge. It was made purely to intimidate me. And the fact that it's not included in the suit verifies that they know it's baseless. The audit was clean and they came up sucking swamp water."

"That's good luck for you," Mitchell agreed.

"It's not luck. I never did anything that was morally or ethically questionable. I want you to know that."

Mitchell walked around in front of his desk and sat on the edge, crossing his long legs at the ankles. "Before you start feeling too good, you need to know that suits like this usually end up being a lose-lose proposition. They're long and drawn out and very expensive. And the outcome is often unsatisfying. If you win, you'll retain all your equity in the company and be yoked to partners that don't like you. If you lose, you'll have to accept the terms of their buyout, and you'll likely have millions of dollars of judgment against you." He shrugged. "Of course, you'd never have to pay it, because you'd be in bankruptcy."

Hal rubbed his temple, trying to massage away the beginning of a headache. "So you're saying, if I win, I keep my equity. If I lose, I'm not out much anyway since I wouldn't own any assets."

Mitchell frowned. "Don't forget the part about losing your house and all your personal assets in the process. To say nothing of your legal bills."

"What are we talking about?"

Mitchell reached for a notepad, wrote down a figure, and handed it to Hal.

Hal whistled. "You've got to be kidding!" Maybe Kathy was right when she said taking on Charlie and Western wouldn't be worth it.

"Nope. That's what it's likely to cost you to defend yourself in this suit." Mitch went back to his desk chair. "Of course, that's if it actually goes to trial. Lawsuits like this rarely make it that far, which I'm guessing your partners are counting on." He tapped his pencil against his desk. "They probably filed just to force you into a negotiated settlement."

Hal ran his fingers through his hair. "What are my options?"

"Well, you can accept their offer to buy you out at your original investment. Or you can make a counteroffer at maybe forty to fifty percent of your equity and hope you reach a settlement of around fifteen to twenty percent. Or you can deny their allegations, submit a response, and appear before a judge at a pretrial hearing."

"What would you advise?"

"Avoid the hearing. You have too much to lose. Make a counteroffer and negotiate with them. You might be able to get as much as twenty percent of your equity."

Hal shook his head. "Maybe I'm naïve, but I can't do that. I rolled over the night I was fired. I'm not willing to do it again. I won't let them put my family's financial future in jeopardy. Write a response denying their allegations. We'll proceed with the suit."

Mitchell heaved a long sigh. "I hope you know what you're doing."

Chapter 31

Intentionality

Telling his family and friends that the lawsuit would proceed created a whirlwind. Kathy was distraught, though she tried to hide it. The kids were deeply frightened. No matter what he said, he could read it in their eyes as they sat around the dinner table.

Susie's chin trembled, and her eyes glistened with tears. "What will we do if you go to jail?"

"I'm not going to jail, sweetie," he said. "My lawyer says Charlie and the board are acting like playground bullies, trying to make me do what they want, even though it isn't right."

"You should stand up to them," added Nicole, lifting her chin in a show of bravery.

"That's what I'm doing." Hal cocked his head and held up a fist in a sign of strength. "My lawyer's setting up a pretrial conference. He thinks there's a chance of negotiating a settlement."

Saying nothing, Derek picked at his food.

Hal put off telling his father about the lawsuit until later in the evening. He expected John Stratton to offer advice, as usual. Instead, he said, "That sounds serious, son. What steps are you taking?" He paused. "How can I help?" Hal couldn't help smiling.

He was communicating with his father, and without feeling defensive. *Amazing.*

A couple of days later, Janine reported that the mood at Western Realty was hovering between outrage and resignation. "Tell everyone to hang on," Hal encouraged. "It isn't over yet."

Oddly, despite the mix of emotions swirling around him, Hal felt calm and confident. Mitch accused him of being in la-la land when he called to tell him a pretrial conference had been scheduled. His mother asked if he was on something. He understood their positions completely. He would have said the same thing himself only two months ago. No matter what irritations presented themselves, he felt an inexplicable deep sense of calm and peace. He didn't try to make it happen. It was just there. A state of grace.

Only Sam asked a question that went to the heart of the matter. "Are you happy?"

"Yeah, I am," Hal responded. "Funny, isn't it?" He then told Sam about Donald Millhouse's views about success and fulfillment. "I feel this lawsuit is a test to see if I can hold onto the peace and fulfillment I feel right now ... and still have what it takes to be a sharp, successful businessman."

"Hmmm." Sam regarded him with frank curiosity. "I must say, Hal, you're not the person I used to know. You're *softer*, yet somehow stronger ... Arrgh." He swatted the air with a sharp, upward motion of his hand. "Forget that. I don't know what I'm talking about."

Hal chuckled and headed to the parking lot. No doubt, he'd changed. He was facing a lawsuit ... and he was happy. How weird was that?

Then he sobered. Where would he be now if he hadn't chanced upon that particular canyon the night he got fired? If Donald Millhouse hadn't walked down that path? If Donald hadn't spoken, or had spoken but Hal had pretended not to hear? What if he had gone home instead of to the cabin? What if he'd written Donald off as an eccentric—and thrown away the opportunity to learn?

He leaned against the pickup, humbled by the complex chain of events that had brought him to where he was in his life now. Pure coincidence? Or was something more at work in his life?

Early the next week, Hal decided to visit Donald again, just because. Every other time he'd gone to visit his friend, he had been working through some issue or facing a crisis. This time, he wanted to enjoy the old man's company and express gratitude for his help over these past two months.

He checked the kitchen clock. If he started now, he would arrive at lunchtime, and Donald, ever gracious, would invite him in for a bite to eat. Hal decided to surprise Donald by bringing a picnic lunch as partial repayment for all the meals Donald had prepared for him. He dug out a wicker picnic basket that he and Kathy had received as a wedding present, but had rarely used, and set out to fill it. Nothing fancy, just the kind of meat and cheese sandwiches Donald often made, along with a couple of oranges, bottled water, a plastic bag of oatmeal-coconut cookies. Kathy had made them, her version of comfort food for a family in distress.

Donald's place was quiet when Hal stepped up onto the porch. His unanswered knock confirmed his suspicion. Donald wasn't home. Now what? Enjoy the sun on Donald's porch while waiting for him? Go back home and make an appointment for the next time? He decided to take a hike and spend the lovely autumn day in the mountains. Donald would certainly be home by the time he returned.

He left the picnic lunch in the truck and set off. Lost in thought, he walked where his feet wanted to go. About a half hour later, he found himself at the old cemetery. Intriguing that he should end up here, he mused.

He stood for a moment, enjoying the lonely beauty of the place. Then he sat down and leaned back against one of the old gravestones. It had soaked up the sun and warmed him. He closed his eyes and thought about the assignment Donald had given him in this exact spot some days earlier. Endings and beginnings. He had yet to define his statement of purpose: Why did he exist? What contribution did he want to make? What would be missing if he were not here?

"Well, don't just sit there. Tell me what's new!"

Hal nearly jumped out of his skin as he whipped his head around. Donald was sitting in the tall grass some twenty feet away. Hal pressed his hand over a thumping heart. "You scared the devil out of me. Where did you come from? I didn't see you here."

"You didn't see a lot of things in your life, my friend." Donald smiled. "But now you do."

Hal squinted in the sun, to be sure it was really Donald sitting there. The old man was clearly not a mirage, but Hal still couldn't believe he just showed up. He'd been certain he was alone. But, then, certainty was something about which Hal was no longer certain.

"What's been going on since I saw you?"

Hal gave him the lowdown: the board meeting, the delivery of the lawsuit papers, his consultation with Mitchell Cross.

"You seem pretty serene about it."

"Something I learned from you." Hal grinned. *"It's not what others do to us, or even what life does to us. It's what we do to ourselves that causes our unhappiness."*

Donald smiled and nodded his acknowledgment.

"Once I really got that, the whole world looked different. I couldn't hold onto my resentment for my partners. I see clearly how what I was doing caused their actions."

Donald pulled up a piece of grass and put it between his lips. "Lots of people would say that's naïve."

"Yeah." Hal chuckled.

"They would assert there are a lot of bad-intentioned people out there that you didn't create by your perspective. Maybe they're right. Maybe Charlie is one of those people. Maybe all he cares about is getting as much as he can for himself, regardless of who he steps on in the process."

It was odd hearing Donald play devil's advocate. Hal pondered his words. "No doubt there are some people like that in the world. But I have to wonder how often I've created enemies in my own mind when they didn't really exist. I tend to view certain people as adversaries, so I interpret their behavior in a way that causes me to take offense and feel resentment." He looked up at Donald. "That's the attitude I put out to them. Then—surprise, surprise—that's what comes back to me."

Donald was quiet.

"Huh, I just realized something," Hal continued. "We judge ourselves based on our *intentions,* which are invisible to others. And we judge others based on their *actions,* which *are* visible to us. We don't see their intentions, so we have to assume them." He took his time thinking through his new insight. "So if I make negative assumptions about people, that's what comes back to me." He grinned. "It all starts with me." Then he laughed. "My fears and suspicions become a self-fulfilling prophecy."

"Trust and goodwill work the same way," chimed in Donald. "They, too, become self-fulfilling prophecies."

Hal nodded. "We don't see people as they are. We don't see what's in their hearts. We see them based on our own unchallenged assumptions and beliefs." He paused again and then added thoughtfully, "My partners didn't change. *I* changed. Once I stopped seeing them as adversaries, I couldn't hold onto my bitterness and resentment. It was something I was doing to myself." He sat up and nodded.

"What caused this change of heart, do you think?" Donald asked.

Hal grinned. "Well, it started with you, forcing me to own up to my responsibility for what's been going on."

Donald laughed. "Force you, did I?"

"That's sure how it seemed at the time."

Donald shook his head. "None of your changes have anything to do with me, Hal. They have to do with your own desire and intentionality. You were ready to change your life. Otherwise, you would never have entered this little adventure. You'd still be blaming your partners and trying to figure out how to rake them over the coals in a lawsuit."

Hal chortled. "No doubt about that." Feeling the need to move, he stood. Donald joined him, and they silently followed a faint trail leading from the cemetery. *Donald is right,* Hal contemplated. *I have been ready—no, desperate—to find a new way to live. I was ready to choose a better way—just like Donald was that day on the bridge.*

They continued down the tree-shadowed trail to a break in the forest that opened into a large meadow with fading fall colors. Donald strolled over to a flat granite boulder, took off his daypack, and sat down. Hal followed and was soon lying on his back, looking up at the deep blue sky and basking in the warmth of the pre-winter sun. "Donald, you used a word back there. Intentionality. What did you mean?"

Donald nodded. "It has to do with the results you're *absolutely* committed to attracting into your life. Knowing your deepest desires and communicating them to the universe. Then being willing to work with all your heart and trust in their fulfillment."

"How's that different from vision, or knowing what we want?"

Donald turned toward Hal, his rugged face graced by a happy expression. "It's more than knowing with the mind. It's knowing from the depth of your being." He paused and looked toward a distant mountain peak. "It's a source of creativity that comes from the deepest level of choice and commitment. One that has the power of Providence behind it." He gave Hal a piercing gaze. "So what do you intend, Hal? Right now, in your life and with the challenges you face? What results are you absolutely committed to attracting into your life?"

The question goaded Hal into a sitting position. The answer was much deeper than buying a new sports car or traveling to Rome. It was connected to the deepest yearnings of his soul, and had more to do with how he lived than what he did. He stood, pondering.

"I choose ..." He stopped, not sure what to say, but he felt something arising within him. "I *choose* to say yes to life and all the challenges and opportunities it brings. I *choose* to be grateful for the countless blessings of life. I *choose* to enjoy my wife and children and make them my highest priority. I *choose* to experience peace and goodwill in my heart, even in the midst of chaos and disharmony. I *choose* to listen to others, to really hear what they're saying. I *choose* to engage in honest dialogue. I *choose* to live in the present. I *choose* to be proactive and make good things happen."

As Hal spoke his intentions, strength flowed through him. He clenched his fists and raised his arms straight above him. He rotated slowly clockwise, east to south, west to north, feeling connected to the earth, the unseen stars in the heavens, and everything around him, filled with the vast power of the universe. A far greater force than the drive for survival or security, far greater than the addictions of the ego. The creative energy at the heart of life, deeper and wiser than his own mind. He lowered his hands and turned to Donald.

"Tell me, Hal." Donald's face was stoic. "What do your intentions have to do with a lawsuit?"

Hal's laugh echoed among the distant cliffs. "Oh, that. It's just an event. My ability to choose gives me a place to stand no matter what." Now Hal knew—his core was solid, like the granite on which he stood. And he knew with his whole being that the origin of his experience was inside. "I choose love and goodwill, no matter what happens in the lawsuit."

The knowledge was absolutely exhilarating.

Chapter *32*

A Turn of Events

The best time to catch up on paperwork in the shared cubicle at Suburban Real Estate was during the lunch hour, when Ray was gone. Hal enjoyed Ray—they shared quite a few laughs— but he needed to be working. So he was enjoying the quiet atmosphere when his cell phone rang. It was the main Western Realty number. *Janine.*

"Hal, did anyone call you about Charlie?"

"What about him?"

"He had a heart attack a couple of days ago, and a quadruple bypass surgery yesterday morning at St. Joseph's."

Stunned, Hal gripped the cell phone. "How is he?"

"Keith's in close contact with his son Travis. Charlie came through the operation pretty well, but he'll have a long recovery." Her voice hinted at suppressed emotion. "It almost makes me regret every mean word I ever said about that man. Even if I meant them all."

"I know what you mean." Hal's mood was suddenly somber.

"What worries me is how this will affect Western. Things are so confusing here. By the way," she added, "you really impressed the partners with the way you handled yourself at the board meeting. They don't talk about anything else. They've actually stopped referring to you as 'Mr. Cowboy.'"

"And here I thought I was the Lone Ranger."

Janine chuckled. "Anyway, I was sure, after the meeting, they would drop the suit, so I was really surprised when I heard you'd been served papers. The only explanation is that Charlie harangued them into going forward. That man!"

"He did what he thought he had to do."

"Don't you go being magnanimous. It makes me feel ashamed to be angry, and I *want* to be angry!"

Hal went back to his work, but thoughts of Charlie kept intruding. He had plenty to hold against the man. Charlie had turned his partners against him, cost him his job, stolen his dream. He was lowballing Hal out of ownership in the company, which also affected his family. Still, he wasn't angry. Unlike Janine, he didn't even want to be angry.

Suddenly, responding to an impulse he didn't fully understand, Hal logged off the computer and drove to St. Joseph's Hospital. He was approaching the information desk when he saw Keith and Larry coming out of one of the elevators. He waved to catch their attention. They both stopped, as if struck by an invisible force. "Wha ... what are you doing here?" Keith asked.

"Same as you. I've come to see Charlie."

"Oh, I don't know," said Keith. "Seeing you wouldn't be the best thing for his health."

Hal's head bobbed. "I guess that's true. I don't want to upset him. But that's not why I came. How's he doing?"

Larry recited what Janine had already told him. "The outlook is fairly optimistic, but he's got a long way to go."

"I'm glad to hear that." Hal was surprised by how sincerely he actually felt his words. "Were you able to talk to him?"

"No," said Keith. "He's on restricted visitation. Family only. We stood at the door a few minutes, then gave his nurse a get-well card to put on his bedside table."

"I'd like to do the same. What room is he in?"

Keith looked at Hal with a furrowed brow. "Why are you doing this?"

"What do you mean?"

"Why are you showing an interest in Charlie? He's your worst enemy right now. You've never hidden your dislike of him, and he certainly doesn't care about you."

It was hard to hear such a blunt but correct assessment. Hal stepped back. "I feel bad for him, that's all. What he's going through is more important than what's happening in Western. I'd appreciate it if you'd let me know what room he's in. I won't disturb him."

Larry and Keith looked at one another. "Four-eleven. I hope he doesn't wake up while you're there," said Larry.

"Thanks, guys. I do appreciate it." He quickly turned and headed toward the elevators. Once on the fourth floor, Hal headed toward Charlie's room. He approached cautiously and peeked in. All he could make out was a form hooked up to a confusion of medical equipment. The sounds of a monitor bleeping and the respirator swishing were noise in the otherwise silent room. A smell of antiseptic cleaner filled the air. Hal stood in the doorway for a few minutes, staring at the shrunken figure lying unmoving on the bed.

He slipped into the room. The human form began to take on the features Hal had grown to know and revile. He thought of the board meeting in August and the imposing man who had exuded so much power, who now looked weak and frail, clinging to life.

Hal crept forward a few steps and stood there, for the longest time, some six feet away, not daring to get any closer for fear of intruding and upsetting his estranged partner. Yet he was unable to turn and leave. He felt frozen in place, incapable of taking his eyes off Charlie in such a fragile and vulnerable state.

The scene brought up a tapestry of emotions, less about Charlie than life itself. Life's harshness. Its fragility. Its fleetingness. Hal felt very small. The hollowness and vanity of the ego were strangely obvious here. He felt, simultaneously, reverence and sadness, gratitude and sympathy.

And suddenly he realized the importance of connection.

Their stories didn't matter. Who was right. Who was wrong. It all seemed so trivial now, knowing that the two of them shared the same hopes and dreams. More than that, they were both part of the dance of life, on planet earth, each with his entrance onto the stage, his exit as well. Another day, another moment, it could just as easily have been Hal lying in this bed.

An unaccustomed compassion welled up in Hal. He wanted to reach out and touch Charlie, take his hand and say, *Hi, old friend. I'm glad you made it. I'm sorry for your suffering. I'm sorry for the part I played in your suffering. I want you to be well.... Not just well—whole.*

Jarring voices interrupted Hal's thoughts. Two people barged into the room. Barely glancing at Hal, they moved purposefully to the foot of the bed, consulting with each other as they studied Charlie's chart. Hal thought he saw Charlie's eyes open as he turned and slipped out the door.

As he exited the room, a tall, well-dressed man in his mid-thirties, escorting a frazzled-looking older woman, were coming in his direction. Charlie's son. The woman had to be Charlie's wife.

The man introduced himself. "I'm Travis White. This is my mother, Irene. You must be a friend of my father."

Hal felt like he'd been caught with his hand in the cookie jar. His instinct was to apologize; but as he looked into their eyes, the sensation of trespassing dissolved. "I'm Hal Stratton. Yes, I'm a business partner ... and friend of your father."

Travis's expression darkened. "You're Hal Stratton? My father has talked about you. Do you know how excited he was to work with you over at Western Realty? I don't know what happened there, but he's been very upset about it."

Totally surprised, Hal couldn't respond.

Irene spoke up. "They fired you, didn't they?"

"Yes, they did," Hal answered, regaining his balance. "But I want you to know I don't hold any grudges. I'd hate to think the stress of dealing with Western has caused your husband's problems."

Travis looked unconvinced, but Irene's eyes filled with tears. "That's kind of you to say. I guess this nasty mess is hard on everyone."

They started to walk away. "Please," Hal blurted out. They stopped, turned, and looked at him. "I hope all goes well. My thoughts and prayers are with Charlie and your family."

"Thank you," said Irene, and they disappeared into the room.

Hal walked slowly down the corridor, confused by what Travis White had just said. *Eager to work with me?* He shook his head. Charlie had it out for him from the beginning. He'd been brought in to do his partners' dirty work.

On autopilot, Hal took the elevator down to the main floor. As he stepped out, he realized he wasn't ready to leave. Instead of turning left toward the main doors, he turned right. Absorbed in thought, he absently followed the signs to the cafeteria. He wasn't hungry, but something was calling him in that direction. At the end of the hallway, there was a large cafeteria to his right. In front of him was a door marked Chapel. He went straight.

He sat in a pew near the front of the intimate room and gazed at the stained glass outer windows and the statue of Jesus hanging in the nave. He had a similar feeling as when he was in the mountains or at Donald's. This was where he needed to be.

In solitude, he contemplated the implications of what Charlie's son and wife had told him. If it was true, there was only one conclusion: he had completely misinterpreted Charlie's motives. He had treated a man who wanted to be his friend with suspicion and disdain, avoided him, and withheld information.

Hal recognized his fallibility and his distorted thinking. He had created a world in which it was easier to do things alone. He had cut people out of his life—Kathy, the kids, his father, the partners … even Charlie White.

Now, Hal longed for connection. He wanted, at that moment, to reach out, to make contact, communicate. Not about trivial things, but about what mattered. He wanted to say to someone, *anyone: We're more alike than different. We have the same fears and sorrows, the same hopes and joys. We want the same things from life—to be happy, to make a contribution, to be loved.*

He thought of the patients in the hospital, and realized he wanted to sit and *listen* to someone, to understand their story. Not to make things better, but to be present. Just to be there—as Donald Millhouse had been there for him.

Despite apprehension that someone might come in, Hal walked

to the front of the chapel and knelt at the altar. He wanted to pray, but wasn't sure how. He recited a prayer from his childhood. Then, at some point, the floodgates opened and he spoke from his heart ... uncensored thoughts and feelings never before spoken, poured forth in a cleansing torrent.

Kneeling in the chapel, Hal suddenly knew his life purpose. Full of excitement, he hurried to his truck and eagerly got his notebook from his briefcase, the one in which he'd written his guiding principles and notes about his life's purpose. He grabbed a pen and wrote:

The purpose of my life:

To be the spark that ignites goodwill and collaboration; to inspire people to break down barriers and work together toward a noble purpose.

He studied the statement. Did it come from his heart? Did it inspire him? Did it give his life a purpose beyond earning a living? Did it help him see his connectedness with the whole? Did it sum up the contribution he wanted to make and the way he wanted to be remembered, in both his personal life and in his career?

Yes.

Maybe it would evolve over time, but in this moment, it resonated through his entire being. It reflected the person he wanted to be, the way he wanted to live. And it would inspire him to be his best self—a hero in his life's journey.

Chapter *33*

Involving the Family

"D addy!" Susie shouted as Hal entered the back door. "Where have you been? We've been waiting to eat dinner."

Hal wrapped his arms around his ten-year-old daughter and, to her laughter and delight, whirled her around a couple of times. She was way too big for this kind of game, but he didn't want to put her down. "I've been visiting a friend in the hospital."

"Who's that?" she asked, back on her feet.

"Charlie White."

Susie frowned. "I thought he was your enemy."

"No, no." *What have I been teaching my children?* "I've said a lot of things that made it seem that way. But you know what? He's my friend, and I'm learning a lot from him. Everyone that comes into our life is our teacher, if we're willing to see it."

Hal grinned at Susie's quizzical look. The words were meant for him, not her.

Kathy entered the kitchen, calling Nicole and Derek to dinner. "I'm glad you're home. Where've you been?"

He could tell she was trying not to sound irritated or worried, but the tone in her voice betrayed her. He put his arms around her and held her close. "Sorry. I've done it again, haven't I? Gone off without letting you know. I went to visit Charlie in the hospital."

"Charlie's in the hospital?" She pulled back from his grasp. "What happened?"

"What if I tell you about it over dinner." During the meal Hal told his family about the call from Janine and his afternoon visit to Charlie, including his outright surprise at what Charlie's son, Travis, had said.

Derek's reaction was like Susie's. "He's a bully. You said so, Dad. Why would he act like that if he wanted to work with you?"

Hal frowned and shook his head. "I know it sounds crazy. But why else would he say that to his son?" He paused. "I didn't welcome him when he joined the company. I made it clear I didn't want anything to do with him."

When he saw that his children didn't know how to react to his admission of culpability, he added, "Haven't you ever thought you didn't like someone when you first met them, then changed your mind?"

Nicole nodded. "Tanya at gymnastics. I thought she was totally stuck up until I got to know her."

"I never took the time to know Charlie. I regret that now."

Hal continued to answer questions as the family ate. As they finished the meal and started cleaning up, Susie asked, "What did you learn from Charlie, Daddy?"

Nicole sat back down. Derek paused from sweeping the kitchen floor and came back to the table. Kathy perched on one of the stools at the center island. Hal began cautiously. "Well, during my visit with Charlie today in the hospital, I began to realize something about my life purpose."

"Your life purpose? What's that?" asked Nicole.

"A life purpose is why we exist, why we're here on earth. It's different for everyone. It's something we discover by looking deep into our heart."

Susie stifled a snicker. Nicole looked thoughtful and intrigued. Derek laughed. "Nicole's life purpose is to boss people around."

"That's not funny. Yours is to be a plague to your sisters," Nicole shot back.

"Okay, okay, you guys." Hal held up a hand. "You interested

in learning more, or not?"

The kids nodded. Hopefully it was genuine interest. "When we find our purpose, we stop going through the motions and begin living with passion and meaning." Hal looked around, sure his kids would be rolling their eyes.

But Nicole spoke up. "What's your purpose, Pops?"

"What I learned today ..." He paused. How could anyone understand? They hadn't lived through the tough lessons of the past several weeks. The visits with Donald. His trip to the cemetery. The compassion he'd felt at Charlie's bedside.

But all eyes were riveted on him. And it hit him. Who had a greater stake in what he'd been through than his family? Who had been more affected by his distance and lack of connection? Who cared more about who he was becoming? And, besides, who was he to decide what they could or could not understand? They deserved an answer.

He glanced at Kathy, who gave him a wink. He took a deep breath and began again. "I learned that my purpose has something to do with caring about others. Really caring, and helping them work together." He choked back emotion as he realized how much his children cared about *him*. He could see it in their eyes and feel it by their rapt attention.

Yet he had almost lost them by shutting them out. He swallowed. "I want you guys to know, I'm sorry for letting other things be more important than you. I've been pretty caught up in my own world."

"It's okay, Dad," Nicole said. "We know you love us."

"Yeah," echoed Susie, and Derek gave a little nod.

Susie waved her hand. "I have a question. Does this mean you're going to become a priest?"

The family erupted into laughter.

"No," said Hal, still laughing. "Why do you ask?"

"Because priests take care of others."

"He said 'caring about' people, not 'taking care of' them," Derek corrected his younger sister.

Hal was impressed that Derek had listened so closely.

"So what are you going to do?" she asked.

"I'm not sure yet. It's not so much that *what* I do will change, but I know *how* I do it will be different."

"What do you mean?" asked Derek.

"Well, I won't go it alone so much. I'll listen to the people around me."

"Did you really learn all that from Charlie White?" asked Nicole. "I thought he was in a coma or drugged up or something."

"Yes, I did, but not because Charlie said anything. But being in the room with him helped me see things from a different perspective."

"But he's the reason you got fired," Nicole said.

"I would never have figured this out if I hadn't been fired. I wouldn't be talking to you like this right now. Losing my job was one of the best things that's ever happened in my life."

All of their eyes opened wide. Hal heard some muffled giggles as the kids glanced around the table at each other. It was like a collective sigh of relief, as if they liked this new, positive dad.

Kathy slipped off her stool. "Hal, I'll bet the kids would love to know more of what you've been going through and what you've learned." Three heads nodded emphatically. "Let's finish cleaning up the kitchen first."

The kids tackled the job enthusiastically, and Hal realized how much it meant to them that he was inviting them into his life. After cleaning up, they all settled into the family room, and he told them about the events of the last few months. The trauma of being fired. His bitterness and blame. How he met Donald Millhouse.

"Is he a guru or something?" asked Derek.

Hal exchanged a humorous glance with a grinning Kathy. "He's not a guru," said Hal with a twinkle in his eye. "But he has been my teacher and opened my eyes to a new way of seeing life."

"What do you mean?" Nicole asked, playing with a braid of her hair.

Hal thought about how he could illustrate the point. "When you look out that window, what do you see?"

"The front yard," said Susie.

"If you look out the kitchen window instead, what do you see?" he asked.

Susie giggled. "The backyard."

"What we see depends on which window we look out, right?"

"I get it," said Nicole. "That's cool, Dad."

He nodded. "In the same way, we can change how we see things that happen in our life—by looking at them in a different way, like out a different window."

"What does looking out windows have to do with Western Realty?" asked Derek.

"Because before I was looking out a window marked, 'It's Not My Fault. They Did This To Me.'" Hal stuck out his lip in a pout, which brought smiles from his children. "But Donald helped me see out a *different* window."

"What window is that?" asked Kathy with a slight grin.

Hal stood and spoke loudly. "The window marked 'I Made Choices, Too. I Am Responsible For What Happened.'"

"But how could you be responsible, Dad?" asked Derek warily. "Did you do something to make them fire you?"

Hal sat back down. "Yes, but not the way you're thinking. I didn't do anything bad or dishonest."

"But you started Western Realty," Nicole countered. "You made the deals. You made it a success!"

"True," he answered, "but I made mistakes, too."

"What kind of mistakes?" asked Derek.

"Like not getting to know Charlie. Making lots of deals without talking to my partners. Not listening to their concerns." He looked at Kathy. "I made those same kinds of mistakes with your mom. You probably heard some of our arguments when she tried to tell me."

An awkward silence fell upon the room as the kids looked down at the floor.

"Hey, there's nothing wrong with making mistakes," Hal said. "We just need to learn from them. I'm making new choices that will work better for me and everyone around me." He smiled. "Including you guys." He tickled Susie and Derek on either side of him and pulled them into a hug.

After settling down from giggling, Kathy spoke up. "Tell them about Key Moments, Hal."

"Hmm. My getting fired was a Key Moment. That's when something challenging or upsetting or disappointing happens." He turned to Nicole. "Like when you want to play tennis, but it rains." He turned to Derek. "Or when you want to just hang out over the weekend, and your teacher gives you an assignment."

"Low blow," said Derek, smiling.

"How about me?" asked Susie.

Kathy jumped in. "Like when you want to be friends with Emma, and she doesn't call you back."

Susie frowned. "Emma was mean."

"How did you feel when that happened?" Hal asked.

"Sad. I went to my room and cried."

Hal gave her a squeeze. "Donald says that when something like that happens—a Key Moment—most of us react automatically. We don't realize we have a choice about what we feel. We just get upset. When I got fired, Susie, I thought the board was being really mean to me. I didn't go to my room, but I did drive up to the mountains and had a good cry there." He grinned. "Then Donald came walking down the path."

Hal pulled out his wallet and took out the folded, tattered paper Donald had given him. He spread it out on the coffee table. The kids crowded around him, and Kathy looked over Susie's shoulder.

Nicole read it out loud. "*Stop - Look - Listen - Choose*. What's that mean?"

"It's how we change when we're in one of those difficult Key Moments. Anyone want to try it?" He walked through the process with the children using the examples they'd already talked about. His heart swelled with love as the kids got into it. "The bottom line is," Hal said as he looked around the room, "we always have a choice when we're in a Key Moment. We can make the easy, automatic, and hurtful choice—or we can make *The Hero's Choice*."

"Hero's choice? That sounds dorky," said Derek.

Hal smiled. "It's when we choose to do the right thing, when it would be so much easier to do the wrong thing. There are heroes besides those who rescue people from burning buildings. Everyday people who quietly make good choices, even though no one else may ever know, are heroes."

Susie yawned and rested her head on Hal's shoulder. He had laid too much on them at once. That last part about *The Hero's Choice* had fallen flat.

But then Derek spoke up. "Can I have that piece of paper?"

"Me, too," said Nicole.

"Why don't I make one for all of us?" said Kathy. "Plus, I'll hang one on the fridge."

Hal smiled with delight. Maybe it didn't fall flat after all. The kids were engaged, and he realized it was probably more due to what they felt from his presence than what he was talking about. They seemed intrigued by his new attitude and comforted to know that he was going to be all right.

It was getting late and they'd been talking for some time. But as Hal looked around the room, he felt an incredible depth of feeling for each of them. He recalled the vivid fantasy of being on his deathbed, surrounded by loved ones, each of them reaching out to him. "There's one last thing I want to share with you tonight," he said.

He knelt down in front of Nicole, looked into her eyes, and took her hands. "Nicole, you are a person who ..." He finished the sentence with all the good he saw in her, one good quality after another spilling from his lips as he held her hands and looked into her eyes. She swallowed hard several times, and tears slid down her cheeks. She flung her arms around him and hugged him the way she used to when she was little. He kissed her cheek and whispered that he loved her.

Then he moved to Derek. Of course, Derek was a little more stoic. But Hal could see the subtle softening of his face and glistening in his eyes. He knew the burden Derek carried, how much he felt the unspoken tension in the family. He affirmed his son's strengths and qualities. Then he gave him a big hug and told him he loved him.

"My turn!" said Susie, bright and eager. No tears from Susie— her face beamed as Hal spoke the qualities that made her special. He gave her a hug and told her he loved her.

Finally, Hal knelt before Kathy, his beloved, and clasped her hands in his. His eyes teared up. He opened his mouth to speak, but couldn't. He thought about the baggage he'd dragged into their relationship and was deeply sorry for his part in their troubles. When he could finally speak, he apologized for leaving the finances and the care of the children up to her. For not listening when she wanted to talk, and disappearing during times of stress. For taking offense too easily, and accusing her of being unsupportive.

"It's okay," Kathy whispered tenderly.

"Let me finish," he said. "You might not ever get a confession like this again." When the kids' laughter died down, Hal acknowledged Kathy's complaints about him one by one. There was a kernel of truth in each. Tears glistened on her cheeks. He gently wiped them. "Kathy, you are a person who ..." He listed the qualities he loved about her. When he added, "Kathy, you are a person who makes the best chili and oatmeal-coconut cookies in the world," the kids applauded.

Then they added their own words of thanks to their mom: doing the laundry, making their school lunches. The evening ended with hugs and laughter.

Later in bed, Kathy thanked Hal for the evening. "We all felt so loved and appreciated." She paused. "I think it's real, Hal," she whispered.

"What's real?" he asked with his arms around her.

"The change in you. I was a little afraid it might be a midlife crisis or passing phase. But tonight I saw that it's coming from your heart ... and it echoed into mine."

Chapter 34

Reconciliation

Hal could not sleep, his words about the importance of connection going around and around in his head. There was someone else he needed to come clean with—his parents. How could he withhold himself from his father and mother after his experience in Charlie's hospital room?

The next morning, he helped his family get ready for their day. After so many years of leaving the house before they were even up, this pattern of spending time with them in the morning was a new pleasure.

Then he headed for the Garage Mahal and felt the familiar surge of energy as he imagined again what the Coupe de Ville would look like when finished. Little more than a piece of junk when he'd hauled it into the garage, it was slowly transforming into a work of art.

How cool it would be to show it off, he thought, like his father had done a few times when he was a kid. Sometimes they'd driven a full day or two to an auto expo show to show off the creation. Even Hal had taken pride in the praise and attention of the expo visitors. Father and son, the car connecting them both.

Hal became excited by his emerging idea. He would call his father and invite him to go to a car show when the Coupe was finished. He was about to call right then, but his hand stopped short of the phone. He felt his old resistance harden. Clearly, a part of him was determined to hold onto old grievances.

Stop - Look - Listen - Choose. The words came back to haunt him. What would he see if he looked his parents in the eyes from the belief that they loved him and wanted the best for him? He pressed his lips together as grief for lost time made his eyes sting.

Without another moment's hesitation, he made the call. His mother answered. Hal could sense her surprise and pleasure when he asked if it was okay to drop by for a visit. He hung up feeling relieved and excited. He'd punished them long enough. *No,* he corrected himself. *I've punished myself long enough.* He immediately got ready and drove over to his parents' house, happy he'd caught them on a morning when they were home.

When Hal arrived twenty minutes later, his mother answered the door. She was dressed as if going to a fancy restaurant with friends, although she assured Hal she was planning on being home all day. "Finally!" she greeted him. "It took you long enough to come over here."

She gave him her typical brief hug and a long once-over. "You look good for someone facing a lawsuit. Not worried at all. I don't know what we've been so concerned about."

"I'm doing great, Mom," Hal said, his eyes smiling. She was still her acerbic self, but Hal could see the warmth and caring in her eyes. "Hey, would you mind doing something for me, Mom?"

"What's that?" She looked at him quizzically.

"Give me a big, squishy momma hug."

Virginia stepped back in mock alarm. "Whatever for?"

"No reason. Just indulge me. Okay?"

She approached him hesitantly, then took him in her arms. Her embrace was stiff at first, but Hal opened himself to receive it. He realized she had hugged him many times over the years, but he'd not let them in. He'd decided long ago that she didn't really mean them. Her stance softened, and Hal felt moisture where their cheeks pressed together.

Up to this minute, Hal had believed, rather self-righteously, that he needed to forgive her for always brushing him off. But he felt her love and now knew the truth. He needed to ask *her* forgiveness for brushing *her* off all these many years. What an irony.

"My, my," Virginia said when she stepped back, a little flustered. She waved toward his father's office. "He's at his desk. Why don't you go back there? He'll be glad to see you."

Hal knocked on the doorframe of the office, and John looked up. "Have a seat," he said in a businesslike tone. "I've got a few things to wrap up."

Hal sat, chuckling to himself ruefully. *He has a funny way of showing me how happy he is to see me.* He studied his father's movements and expressions as the older man completed his task.

"Done," John pronounced after about five minutes, setting the papers aside. "It's good to see you. I've missed our Saturday breakfasts. I've been wondering why you haven't returned my phone calls."

"That's why I came over, Dad." Hal looked away from his father's gaze. "I've been avoiding you."

John leaned back in his chair and crossed his arms. "Would you mind telling me why?"

The *yesterday* answer was: *You belittled me when I needed your support. You told me that everything that happened at Western Realty was my fault.* The true answer went much deeper: "Because I've misjudged you," he said. "I interpreted everything you said as critical and unsupportive."

Even as Hal spoke, his old complaint shifted, reminding him how he'd turned his complaint about Kathy around. The impact was immediate. "But I now see that *I* was the one being critical and unsupportive—of both you *and* myself." Humbled, he added, "I'm sorry for misjudging you."

His father turned away and rubbed a finger under his eyelid.

Is that a tear? Hal had never seen him cry.

"I felt terrible when you told me you'd been fired," John admitted. "I didn't know what to say, but I wanted to help you, somehow."

"I didn't take your advice too kindly," Hal quipped.

They both laughed, not as much because of the humor in the

statement but as an acknowledgement of the weeks of tension between them.

"I was *shocked* when you walked out on me," John said.

Isn't it amazing that two people can look at the same event in such different ways? Hal thought. "Sorry. A lot of what you said was true, but I was too defensive to see it then."

"I probably came on too strong." He puckered his lips and looked at Hal over the top of his glasses. "Your mom says I was doing my dad thing—trying to figure out what went wrong and how to fix it. She tells me it's not very helpful. But I really was trying to do whatever I could for you."

Hal heard the apology in his father's voice. "I know you were. I was too upset and angry."

"I can understand that." He nodded and smiled.

Hal's face became animated. "I'm ready to listen today, though. If you have some words of wisdom for me. I can use all the help I can get, with the lawsuit coming up."

"You'll be going head-to-head with that Charlie White. I've had experience in some pretty tough negotiations, and I've learned a lot about how to deal with the Charlie Whites of the world." John began telling Hal of his experiences in the corporate world, outlining some strategies he thought might be useful.

This time, Hal didn't hear his father's advice as criticism. He listened eagerly. More important, Hal noticed that each time he responded to his father's point of view openly and with compassion, rather than defensiveness, he felt lighter and more whole. But nothing affected him more than what his father said next.

"I don't think I've ever told you, but I'm proud of you."

"Sorry. What was that?"

John laughed. "Yeah. You heard me. I played it pretty conservatively my whole career. I was successful but always within the safety of a large corporation. I never took risks like you. Like starting your own business. I respect your audacity and willingness to go for it."

Hearing these words was like eating a feast after long days of fasting. For years, Hal had hungered for his father's praise. Tears dampened his eyes. "Dad … Thank you. That means a lot to me." Suddenly Hal realized that all his life he had distanced himself by thinking of John Stratton as his father, less personal. Hal now looked upon his father with a new heart. *Dad.*

John grabbed a tissue and made a great show of coughing into it, but Hal knew his dad was as moved as he was. John seemed relieved when Virginia knocked discreetly at the open door.

"Anybody hungry?" she asked.

The three of them sat at the kitchen table, eating tomato soup and grilled cheese sandwiches and chatting like old friends. Hal again expressed thanks for the loan. "It means a lot to me that you stepped in when we needed it." He turned to his mom. "Mom, I've apologized to Dad for how I've been acting. I owe you one, too."

She waved it off. "I knew you were under a lot of stress, Hal. I can't imagine what it must be like not knowing what's ahead."

They discussed the lawsuit, and Hal reassured them of Mitchell's belief that it would never go to court. As he left, Hal said, "Dad, I need your help with a project."

John squinted. "What might that be?"

"The Caddy. I've been trying to finish it on my own, but I could use your help. What would you think about lending me a seasoned hand?"

John's face gleamed with surprise and delight. "I've always wanted to rebuild a '59 Coupe. It's one of my favorites. I'd love to work with you on it. Just name the time."

"I'll be working on it tomorrow morning, but you can come over any time you like." Hal pulled out a set of keys and removed one from the chain. "Here's a key to the garage. From now on it's not my project, it's *our* project." He paused. "What would you think about taking it to a show when we're finished?"

"That would be great. Just like old times." He couldn't stop smiling.

"Exactly. And you can decide where."

"Las Vegas," John said without missing a beat. "There's a great show there every spring. Think we can finish it by then?"

"It's possible. But we might need a little help…"

Hal got home in time for the kids' return from school. "Derek, there's something I'd like to talk to you about. Can you come out to the garage with me?"

Derek flashed an *oh-no-I-must-be-in-trouble* look at his sisters and dutifully followed his father from the kitchen out to the shop. "I didn't do anything to your car, Dad. I'm always really careful around it."

"I know you are. That's why I want to ask you a favor. What would you think about helping me and your grandfather get it ready for an auto show in Las Vegas?"

Derek's jaw dropped. "You mean it, Dad? You'll show me how to use the tools and everything?"

"You bet. I'll teach you everything I know."

Chapter 35

A Reckoning

Charlie White had been home from the hospital for over a week when Hal called to ask if he might come for a visit. He was surprised when Charlie consented.

It was an early November day when he drove to the Whites' Cherry Hills mansion. He was greeted by a woman who identified herself as the personal assistant. She led Hal to a pleasant sitting room on the south side. *Charlie could certainly weather a lawsuit far better than me,* Hal thought as he walked through the spacious and elegant home.

The sun bathed the sitting room with warmth and light. Hal looked at the family photos, the titles of glossy coffee table books, and the collection of mineral specimens strikingly arranged in a display case.

He heard sounds coming toward the room and turned. Charlie was slowly approaching and leaning on a walker. He had lost a lot of weight, and his face was gray and drawn. Hal was struck by how quickly such a powerful man had been brought to the physical brink.

"Charlie, it's good to see you," said Hal, not sure whether to extend his hand.

Charlie let the assistant help him to a firm chair. He lowered himself partway, then dropped into it and fell against the back. "Have a seat." Charlie gestured toward a sofa.

"Thank you. How are you feeling?"

"Not bad. They tell me the surgery went well, and I'll be good as new in another four weeks or so."

"I'm glad to hear it. I was pretty concerned when I saw you in the ..." He cut himself off.

"In the hospital? You saw me in the hospital?" Charlie raised an eyebrow. "When?"

"The day after your surgery."

He scowled. "They weren't supposed to let anyone but family near me."

Hal was about to apologize when he realized he wasn't sorry. The few brief minutes standing near Charlie had been among the most profound of his life. The feelings came flooding back just thinking about it. "I'm glad I didn't disturb you. I just wanted to pay my respects."

Hal heard one of the first laughs ever from this austere man. "Someone must have told you I was at the edge of death. No such luck for you, Stratton."

Hal chuckled. "I didn't mean it like that. Back in August I might have felt that way. But the truth is, that day in your hospital room ... I hesitate to say it, because it sounds so false, but I really felt horrible that you'd had a heart attack. The lawsuit and our business differences seemed trivial. I just wanted you to pull through." He paused. "I was hoping and praying for you, Charlie."

Charlie harrumphed. "Well. I guess I should thank you. I am doing a little better each day. Now, what brings you here only a couple weeks before our pretrial conference?"

"I wanted to come by and wish you well. And I have a question for you, if you're up to it. The last thing in the world I want to do is cause you distress, so you can ask me to leave."

Charlie regarded him with frank curiosity. "Okay. What is it?"

"I ran into your wife and son, Travis, at the hospital. Travis said something that surprised me. No, it shocked me, and I don't know what to make of it. He said you had looked forward to working with me when we brought you on board at Western."

Charlie shifted and eyed Hal speculatively. "That's true."

"I can't believe how wrong I am in my assumptions," Hal murmured.

"I missed that."

Hal repeated the comment, then asked, "Can you tell me why you looked forward to working with me?"

Charlie eyed him closely. "As long as you know it won't make any difference." When Hal nodded, he continued. "I'd been watching you for some time before the board approached me. I was impressed with the way you'd built the company. You were ambitious and hard-working. And you have a nose for a good deal. Truthfully, you reminded me of myself, when I was a little younger, and I thought we'd make a formidable team."

"Really?" Hal was flattered by this man who was a pillar in the business community. "I'm sorry to say, I read you completely wrong. I thought you wanted to get rid of me from the start."

Charlie gave a ghostly laugh. "I was surprised—offended, actually—by how unfriendly and arrogant you were around me. You made it perfectly clear you were happy to have my assets, but you wanted as little to do with me as possible."

"You're right," Hal admitted. "I wasn't happy to have you on board, even though I was party to the decision." He raised a hand to his forehead. "I feel small admitting this, Charlie, but the truth is I resented you—your money, your power, your prominence." Hal wondered if he should proceed so openly. *But if I don't, we're still playing games. It's risky, but it's the only way we'll get to bedrock.*

Charlie scoffed. "Your attitude put me off, to put it mildly. Especially after the investment I made to become a partner in the company."

Hal sighed and nodded. "I can see why, given my arrogance." He paused; this was tough. "I guess I thought of Western as my company and didn't like the idea of someone like you coming in and telling me what to do or pointing out my mistakes in running the business."

"That was obvious." Charlie called to his assistant for a glass of water. After he took a drink, he put the glass on the side table and turned to Hal. "It was your attitude and the way you kept information to yourself that made me wonder if you had something to hide."

Hal closed his eyes. He'd never imagined his lack of communication could have such a consequence. Although it was difficult to listen to Charlie, Hal knew he was telling him the truth. At least it was Charlie's truth and needed to be expressed.

"I was also concerned about how much power you had as a general manager. Your partners had deferred to you for a long time. They rubber-stamped everything you wanted to do. It was clear you liked it that way. You didn't let them act like partners."

All Hal could say was, "You're right, Charlie."

With some effort, Charlie moved to the edge of his seat and fixed his gaze on Hal. "But more serious than your treatment of me or the partners is that you made some bad decisions. Your investment in the McFee Ranch left the company depleted of cash and created some serious debt. That was irresponsible and left you and the partners no choice but to bring me on board."

Hal was impressed by Charlie's sincerity. Previously he'd seen him as a bully—a ruthless, power-hungry, self-serving tyrant. He felt humbled at how badly he had misjudged this man. He didn't agree with Charlie on this last point, but it was clear the man wanted what was best for the company. He'd obviously come to believe that Hal was a detriment and needed to go.

Hal asked Charlie for a pad of paper and a pencil and was directed to a desk in an adjoining room. Then he sat beside Charlie and drew a sketch in the middle of a page. "This is the McFee Ranch." Then he drew a rough outline of another piece of property that bordered the southeast side of the ranch. "Do you know who owns *this* property? The Carlson family."

Hal drew another piece of property, on the east side of the ranch. "This one is owned by The Madson Group in Colorado Springs." He continued sketching around the McFee Ranch so Charlie could see the seven tracts of land that bordered it. Then he drew outlines of the properties contiguous with those. "Do you know what *this* property is worth today?" Hal asked, pointing to a large plot to the north.

Charlie shifted his body slightly. "Can't say I do."

Hal wrote a number inside the property boundaries. He continued writing numbers, representing the acreage and gross value of each property, until he'd filled up all the rough-drawn sketches on the entire page.

"These are today's values," he said, "but the McPherson Corporation has been talking about building a fifty-thousand-square-foot manufacturing plant about three years from now." He pointed at one of the plots. "And the county plans to put a high school right here in four years." He pointed to a bordering tract. "Do you know what that's going to do to the value of this property? And the piece next to it? Can you see what all of this will mean regarding the value of *this* property?" He placed his finger square in the middle of the McFee Ranch.

Charlie whistled. "I had no idea."

"Of course, these developments are not guaranteed. McPherson could fall through. But the McFee property is prime land, maybe some of the best in the entire state. At least that's how I read it. That's why I didn't pass on the deal."

Charlie leaned forward slightly, his hands resting on his walker. "When were you planning to let us in on this little secret?"

"At the August board meeting, the night I was fired. I tried to tell you all I had a plan to get us out of the financial difficulty, but no one wanted to hear me out. You kept cutting me off." Hal was glad he could make this statement without rancor.

Charlie wrinkled his brow.

"And, of course, this information was available to any of you if you'd researched it. But you'd made up your minds that it was a poor investment and so didn't bother."

Hal stood and walked to the window, taking in the southern exposure of Charlie's property. "I have made mistakes in running the business, but I took my role as managing partner very seriously. Most of my decisions were sound, and they made the partners a lot of money—which is one reason they didn't often question my deals." He watched a couple of bicyclists head up the High-Line Canal trail that ran along the border of the property.

Then he turned back to Charlie. "I've searched my conscience, and I can unequivocally state that as president and managing

250

partner, I never did anything unethical, illegal, or immoral. And I welcome the opportunity to assert that in a court of law."

Charlie gazed at Hal for a moment before speaking. "You always were a good speech-maker, Stratton." He reached for his walker, indicating the end of the interview.

Hal watched Charlie get to his feet, wondering whether to say what was on his mind. He'd gone this far—might as well go all the way. "You've given me important feedback today, Charlie, and I appreciate it. I need to give you some feedback, too. What you said about me riding roughshod over the partners? You're doing the same thing to them now."

Charlie straightened and glared at Hal. "How so?"

"You have a dominant leadership style—"

"So?"

"So the partners defer to you. They don't speak up or offer their own opinions. I've seen it every time we're all together. To me, that's a far bigger problem than any mismanagement or poor decision-making on my part."

Hal stopped. He'd said enough. He'd listened to Charlie give him his own comeuppance, and he'd deserved it. And he'd said what he needed to say back. The next move was up to Charlie and the other partners. He thought he saw a glimmer of humor in Charlie's eyes.

"I'll say one thing for you, Stratton. You've got guts."

Chapter 36

Day in Court

The pretrial conference was scheduled for mid-November, a little over twelve weeks after Hal had been fired. He eagerly anticipated the day. He and Kathy talked a long time with the children the night before. Despite Hal's reassurances, the idea of their parents going to the courthouse made them nervous. Derek wanted to stay home from school so he could hear the outcome as soon as possible, but Hal and Kathy convinced them all it was better to go about their normal routines.

"We'll be here when you come home, I promise," Hal said. He embraced each of them, hoping they felt his calm and his love for them.

He did feel calm, and it amazed him. Kathy was stressed enough for both of them. On their way to the courthouse, she asked him for the umpteenth time how he was feeling. "Aren't you even a little nervous?"

"A little," he said. "You never know what might happen. But, overall, I feel great."

"What's it going to be like to see your partners?"

He kept his eyes on the road. "I know it sounds odd, but I'm looking forward to seeing them."

"I don't know how you can say that." Kathy huffed. "I'm not."

He gave her a quick glance. "What can I do to make it easier for you?"

She sighed, twisting the strap of her purse. "Just don't forget about me when things get hot. Look at me once in a while and hold my hand."

Hal reached over and gave her hand a squeeze. "I can do that. I really appreciate you taking a day off to go with me."

They arrived thirty minutes early, to meet with Mitchell Cross before the proceedings. When they turned the corner and headed down the corridor toward the courtroom, Mitchell was waiting on a bench. At the other end of the corridor, the partners were grouped around their attorney, William Gutierrez. To Hal's surprise, Charlie was with them. He looked stronger than when Hal visited him, but he was still using a walker, and his personal assistant was off to the side.

"Over here." Mitchell motioned Hal and Kathy to join him. They sat and he went over the protocol and procedures for the conference. Afterwards, Hal closed his eyes for a few moments. *This morning, I choose ...* He finished the sentence in a number of ways, visualizing the outcomes he desired. More importantly, the way he wanted to feel and *be* throughout the morning—no matter what happened. Then he stood.

"Where are you going?" Kathy asked.

"I'll be right back." He walked down the hallway and up to his partners, who were engrossed in conversation. They stopped talking when Keith noticed Hal approaching and alerted the others.

"Hi, everyone," Hal said. "I just wanted to say good morning. It's good to see you all."

They stared and smiled at him awkwardly. Except for Gutierrez. "Whatever you have to say, save it for the meeting."

"I'll see you inside, then." Hal turned and walked back to Kathy and Mitchell.

Several minutes later, both sides were invited into the courtroom, and the hearing began. Sylvia Johnson, a judge with a no-nonsense reputation, presided. She allowed the parties to introduce themselves and listened as the attorneys presented the background of the case. For most of the introduction, she reviewed the written documents before her. Hal watched her, hoping to get an indication of what she was thinking, but her expression was enigmatic. When she finally set the papers aside and looked up, he felt a shiver of anticipation.

"I've looked over the allegations of the plaintiffs and the response of the defendant," she said. "Frankly, I'm surprised you haven't settled this matter. It's not easy managing a business and working out issues with partners, but that's exactly what you signed up for when you formed this corporation. You can move ahead with your suit if you wish, but I'm not reading anything here that would lead me to believe that gross misconduct has taken place."

She continued, "You, the partners, obviously didn't like some of the decisions Mr. Stratton was making, so you fired him. But you had a responsibility to know what was going on in your own company and to speak up if you were unhappy. You're grown men and women, for goodness sake. I suggest that you get together and work out a settlement that is fair to all parties. You can schedule a settlement conference and keep paying your high-priced attorneys, if that's what you want; or you can get together right now and see what you can come up with. If you wish, I'll have my clerk find an empty room you can use." With a bang of the gavel, Judge Johnson closed the proceedings and retired to her chambers.

Hal came so close to laughing that he had to cover his face with his hand. The feeling was not one of revenge, but relief. Someone had finally seen through the lawsuit and encouraged his partners to find a sensible solution. He turned, grinning, to Kathy, and she gave him a big hug.

"Don't get too excited," Mitchell said. "It isn't over yet."

"But it certainly bodes well for us," Hal said.

"That it does." Mitchell chuckled. "I've never heard her offer an opinion so bluntly in a pretrial conference. The pressure is definitely on your partners to negotiate a fair deal."

"What do we do now?" Hal asked.

"Wait. Your partners are probably shell-shocked. It's going to take them a few minutes to decide what to do. My guess is, Mr. Gutierrez and I will probably get together to begin discussing a settlement conference."

The judge's clerk approached Mitchell to let him know where they could find an open room. He then went to deliver the same message to Gutierrez, who immediately went there with the partners to continue their discussion. Hal, Kathy, and Mitchell waited in the hall.

Mitchell turned to Hal. "Your partners might be ready to negotiate a settlement this morning, so let's review our position and what you want from these negotiations."

"I've already got what's important to me." He put his arm around Kathy. "A fair opportunity for a fair deal. I just want what's reasonable and equitable for everyone."

Mitchell rolled his eyes. "You've still got to negotiate a financial settlement." He shook his head and tried to sound serious. "Just don't settle for a Hallmark Card and a gift certificate to a nice restaurant."

Hal laughed. "I guess we could counter at seventy-five percent and see if they're willing to settle at fifty."

"Fifty percent is a long shot, despite what the judge said. They're probably assuming they can get thirty. That's a far cry better than the original offer."

"Maybe so. But as I see it, fifty gives them a pretty sweet deal. They get rid of me, and they split half my equity among the four of them. A nice little windfall. How could they not feel good about that?"

"Because they know they can get more."

Hal's countenance changed. "I hope there's more at play here than greed," he said. "Look, Mitch, I feel good about fifty percent. That's six million dollars in a buyout to me and the same amount in their collective pockets, a million and a half each. They lose me and still collect a hefty bonus. Not too shabby."

Ten minutes passed, then fifteen, then thirty, then forty-five. Kathy expressed her worry that Mr. Gutierrez hadn't come to get them yet. Mitchell reassured her. "The longer they take, the more serious they are about getting to a settlement today. But I'll go see what's happening if you like."

He returned ten minutes later, grinning ear to ear. "It's show time. Follow me." He led them to a small room with a long conference table. The partners and Gutierrez were seated on the far side; Hal, Kathy, and Mitchell sat on the near side.

Gutierrez said formally, "The partners have already made you an offer, Mr. Stratton. Protocol dictates a response from you."

Hal hadn't expected to be put on the spot immediately. He looked at Mitchell, who raised a warning eyebrow, but he went ahead and spoke what was in his heart. "A few minutes ago, Mitchell asked me to tell him my counteroffer, and I gave him a number. He told me how he thought you'd respond and how that would set off a process of haggling and negotiating to get to something we can all agree on."

Hal looked at his partners. "I don't feel good about playing that game. Throwing a phony number out there isn't the way to do things when trust and goodwill are present. Now, I think you all have a sense of what's right in this situation, not just for yourselves individually, but for the company as well. It would be unfortunate if any of us walked away from this meeting today feeling bitter or disappointed with the outcome. Then we would all have lost, and much more than money."

He paused, but no one spoke. "The lawsuit states that I'm guilty of usurping authority, negligence, and breach of fiduciary duty. I agree that I've made some mistakes. I've done my best to be honest about my failings with myself and with each of you. The question is, do you believe my sincerity? If so, we arrive at one settlement. If not, we arrive at another. So I need to know, what are your most serious allegations against me?"

He scanned the room, trying to read their faces. When he got to Charlie, he grinned. "I hope my speech didn't sound too preachy."

"That's quite all right," said Charlie. "You're an okay speech-giver." Hal noticed Charlie seemed to be trying to suppress a smile. He relaxed a bit. "So, what are your complaints?" he asked the group.

Larry, Patricia, and Keith exchanged glances. Then Larry said, "Our biggest complaint is that we had to wait seven long years to know the real Hal."

Hal's jaw dropped, and they all burst into laughter, followed by relieved chatting. Gutierrez brought them to attention by clanging on his water glass with a pen. "All goodwill aside, we still need a number, Mr. Stratton. What will you settle for?"

"Fifty percent of my equity. That's an honest figure, not a negotiating stance."

"We can't live with that," Keith said. "That wouldn't feel like a win to us."

Hal's exuberance faded. He'd hoped to avoid posturing and bargaining. "What *would* be a win for you?"

"Well ..." Patricia paused dramatically, "we're sorry if you consider this an insult, Hal, but we want to withdraw our suit and offer you your job back as general manager."

Kathy let out a sharp squeal of delight and grabbed Hal's arm.

Stunned, Hal shook his head. "Did I hear you right? You're offering me my job back? Why would you do that, given all the complaints you have about how I ran the business?"

"We've been doing a lot of talking since our last board meeting," Keith said. "We've had to admit we were party to everything you did. We deliberately turned our heads when you made decisions. We let you take all the risks. Then we complained when things didn't turn out the way we wanted them to."

Larry added, "We even secretly wanted you to screw up at times so we could be justified in our complaints against you."

The two attorneys looked at each other as the meeting veered out of their control. Gutierrez shook his head. "I'm confused. Who's the plaintiff and who's the defendant here anyway?" The parties ignored their attorneys and kept talking—about what went wrong at Western, and how they'd gotten themselves into this mess in the first place. They talked about their lack of communication, the differences in their personality styles, the state of the business now, and what they could do to move forward.

Eventually, their talking ran its course, and they started gathering their belongings. Hal stood and cleared his throat. "You still haven't heard my response to your offer."

An immediate hush came over the room.

"From the depths of my heart, I thank you." Smiles appeared on everyone's faces. "But I cannot accept it."

Stunned expressions instantly supplanted the smiles. Kathy stood and faced her husband, incredulity in her eyes. "But Hal, what do you mean you can't accept it? You were so depressed when you got fired. You love Western. It's your life."

"It *was* my life," he said simply.

Larry was shaking his head. "I don't understand."

"*I* do." Everyone turned toward Charlie. "Sometimes life pulls the rug out from under us and completely changes how we see things. And I'm not talking about myself. I'm talking about Hal."

He smiled at Hal and continued speaking as if they were the only two in the room. "I've watched you closely these last few months, Hal. At first, I thought your new attitude was pure BS, manipulation. I thought you were trying to weasel your job back or get us to drop the lawsuit." He held his arms up in an open gesture. "But I was wrong. You apologized to me when you came to visit last week. I was pretty harsh in my criticism, yet you took it without defending yourself. Now, I owe *you* an apology. I had accused you of pocketing the company's money, but the audit revealed that you've done nothing wrong. I misjudged you and falsely accused you, and I'm truly sorry you won't be leading our team."

Charlie's words touched something deep within Hal, but all he could muster was, "Thank you. That means more to me than I can say."

Charlie opened his briefcase and pulled out a sheet of paper, the one with Hal's sketches demonstrating the potential value of the McFee property. Charlie placed it on the conference table where everyone could see it. They all gathered around as he reviewed the value of each adjacent property and the long-term implications for the selling price of the McFee Ranch. "If we're smart enough," he said, "we can turn this purchase into our biggest moneymaker ever."

"I knew it," crowed Patricia. "I tried to tell you guys, but you didn't believe me. Hal knew what he was doing when he bought that land."

"I always said you had a nose for a deal, buddy," Keith said.

Hal watched incredulously as his partners high-fived each

other. He hadn't conceived that Charlie had not shared this information with them.

"You put a lot of research and forethought into that deal, Hal," Larry said. "Why didn't you tell us this earlier?"

"He tried," Charlie said. "The night he was fired. It's my fault he didn't have the chance."

Larry gave Hal a pat on the back. "It'll be good to have you on our team, even if you aren't managing partner."

Hal held up a hand. He spoke slowly, almost thinking aloud. "I've learned a lot about myself these past three months. I'm not the man I was at the August meeting. I don't think it's best for me to come back, even as a member of the board." He drew a breath. "Life is inviting me to move on."

"What do you plan to do?" Patricia asked.

"I don't know yet. And don't get me wrong. The real-estate development business has been good to me. I just feel called in another direction."

"Ohhh." Everyone looked toward Keith, whose head was bent. He looked up. "This means we still have to buy you out."

Hal held back to let the idea sink into his partners' minds. "But not at my full equity," Hal assured them. "That wouldn't be fair to all of you, especially during these tough financial times. I meant it when I offered fifty percent. That's a pretty good reward for my seven years of service to the company."

They looked around at one another. "To tell the truth, Hal, your service is worth more than that," Larry said thoughtfully. "You built the company."

"Thanks, Larry. But I don't want to bankrupt your ability to grow because of payments to me. Fifty percent *is* a good settlement. And I'm willing to defer a good part of the buyout until the McFee property begins to pay big dividends."

The room was quiet. Then Patricia said, "That seems fair to me. If you work with us, we might even be able to start making some monthly payments to you right away, like some percentage of your salary. Then agree on a date to make cash payments at some point in the future."

"I can live with that if you can," Hal said. He held Kathy's hand tightly while the partners leaned toward each other, speaking softly. When they broke, Charlie said, "Okay, Gutierrez. We agree to Stratton's terms. Now it's time for you and Cross to do what we pay you for."

The relief in the room was palpable. There was even a moment of humor when Judge Johnson stopped by to ask how they were doing. Her eyebrows rose at the eagerness with which both sides told her about what had happened. "This is definitely one for my memoirs," she said. After congratulations and handshakes, she went on her way.

"Well, I guess we're done here," said Patricia. "I'm sorry about all the … well, you know. Hal, I don't know how we'll replace you."

Hal looked at Charlie, who shook his head. "Life's calling me in another direction, too." He waved to his personal assistant, who quietly came over. "I'll say goodbye now." He shook hands with everyone and headed for the door. He shook Hal's hand last, and gripped it a little longer than was custom. "Drop by once in a while, you hear?"

They all watched Charlie leave the room. "I think I'm beginning to like that old codger," Larry said. "I almost wish he would take over as managing partner."

"You don't need him any more than you need me," Hal said. "Every one of you is capable of standing in our shoes. That's why I invited you in as partners in the first place."

"Thanks, Hal," said Keith and Larry, in unison.

They started their goodbyes, but Keith spoke up. "Before we go, I, for one, would like to know what happened to you. What changed you, Hal?"

"You guys firing me," he said matter-of-factly. "It forced me to look at myself and my life in a way I never had before. And I can tell you that's not easy." He shook his head. "I'm not sure I would have been able to do it if I hadn't had the help of a very special friend. He helped me get honest with myself and to accept responsibility for my life." Then he chuckled. "It may sound simple, guys, but it took a lot of work and a boatload of humility. Just ask Kathy." He turned to her with a smile. She nodded.

Hal figured that was enough. He took Kathy's hand, ready to leave, but the partners made no move. What were they waiting for? Suddenly he knew. The hunger was universal. People everywhere were seeking a better way. They wanted more than life was offering on the surface. Hal knew that words were inadequate. The greatest gift he could give them wasn't spoken but lived. But there they all were, staring at him ... and waiting.

So he told them about the Key Moments—*Stop - Look - Listen - Choose*. He explained how he was learning to challenge his core beliefs. He told them about his day in the cemetery. And he did his best to explain survival, security, success, and serenity. He expected them to laugh out loud or show boredom, but they didn't.

"I've learned that I can choose how to see and feel and act in every moment. My friend calls it *The Hero's Choice*—learning to make choices that reflect our deepest values. When we do, we experience serenity. At that point, life is no longer about what we can get ... but what we can give."

It was a solemn group that left the conference room. In the hallway, they still lingered, clustering around Hal and Kathy, shaking their hands, offering their best wishes. After several minutes, Hal and Kathy walked out of the courthouse with their arms around each other's waists. Kathy shook her head. "I still can't believe today turned out the way it did." She laughed. "When you told me what you wanted out of this meeting, I thought you were crazy. Do you really think it was your change of attitude that made it happen?"

"I know it was."

"What do you call it? Living from the inside out?"

"That's what Donald calls it, yes."

"Well, I'm beginning to see that anything is possible, living that way."

Hal pulled Kathy close and kissed her forehead. "Not only is anything possible," he said. "*Everything* is possible."

He took her hand. "Come on, Kath. Let's go home."

Chapter 37

A Last Visit

A chill was in the air as Hal marshaled the kids to do some yard work. Indian summer had kept temperatures mild throughout September and October. Now, the Saturday before Thanksgiving, the standoff against winter could not hold out much longer.

Kathy and Nicole raked leaves into piles. Derek held a big plastic bag that Hal and Susie filled with leaves.

"Hey, Dad," Derek asked, "is Donald a real guy, or did you learn all that stuff from some book?"

Hal stopped, arms full of leaves. "Why do you ask?"

"Because no one else ever sees him. You go off, then come back with all this goofy wisdom. It seems a little weird, that's all," he said with a teasing glint in his eye.

"Yeah," Susie chimed in.

Hal called to Kathy and Nicole. "Okay, everybody. Tools back in the garage. We're going to the mountains for a visit."

"Where?" Kathy asked. "Oh. I get it. Mohammed."

"Shouldn't we call first?" asked Nicole.

"Donald's usually home," said Hal. "Besides, it would be fun to surprise him. And on the way back, we'll stop for hot cider at Valley View."

They all piled into the SUV, Hal driving. During the ride westward, Hal repeated the story of how he met his elderly mentor. Susie wanted to know what he looked like. Nicole was interested in how his place was furnished. Derek asked if he had any kids. Hal briefly recounted what Donald had told him about losing his family.

"Wow. That's sad," said Susie.

Hal sniffled. "It is. He misses them a lot, but he's learned how to find joy in life even so. That's the biggest lesson I learned from him. No matter what happens, we get to choose how we experience it."

Derek poked Nicole. "Write that down. We can make a book, *The Wisdom of Donald,* and make a fortune."

Kathy fidgeted with a button on her jacket. "I have to admit, I'm nervous about meeting him."

Hal glanced at her. "Why is that?"

"Because he means so much to you, Hal. I don't know what he'll think of me, or what questions he'll ask."

"Don't worry, he can't read minds, and he won't probe into your life. He's just a guy. A really nice guy. A really *normal* guy."

Hal hadn't thought about what it must have been like for Kathy and the kids, hearing him talk so much about Donald. And he'd never thought about asking Donald if they could come for a visit. He'd been too focused on his own problems. *Another example of being wrapped up in myself,* he thought wryly.

Kathy and the kids were subdued as they drove up the lane and parked in front of Donald's cabin. "Here we are," Hal said, but nobody moved. "Hey, come on. This is supposed to be fun."

Slowly the family got out of the SUV. Kathy walked around the car to Hal and gripped his hand tightly. Susie reached for his other hand. He motioned them into a group hug. "You guys are the most important people in my life. Even more important than Donald. Remember that. Come on, let's go meet the man."

The minute Hal stepped up onto the porch, something felt different, but he wasn't sure what. He stopped and the rest of the family stopped behind him.

"Are you sure we should be doing this?" Kathy asked.

"Don't worry, Donald will be thrilled to meet you," Hal said, trying to keep uncertainty from his voice. Then he realized what was wrong: the Adirondack chairs that had lined the front porch were gone. He felt a hard thump in his chest, but he told himself that Donald had just put them away for the winter. Still, he was anxious as he knocked on the door.

He waited a few moments, then knocked again, more loudly. Still no response.

"We should have called first," Kathy said, the agitation apparent in her voice.

Hal walked up and down the porch but drawn shades prevented him from seeing in. He looked around the yard and up the paths that he and Donald had so often taken. "I don't see him, but that doesn't mean anything. He sometimes pops out of nowhere."

They milled around the porch a few minutes, then Hal knocked again. Feeling his family's unease and disappointment, he tested the doorknob. It turned easily and he peered inside.

Kathy grabbed his arm. "We can't just barge in."

Ignoring her, he stepped partway into the room. "Donald," he called, "you have company."

His voice echoed back to him and instantly he knew. The stillness he'd felt on the porch was that of an unoccupied house, empty and lifeless. He pushed the door open further and walked inside, pulling Kathy with him. The kids followed. They stood in the middle of an empty room.

"I don't understand," Hal said, feeling strangely disoriented. He walked through the great room and past the kitchen, to the back of the house, calling Donald's name. All of the rooms were stripped of everything that had given them warmth, charm, and life.

He returned to Kathy, numbed. "I don't understand. The house is totally empty. Here's where the comfy chairs were. Over here's where he had his big table." He strode about the place, looking in corners and closets, hoping to find something, anything.

"I can't believe he'd up and leave without telling me."

He saw fear in Kathy's eyes. She was wondering if he'd created Donald and furnished this room in his own imagination.

She moved toward the door. "No one's here, Hal. We should leave."

"Daddy, where did your friend go?" asked Susie.

"Nowhere," Derek said, smirking. "I told you, Dad made him up."

"No, he was here just a couple days ago, when I called him to tell him about the court hearing."

"Well, he's not here now," Kathy spoke quietly.

For a moment, Hal wondered if he had indeed conjured Donald. Had the crisis of losing his job unhinged him? Had all of Donald's lessons been hallucinations? The thought frightened him to his core.

He paced from the kitchen to the bedrooms and back into the vacant great room again. "I can't believe it. I can't believe it," was all he could say. His family hung back, not sure how to react.

Finally, Hal sat on the great room floor, in the very spot where he'd spent so many hours sitting in the recliner and talking to Donald. He felt a devastating pang of loss. Kathy approached tentatively and wrapped her arms around him. "I don't understand," he said in a husky voice.

"Hey, look." Derek pointed to the mantel, which was bare and dusty—except for a wooden plaque.

Hal jumped to his feet and rushed over to be sure of what he was seeing. The plaque bore the words *The Hero's Choice*. "Thank goodness." His fingers trembled as he took it down.

"Hal, you shouldn't do that," Kathy said. "It's not yours."

"Oh, but it is," he said with a huge smile. He displayed the plaque to her excitedly. "Don't you see? These words are the summation of everything Donald taught me. He left it for me."

Abruptly the darkness and heaviness lifted, and Hal was flooded with a feeling of lightness and peace. He burst out laughing. The joyful sound echoed off the walls of the empty great room, bringing the place to life once again.

"Don't you remember me telling you about the plaque?" he said as he motioned his family closer. He saw recognition in their eyes as each of them reached out and touched it.

"Maybe this Donald *is* real," said Derek buoyantly.

"But where'd he go?" asked Nicole.

"I don't know," Hal said, staring at the plaque. "But it doesn't matter." He looked up at his family. "Have you heard the saying, *When the student is ready, the teacher appears*?"

Kathy and Nicole nodded.

"Well, maybe there's a corollary. *When the student graduates, the teacher disappears*," he said with a grin.

Nicole moved close to her father. "Do you think the plaque is your graduation present?"

Hal nodded vigorously. "I think it is."

Derek carried the plaque as the family stepped back out onto the porch. Hal shut the door behind them, then paused for a last look at the lush forest surrounding the cabin and the snowcapped mountain peaks glimmering in the distance.

He smiled at his family and felt the fullness of the moment, of life as it was. Even of Donald not being there. "Today," he said with an expansive gesture, "is a beautiful day."

The kids chatted excitedly as Hal drove down the lane and onto the road. Kathy smiled back at them over her shoulder. Hal reached out and gave her hand a squeeze. They had only gone a few miles when Kathy said, "Slow down, Hal."

A young man, not more than 24 or 25, was trudging along a narrow footpath that paralleled the road. His head was bowed and his shoulders slumped. Even from several yards away, Hal could see in the young man's eyes a lost and frightened look. He shot a questioning glance at Kathy. She simply nodded.

Hal parked the SUV on the shoulder and strode up to the footpath. The young man, dressed in city clothes rather than hiker's gear, stopped on the trail and regarded Hal with curiosity and suspicion. "Don't see many hikers in these parts this time of year," Hal said. "Everything okay?"

Your journey continues…

H al Stratton learned how hard it is—but how rewarding and good it feels—to make the hero's choice in the key moments of life.

Now it's your turn. Join the dialogue about key moments and learn more about embracing reality, exercising responsibility, and achieving the results you truly desire, by visiting our website: www.abouthdi.com

About the Author

R oger K. Allen, Ph.D., is a highly respected expert in leadership, communication, team development, and personal and organizational change. Using his engaging style, Roger has delivered hundreds of workshops, retreats and seminars around the country which have been acclaimed as among the most powerful learning experiences available anywhere.

Roger founded and served as President of the Human Development Institute beginning in 1981, providing thousands of hours of individual, marriage and family therapy to a diverse client population and supervising the work of other members of the professional staff. During this time he created and taught, along with other HDI staff, experiential programs in personal development and interpersonal relations in a number of cities around the country. These programs have been noted for their life-changing impact on the lives of thousands of people.

In 1992, Roger began consulting to businesses to help leaders create high performance/high commitment organizations. Roger offers a rare set of skills to help leaders do the deep work required to become a cohesive team capable of defining the direction of the organization and rallying employees behind them to achieve outstanding and sustainable business results. He has spearheaded major executive and organizational development projects with such clients as AT&T Capital, Ashland Chemical, Coach Leatherware, Denver Museum of Nature and Science, Honeywell, Merck Pharmaceuticals, Proctor & Gamble, The US Forest Service and US West. The personal, team, and organizational development products offered by Roger K. Allen, Ph.D., have helped tens of thousands of people and dozens of organizations transform the way they work and live.

An outdoor enthusiast and father of three adult children, Roger resides in metro Denver, Colorado with his wife Judy.

To learn more about Roger Allen and the services of HDI, visit www.abouthdi.com or send an email to info@abouthdi.com. You can also call, toll free, 1-877-205-9207.

To learn about Roger Allen's business consulting, including workshops related to *The Hero's Choice,* call 1-877-205-9207 or visit www.executiveteamsolutions.com.